UFO LANDINGS UK

C000101944

Philip Mantle

First edition published in 2020 by Flying Disk Press

FLYING DISK PRESS
4 St Michaels Avenue
Pontefract
West Yorkshire
England
WF8 4QX

Published by FLYING DISK PRESS

Cover design by Mark Randall

CONTENTS

Acknowledgements

I have been greatly assisted with this book by a whole number of people, organisations and publications. I would like to thank everyone for their kind cooperation and apologise now for all those that I have missed. A special thanks goes to:

MUFORA, British UFO Research Association, Flying Saucer Review, BUFOG, MAPIT, UFOIN, BEAMS, John Hanson (Haunted Skies), Bob Tibbitts, Andy Collins, David Haisell, Clive Potter, David Sankey, Nigel Wright, Steve Mera, Jenny Randles, Dr David Clarke, Carl Nally, Dermot Butler, Nigel Watson, Janet & Colin Bord, Dave Hodrien, Ron Halliday, Steve Wills, Andy Roberts, Steve Coop, Janet and Colin Bord, Robbie Graham, Nick Redfern, Brian Allan, Malcolm Robinson and John Steiger.

Although I have mentioned the following above, I feel I must emphasise that without the following this book would simply not have been possible. The man who persuaded me and helped me launch Flying Disk Press in 2015 in my friend and colleague John Hanson. John, under his HAUNTED SKIES banner has published his own series of excellent books. During the writing of this book, he has been a constant source of information. What I would have done without him I honestly don't know. Although the Flying Saucer Review (FSR) magazine is no longer in print I would like to thank the publishers and various editors down the years. The FSR is a primary source for a great deal of information in this book and it is sad that it is no longer being published. I would also like to thank the British UFO Research Association. I am proud to say that I was part of BUFORA for a number of years and served them in many different ways. I have been fortunate enough to obtain access to their various publications down the years and have used a number of their investigations in this book. Last but not least is the long down defunct UFO Investigators Network (UFOIN). The various investigators at UFOIN were involved in some fascinating and remarkable UFO cases and again I have accessed some of these for this book. Last but not least, I would like to thank all of the witnesses who have gone on the record down the years as without them nothing in UFO research is possible.

Philip Mantle.
2022.

INTRODUCTION

I have now been a UFO researcher and investigator for over forty years. My interest in the UFO phenomenon began in the late 1970's and was compounded once I watched the Steven Spielberg movie 'Close Encounters of the Third Kind'. For most of my teenage years I had been fascinated by all things 'paranormal'. My life would change forever when an aunt of mine showed me a small advertisement in our local evening newspaper the Yorkshire Evening Post. The advert was for a meeting of the Yorkshire UFO Society (YUFOS). This was now 1980 and the meeting was for a Sunday afternoon in the city of Leeds in West Yorkshire, just five miles or so from where I lived. That Sunday I took the bus into Leeds, found the location of the meeting and in I went. YUFOS was set up by brothers Mark and Graham Birdsall. Many years later Graham Birdsall went on to publish and edit the highly successful newsstand publication UFO MAGAZINE. Sadly, Graham passed away in 2003. Little did I know that Sunday that my life would never be the same again.

I feel very fortunate to have joined the Yorkshire UFO Society when I did and for meeting Mark and Graham Birdsall. I was also fortunate in joining YUFOS at that specific time as areas in and around Yorkshire saw a very high amount of UFO sightings, many of which were reported to us. It was the best place and the best time to become involved in active UFO research.

Before long I had quickly learned that the vast majority of UFO sightings had a conventional explanation. Stars, planets, aircraft, birds and balloons, all had been misidentified as a UFO. There was, however, a very small residue of UFO sightings that remained that, unidentified. Among this small portion that remained there was a few cases that were labelled as 'high strangeness'. This was a term used by astronomer and UFO researcher Dr. J. Allen Hynek. Dr, Hynek was also responsible for the phrase 'Close Encounters' and he worked on the movie of the same name as a consultant. Dr. Hynek basically made all UFO researchers aware of the fact that the more bizarre (strange) a UFO close encounter is, the more likely it is to be the genuine article. By this he meant not a misidentification of something conventional, but something out of the ordinary. Hence a case that had all the hallmarks was labelled 'high strangeness'.

Under the heading of 'high strangeness' is a section of UFO accounts that surely cannot be the result of misidentification of something conventional, and that section are encounters with UFOs on the ground. UFO landings. From a witness point of view, you have to be relatively up close and personal to observe such an event. It is not some small light in the sky that in all likelihood is an aircraft of some kind. No, this is something that seems to defy logic and is only a matter of meters from the witness/witnesses and is the ground or just above it. Added to this such reports may also involve the observation of humanoid beings in conjunction with the landed UFO and even more bizarre there are accounts of 'abductions' where the witness even boards the landed UFO either by there own accord or not. It is difficult to label such cases as anything else other than 'high strangeness' accounts.

I was fortunate to investigate one such UFO landing case in my early years at YUFOS and it will feature later in this book.

I have since that time always had a fascination for such UFO landing reports and this book will look at such cases from the UK only. This book is not meant to be definitive in any way and it will not cover what many describe as Britain's best UFO landing case, which is the events in Rendlesham Forest, Suffolk in December 1980. Whole books have been written about this account, so I have decided not to cover it here. A small account of it in this book simply couldn't do it justice.

Most UFO researchers would agree that the modern era of UFO research began on June 24th, 1947, when private pilot Kenneth Arnold observed a formation of unidentified objects flying over the Cascade Mountains in the USA. Arnold reported the movement of these object as looking like a saucer skipping on a pond and the term 'flying saucers' was born. I agree entirely with this but there will be no starting date when it comes to reports of UFO landings in the UK. There are a number of such accounts in this book that will pre-date the Kenneth Arnold sighting.

What follows are UFO landing accounts from the UK. Will you the reader agree with me that these cases cannot be the result of misidentification and that they really do fit into the 'high strangeness' category as outlined by the late Dr. J. Allen Hynek. I will feature UFO landings of all types including some where humanoids are also observed and what some people claim are alien abductions. You can decide for yourself whether I am right or not and that the following cases are the result of something extraordinary and not the ordinary.

Philip Mantle

CHAPTER ONE

UFO LANDINGS PRE-KENNETH ARNOLD AND THE 1940's

It might not be that surprising to learn that my files are not bulging with cases that pre-date the Kenneth Arnold sighting in 1947. There are, however, a small number of UFO landing cases from the 1930's and 1940's that serve to set the scene for what was to come and some what we might call 'folklore' stories going back even further in time.

Extract from the British Magazine 8 (1767), p. 500.
"Domestic Intelligence":
Saturday, September 12
Extract of a letter from Edinburgh, Sept. 8.

We hear from Perthshire, that an uncommon phenomenon was observed on the water of Isla, near Cupor Angus, preceded by a thick dark smoke, which soon dispelled, and discovered a large luminous body, like a house on fire, but presently after took a form something pyramidal, and rolled forwards with impetuosity till it came to the water of Erick, up which river it took its direction, with great rapidity, and disappeared a little above Blairgowrie. The effects were as extraordinary as the appearance. In its passage, it carried a large cart many yards over a field of grass; a man riding along the high road was carried from his horse, and so stunned with the fall, as to remain senseless a considerable time. It destroyed one half of a house, and left the other behind, undermined and destroyed an arch of the new bridge building at Blairgowrie, immediately after which it disappeared. As few appearances of this kind ever were attended with like consequences, various conjectures have been formed concerning it.

1896:
Folktale Possible UFO/Abduction Portmeirion,
Gwynedd,
North Wales

A Portmeirion fairy story. Or was it a UFO close encounter?

Elias Owen, Welsh folk-lore: a collection of the folk-tales and legends of North Wales; being the prize essay of the national Eisteddfod, 1887, published 1896: Penrhyn Isaf was the farm just behind Portmeirion and Tyddyn Heilyn, near where the railway crosses the river. Big David's strange experience must have happened somewhere near where Castell Deudraeth is now.

'A three-hour fairy dance seeming like a few minutes. The Rev R. Jones mother, when a young unmarried started one evening from a house called Tryddn Helyn, Penhyndeudraeth to her home Penrhyn isaf accompanied by their servant man, David Williams called on account of his great strength and stature Dafyd Fawr (Big David). David was carrying home on his back a filtch of bacon. The night was dark but calm. Williams walked somewhat in the rear of his young mistress, and she, thinking he was following went straight home. But three hours passed before David appeared with the pork on his back.

He was interrogated as to the cause of his delay, and in answer said he had only been about three minutes after his young mistress. He was told that she had arrived three hours before him, but this David would not believe. At length, however, he was convinced that he was wrong in his time, and then he proceeded to account for his lagging behind as follows:

He observed, he said, a brilliant meteor passing through the air, which was followed by a ring or hoop of fire, and within this hoop stood a man and a woman of small size, handsomely dressed. With one arm they embraced each other, and with the other they took hold of the hoop, and their feet rested on the concave surface of the ring. When the hoop reached the earth these two beings jumped out of it, and immediately proceeded to make a circle on the ground. As soon as this was done, a large number of men and woman instantly appeared, and to the sweetest music the ear had ever heard commenced dancing round and round the circle. The sight was so entrancing that the man stayed, as he thought, a few minutes to witness the scene. The ground all around was lit up by a kind of subdued light, and he observed every movement of these beings. By and by the meteor which had at first attracted his attention appeared again, and then the fiery hoop came to view, and when it reached the spot where the dancing was, the lady and gentleman who had arrived in it jumped into the hoop and disappeared in the same manner in which they had reached the place. Immediately after their departure the Fairies vanished from sight, and the man found himself alone and in darkness and then he proceeded homewards. In this was he accounted for his delay on the way.'

Mr T.W. (name on file)
1908 (approximately)
West Midlands

Mr W wrote to UFO researchers when he was 85 years of age. He went on to detail his account of an encounter with a landed UFO when he was just 10 years old.

Seventy-five years ago, when I was a boy of about ten years of age I was walking along a path at the back of the house where I lived when I saw a vehicle in the garden. I did not see it or hear it land. It was made of metal and was a greenish-blue colour. It was about five to six feet long, four feet high and three feet wide with a turret on top and a door at the side.

The door opened and I saw two men step out. One stood by the door. The first one out came toward me and was waving his outstretched arms and shouting warning me to go away. This man went back and both men went back into the vehicle.

Then immediately there was a switching on of what seemed to be an electric current but bright around the vehicle. It (the vehicle) went up with a loud noise and a red light was flashing at the back of the vehicle. The red flashing light seemed to be the power and it went up at great speed.

The little men who came out of the vehicle were about four feet six inches tall. They did wear a loose-fitting uniform and on top of their helmets were two pieces of metal or something about a quarter of an inch thick and nine inches long. Their uniform was a greenish-blue colour. Their faces were very much the same colour of white people.

I remember asking two boys if they had seen it in flight and they said they had seen it in flight and they also said that they had seen the red flame at the back of the vehicle. About the same time, in our daily newspaper, I had seen a picture of what we were likely to see in the future.

It was a cigar-shaped object with a propeller, but I had not seen anything like what I have tried to describe or heard about UFOs. Well, how ridiculous this story was if I told it seventy-five years ago and also at the present time. However, it was all real to me. The stories in the Daily Express are mostly about flying saucers. Perhaps they are an improvement on the vehicle I saw. You will understand why I wish to be anonymous and my name and address not to be published.

The sighting was remarkable because I had never heard of people from another planet. It was before I saw another picture of the first airplanes to one circular mile. I have never seen a flying saucer or UFO which the people write to you about but my daughter, her husband and others in our street saw something recently.

Have a good laugh at the drawing. Mr. T.W.

Of course, there is no way of checking such accounts that happened such a long time ago. However, I think it is fair to say that this account from Mr. W has indeed set the scene for what was to follow down the decades.

Mr. W even has a sense of humour and asks us to have a laugh at his drawing of the vehicle and one of the men. Mr. W was responding to an article in the Daily Express newspaper here in the UK in 1978. Little did he know that his words were a tad prophetic when he said, "Perhaps they are an improvement on the vehicle I saw." How things were indeed going to change.

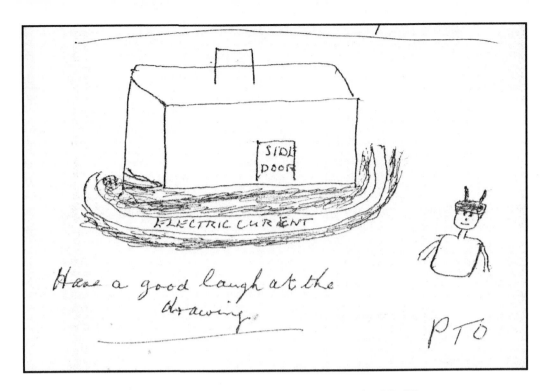

Inside drawing: SIDE DOOR

ELECTRIC CURRENT

Have a good laugh at the drawing

PTO

Drawing of the vehicle and little man by Mr.W.

Mr. C. Lethbridge
Caerphilly Mountains
Wales
Date: May 18, 1909

Mr. C. Lethbridge, a dockworker was walking home over the mountain when, at the summit, he came across a tube-shaped contraption on the grass, and two men working on something nearby, they wore "big, heavy fur coats, and fur caps fitted tightly over their heads." Mr. Lethbridge went on, "I was rather frightened, but I continued to go on until I was within 20 yards of them. The noise of my little spring cart seemed to attract them, and when they saw men, they jumped up and jabbered furiously in a strange lingo."

Mr. Lethbridge became even more alarmed when the long object rose from the ground, and he was amazed when he saw the two "men" jump into a little carriage suspended from it. Tube, carriage, and "men" rose slowly into the air in a zigzag fashion. When it was clear of the telegraph wires, two great lights shone out and the object sailed away towards Cardiff.

The astonished witness said later he could clearly see two wheels at the bottom of the carriage, and a whirling fan at the tail. The next day trampled grass, torn newspapers, and a quantity of a substance like papier-mâché was found on the scene.
(HC addendum Source: Charles Bowen, The Humanoids)

Mr. C
Killary Harbor
Ireland
Late February 1913

A Mr. Collins was aboard his yacht when he saw a strange "aero-plane" like object approaching from the sea. It suddenly ditched into the water near the shore. Collins then approached the craft, which was now apparently at the shore. He saw three occupants apparently working on the object. Two were tall, heavy set, blond haired and light complexioned. Thinking they were or German origin he asked if they needed any help in German. One of the men responded in French, claiming he could not understand, and then in no uncertain terms told the witness to leave the area. Collins quickly left and did not see the craft depart.
HC addition # 3425 Source: Nigel Watson.)

West Yorkshire
England: (exact location not specified)
1933

A five-year-old girl was living in a cottage in West Yorkshire when one afternoon she saw a dome-like vessel land nearby. The craft contained two little 'people'. One of them came out and explained to the little girl that she should not be afraid. The creature was a human-like midget wearing a dark green jumpsuit. The girl could also see what looked like an 'instrument panel' inside the strange vehicle. No other information.

Dollis Hill
London
England
February 1934

On a cold rainy evening a married couple observed a metallic cylindrical object on the ground with two men wearing peaked caps standing near it. The couple approached but the object moved quickly away and the two men with peaked caps had vanished. (HC addition # 1756 Source: Peter Rogerson, MUFOB Vol. 6 # 1)

Near London
England
1937

An eight-year-old girl was walking alone in a meadow when she saw a huge silvery object with stilt like protrusions hovering above her. A platform of some kind descended from the object and three tall men, dressed in red stepped down. One carried her onboard the object as she realized she was unable to move. The interior of the object appeared much larger, and she recalled being placed on a molded chair facing a dazzling bright light. She then experienced unique thoughts and visions. Later she was taken to an enormous pyramid and wandered inside dark corridors until she found a door that opened to the meadow where she was originally taken from. HC addition # 1374 Source: Lillian (Crowner Desguin, UFO's Fact or Fiction.)

Jack Quinn
Roseberry Topping,
Guisborough
England
August 1939

Ten-year old "Jack Quinn" and his mother were taking a walk on a local hill when they heard a strange humming sound under their feet, which seemed to be vibrating. Scared his mother grabbed his hand and pulled him across the heather, but in their haste, he fell and hurt his ankle. As his mother knelt down to check, there was a strong smell of "something burning" like burnt paper. Then a big white globe of light suddenly appeared from nowhere, in the middle of the field. The sphere of light did not move at first, it just sat on the heather about 4 or 5 yards away. They estimated it to have been about 6 feet across. Then two little men appeared on the brow of the hill. Even though they were about 30 yards away, the witnesses could see that they were tiny, about 3 ft in height. They wore some kind of shiny material, a sort of light greenish color, and had close-fitting helmets made of similar kind of material. The little men were jabbering away to each other in high-pitched voices. They then looked across at the witnesses, pointed, getting excited. The globe of light the moved closer to the witnesses and the mother, now terrified began to pray. The light rolled right around the witnesses very slow. Then it stopped, the humming sound getting louder. Then suddenly everything stopped. The humming noise and vibrating disappeared, and the globe of light and the little men seemed to dematerialize. Both witnesses got up and as they made their slow and painful progress across the field to the path, they distinctly heard some weird high-pitched laughter, which seemed to come from the air. Then there was a sudden, unnaturally complete stillness. Both felt very tired. They seemed to have become disoriented and lost as they stumbled around the field for about half an hour. Soon, inexplicably they found themselves back in the path totally unaware how they got there.
(HC addendum Source: Lynn Picknett, The Mammoth Book of UFOs.)

Cathie Connolly
Meriden (near Coventry)
Warwickshire
England
Summer, 1940

Eighteen-year-old Cathie Connolly waited over thirty years before she told her story. In the mid-1970's she related her teenage encounter to UFO researcher Bob Tibbitts who was then the head of the Coventry UFO Research Group. It was at a public meeting of CUFORG that Bob Tibbitts met Cathie Connolly. Cathie went on to relate the following account to Bob Tibbitts:

"One Sunday afternoon, in the summer of 1940, I was walking along a country lane near Meriden, Warwickshire, when I came across a metallic dome-shaped structure that I took to be a new building, next to a row of smoking chimneys poking up through the grass, around which were a number of tall men gathered apparently adjusting something near this structure.

As I walked past, I noticed they were all dressed in one-piece garments with unusually high foreheads, strange eyes and tanned coloured skin, very unusual in those days as most people had pasty (white) skins.

I carried on walking, noting the structure was giving off a blue-grey light. When I glanced around again, I was staggered to see no sign of the structure or the men. A few months later I was working in the chain room at Reynolds Chains, Coventry, examining metal links, when all of a sudden, I became aware of a man next to me whom I instantly recognised as being similar in appearance to one of the people I had seen near the structure. He said, 'It's your war as well. Take me to your King and Queen'. I was stunned. I told him I couldn't do that. The next thing I new I was aware of was lying on my back in what I took to be a spaceship. I tried to move but couldn't, as I was being held down by a number of strange men who had slits for a mouth, stretching almost to their ears, with cat-like faces and eyes devoid of the white part. One of them said, 'We are not going to hurt you. We just want to know if you are pregnant.' He then invited me over to what he called a scanner (a window), set into the side of the 'ship' and asked me to look into it. I was shocked to see an air battle in progress over the sea underneath us, with a number of boats crowded with people, accompanied by the excited voices of the pilots being broadcast into the room. One of the pilots looked at us and shouted out, 'They've got a captive. It's a woman. Don't open fire'. As we passed alongside of the aircraft, I saw the pilot making the sign of the cross and then everything faded away."

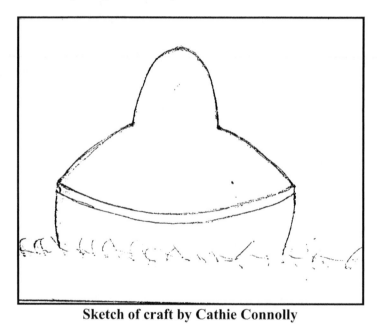

Sketch of craft by Cathie Connolly

Bob Tibbitts went on to add:

"I remember her telling me that one of the entities had something in their hand, apparently occupied with some sort of device they pointed towards her."

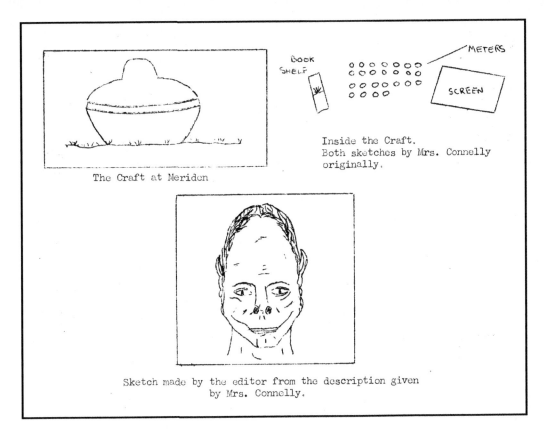

The Craft at Meriden

Inside the Craft.
Both sketches by Mrs. Connelly
originally.

Sketch made by the editor from the description given
by Mrs. Connelly.

Again, like the case of Mr.W. there is little in the way that any researcher can do much about such an account apart from writing it down and preserve it for posterity. This case is very different to that of Mr. W. It had multiple entities and is probably one of if not the first alleged accounts of alien abduction in the UK. This is a| very curious tale indeed and it is easy to see that the 'strangeness' factor has gone up drastically. Whatever you believe is the nature and origin of such experiences there is little doubt that it was not caused by the misidentification of a common object.

Emily Crewe
Stansted
Essex
England
1940

My name is Emily Crewe, I live in Kempston, Bedford and I am recounting here a strange experience that I had one morning in 1940 whilst working in the ATS... the Women's Auxiliary Territorial Service in Stansted, Essex. I was aged 21 and had only been employed at the army camp for seven months but was already used to the hard grafting of kitchen work, preparing meals for nine hundred men and women. This particular morning in question, just around 12 o'clock to be exact, I was taking my turn at mopping the large, greasy, concrete floor in the kitchen, when something very odd took place.

"As I worked there all alone, I suddenly heard an almighty racket going on." I looked through the large kitchen window and saw pandemonium out there, everybody running for their lives and shouting "get under cover!"

13

Pretty soon the parade ground was emptied but hovering in the sky was the weirdest sight I had ever seen. It was truly terrifying, and I stood, frozen to the spot with shock as I looked on. There was a huge golden ball hanging there, with sparks coming off it!

I don't know if it was silent, but next the object floated down over the parade ground, descending to foot level, then appeared to make for the kitchen area where I was. All of a sudden, it came right up to the window and pressed itself up tight against the glass. Snapping out of my shocked state, I quickly locked the kitchen door, just in case it tried to get in. Although big enough to accommodate a large hut in its size, the glowing 'thing' seemed less menacing to me as I got a better look.

"It's 'skin' seemed smooth, rather like rubber but transparent, and I could see something bright moving inside the object. Then it began behaving like a jelly, shaking and wobbling. Quite comical really." My initial fears cooled down somewhat as I saw it perform these peculiar motions. Then it moved sideways against the outside wall and gradually moved away...to my great relief! Unable to see this object anymore, I remember that I made for the door, unlocked it and found outside that some of the girls had come over to see if I was alright. They told me that the 'thing' had jumped the wire fence surrounding the camp, over the road and shot into the forest.

"Afterwards we were called to assemble to be admonished and instructed that the matter was not to be discussed or speculated about, but simply forgotten." What was it? A weather balloon perhaps? But there was nothing attached to it; it was perfectly round and floated sedately over the parade ground to begin with, rather than something being blown about in the breeze. Ball lightening even?

Yet how could it have behaved so intelligently, first heading to where I was watching then making its escape into the forest and beyond? "I should add that there was no trouble, no shots were fired or even any guns raised, come to think of it. I will leave it up to you dear reader to figure this one out."

It was a long time ago, the ATS camp has gone and now Stansted Airport has taken its place, but it is an event that is not easily forgotten, certainly not by me.
Emily Crewe.

Mr. W.
Radway Green
Cheshire
England
October 1942

Mr. W. Harper and six others, including James L. Toft, were looking towards Alsager when they saw a large object like a double parachute, giving the impression of a cigar-shaped object with a dome on top and lights on either end, floating and swinging side to side. The men, believing it was an aerial mine, flung themselves down. When they looked up, they saw the object moving towards Alsager at terrific speed. Mr. Bradshaw and members of his ARP muster saw, through binoculars, the object descend into a field 2 km away. Bradshaw thought he was seeing an aircraft crashing.

The area where the object came down was said to be scorched for some time afterwards. Mr. Toft investigated and found a discolored area, footprints and some burnt patches that could have been caused by anything.

(HC addendum Source: Michel Bougard "La chronique de OVNI" 1977 & James L. Toft in BUFORA Research Bulletin 4-1 p-3).

John Warren
RAF Ludham
Norfolk
England
May 1943

Mr Warren was serving in the Royal Air Force (RAF) during WWII. He was stationed at a small airbase near the village of Ludham which was just a few miles away from Norwich in Norfolk. Mr Warren was responsible for arming the two squadrons of aircraft stationed at the base and also the anti-aircraft guns.

One night in May 1943, Mr. Warren was returning back to base rather late after attending a dance at a local village some twelve miles away from the base. He had missed the last train, so he had no option but to walk the twelve miles back to base. Once he had left the village there was nothing but open fields in front of him.

After walking for several miles, and just on the outskirts of the village of Ludham, Mr. Warren observed a 'green glow' in the road up ahead of him. On getting nearer to this strange glow he noticed that it was coming from a 'man' standing at the side of the road. This man had a peculiar sort of 'diver's helmet' on his head and an oblong-shaped thing on his chest.

The green glow was coming from this thing on his chest and fanned upwards into the mans face. The man had a peculiar 'grin' on his face and this expression never changed. The man never moved nor acknowledged the presence of Mr. Warren. Behind the man was a hedge or fence which bordered the field. In this field stood an object which was the shape of a 'bell tent'. Beside this stood two more figures who seemed to be wearing some kind of white 'boiler suit' and were moving around to the left-hand side of this object.

Mr. Warren was very frightened by this sight and walked past the strange man at the side of the road and never looked back. At no time did this man at the side of the road move or talk or anything, he simply stood there with a grin on his face and this green glow from his chest shining up into his face.

Mr. Warren made his way back to base and went to bed still puzzled and frightened by what he had seen. His initial reaction, being war time, was that the German were invading, but if that was the case surely, they would have killed him. Not long after he got into bed a friend climbed in through the window (Mr. Warren had locked the door) and he too was in a frightened state and suggested that he had come across the same thing although he would not go into any great detail. Mr. Warren was so frightened by the event that he stayed well clear of the area in question for over two weeks. On visiting the area, he could find nothing that could account for what he had seen.

I personally interviewed Mr. Warren in August 1987 at his home in West Yorkshire. He still remembered the event with great clarity and told me that he was still very puzzled by the whole event. He was de-mobbed in 1947 and he had reached the rank of Leading Aircraftman. I have a full type written transcript of my interview with Mr. Warren on file. Mr. Warren contacted me after seeing me in a local newspaper in the area. I found him to be a sober, sensible and reliable witness. He had previously reported his encounter in 1966 and he was contacted in 1973 by the British UFO Research Association (Yorkshire Branch) and a copy of their letter is reproduced here. I speculated with Mr. Warren if he could have misidentified some kind of military test or manoeuvre of some sort, but he was sure this was not the case. He had seen many things during his service with the Royal Air Force during WWII but nothing like this event in May 1943.

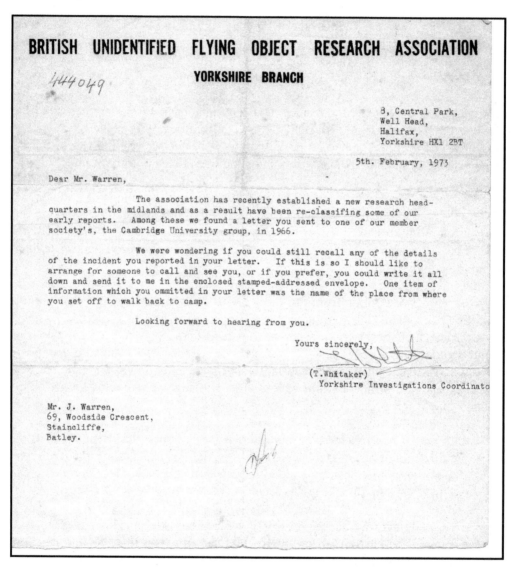

Letter from the British UFO Research Association to Mr. J. Warren

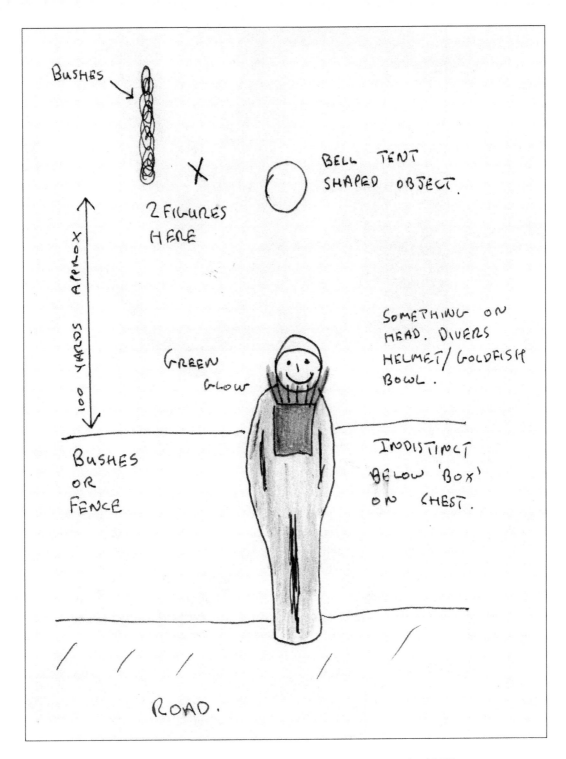

Drawing of the encounter by Mr. Warren done in 1987

Mr. John Warren photo taken in 1987 by the author

Mr. S.
Island off the West Coast of Ireland
Republic of Ireland
Christmas 1945

Mr S. (name kept confidential) told the British UFO Research Association in 1976 of an event that had happened in 1945 on one of the islands off the west coast of Ireland. The investigator in question who dealt with the following is Larry Mahoney and little did he know what to expect when he answered a letter he received from Mr. S.

The witness had been to a family celebration and at around midnight at Christmas of 1945, he left the party to go home. As he lived on the mainland, he had to wait for a local man to come and take across the water in a rowing boat.

While sitting on some rocks on the beach his attention was drawn to a light in the sky some distance away from him. He had only occasionally seen aircraft in this area and wondered if what he was seeing might be an aircraft off course. Just before the 'plane' came into view he saw bright flashes of light like those from a camera.

Within no time at all the craft was just a few hundred feet away. He could make out that it was square-shaped underneath while its upper surface was dome-shaped and a silvery colour. Purple lights could now be seen around the dome section. He could see that it was obviously no ordinary aircraft, especially as he had served in the air service during the war. He became nervous and his fear worsened as the object, now making a noise 'like a drill' settled onto the water just offshore.

Sensing that perhaps he should not be there he jumped up and ran behind the rocks he had been sitting on. After just a short time he peered over the rocks to get a better look at the object. Almost immediately the object lifted off from the sea and flew a short distance inland, landing in a nearby field. Even at the point, he wondered if the craft belonged to some foreign military power. He thought that he might soon find out as the craft had landed closer to his location than when it was on the water. If anyone climbed out of it he would have a good view of them. However, he lost his composure completely when a hatch opened in the dome and someone emerged, followed by a second crew member. By the light given off by the object he could make out that the people who climbed out were not, in fact, people at all. He was terrified that he would be discovered so he crouched down as low as he could. The crew members walked about the craft and a short distance along the beach, picking something up from time to time. One of them filled a large vial with sea water. The witness felt that they were collecting samples of seaweed and plant life that was growing in the sand.

At one point on the beings stopped what it was doing and looked directly at the rocks where the witness was hiding. It then carried on as before occasionally looking back at the rocks and the witnesses gave a huge sigh of relief. He felt that the beings were aware of his presence but just kept an eye on his so that he couldn't get too close to them. He was just glad that they had left him alone. After just a few minutes the beings got back into the craft which lifted off and sped away into the sky.

In 2005 UFO researchers Dermot Butler and Carl Nally located the witness and interviewed him. He recounted his story to them but requested that his name remain confidential. This account is featured in the book 'Conspiracy Of Silence – UFOs In Ireland'.

Aylesbury
Buckinghamshire
England
1946

A man walking along a country road sighted a huge dome shaped structure on a field across from him. As he watched several glass-like doors seemed to open and shut. The witness approached the object and saw several men in silvery suits apparently working around the object. One saw him and was heard to say, "How did he get here"? "His clothes are at least 100 years old"? Two of the men then seized him and dragged him inside the object. He managed to break away and ran through some doors. He ran for a while, turned around and the craft had disappeared.
(HC addition # 189 Source: Norman Oliver, Quest UFO Magazine Vol. 11 # 4).

Frank Handford
Fishpool Hill
Hereford
July 1947

Mollie Tilley from Tamworth, Staffordshire told of her uncle's account of a UFO landing as Fishpool Hill in July of 1947. Aged 70 Mollie told John Hanson of the Haunted Skies series of books about the UFO landing on the family farm. Her account was as follows:

"My uncle and mother were not the sort of people to make up wild stories. They were the exact opposite, not given to flights of imagination. My mother told me his story many times over the years and was adamant Frank was telling the truth."

According to Betty, Mollies mother, Uncle Frank and Mrs. Newman, his housekeeper, were disturbed by dogs barking in the middle of the night. Frank loaded a pair of shotguns ready to defend them both. When the pair went over to the window overlooking the apple orchards, they saw something that neither of them could ever expect:

"We saw the incredible sight of a dome-shaped craft, glowing with light, descending onto the ground and watched as a pair of steps slowly came out of the craft, followed by the entrance of three silver-suited 'beings' who stood next to the spaceship, picked up some apples and a piece of turf before re-entering the 'ship' and leaving."

The next morning, they ventured outside and discovered a large circular impression burnt into the ground and scorching to a nearby wicker gate. Frank telephoned the police who later arrived with men from the Air Ministry as well as military personnel. These conducted a search of the area with a Geiger counter; 2which revealed high levels of radiation."

The men then left after threatening Frank with dire consequences if he told anybody what had happened. Despite publicity in the Hereford Times newspaper about this incident and searches through local newspaper archives, John Hanson was unable to find any other witnesses but was able to confirm that a Mr. Frank Handford was living on Fishpool Hill in July 1947.

Sadly, this account is third hand at best but still it remains labelled high strangeness. One might ask why the witness waited until the following day to telephone the police, why not immediately? If Frank Handford did indeed have two loaded shotguns, then why not use them? If he, had it could have finished the argument once and for all regarding whether or not we are dealing with extraterrestrials. The strangeness factor of this case is quite apparent. The 'beings' land, pick up an apple and a piece of turf and then leave. We must also remember that in the summer of 1947 across the Atlantic near Roswell, New Mexico in the USA, we had what is undoubtedly the most famous UFO case in history, the UFO crash at Roswell. Would someone living in rural Herefordshire have heard about the Roswell incident? I personally doubt it but I can't rule it out.

There are echoes of the Roswell incident in this account. The men from the ministry and the veiled threats to keep quiet. A number of the witnesses of the Roswell UFO crash also claimed to have been threatened by the military and were ordered to keep quiet and not tell anyone. Mollie Tilley was in her late 70's when she related this account via her mother. Could she have been influenced by seeing or hearing about the Roswell event? We will never know but like the previous accounts in this chapter it surely could not have been classed as misidentification of a conventional object.

John Lewis
Near Shipdam Airfield
Near Norwich
Norfolk
England
Summer 1947

A young boy, John Lewis, (pseudonym) was playing in a wooded field when he caught sight of a silvery torpedo shaped craft in a clearing. Several four-foot-tall humanoid figures stood next to the object. These were described as well built, wearing dark green close-fitting coveralls. They had what appeared to be glossy black hair and seemed to be wearing dark wrap around visors. The beings seemed to be inspecting the craft and were moving about quickly.
(HC addition # 789 Source: Sheridan Lane, Quest UFO Magazine Vol. 11 # 2)

Frank Handford
Fishpool Hill
Herefordshire
England
July 1947

Frank Handford and his housekeeper Mrs. Newman were awoken by the barking of their dogs. Fearing intruders, Frank and Mrs. Newman went to investigate. Through the window overlooking their apple orchards they saw a luminous dome-shaped object descending to the ground. From it emerged a ladder, down which three beings in silver suits, who picked up apples and some turf and then re-entered the craft. The next day they found a large circle burned into the ground and scorching on a wicker gate. The police were called, and they came with military personnel, who claimed that a search with Geiger counters revealed a high-level of radiation and warned the witnesses not to talk. (HC addendum Source: John Hanson and Dawn Holloway 2010a p50 citing investigations by themselves and Robert and Marilyn Aldworth.)

Brenda
Wiltshire
England
Summer 1948

The following story has nothing to do with Hollywood, rather, it's one from my own back-catalogue and, until now, it has never appeared online. It was originally published in 2007 in Issue 25 of the now-defunct UK publication Paranormal Magazine.

"On a summer's afternoon, in either 1948 or 1949, my mother, Brenda, was walking with our dog and myself in the area we called simply 'The Field' at the back of our housing estate… in what was then the outskirts of Chippenham in Wiltshire [England]. Whilst there, she saw an unusual, occupied aircraft."

So began a handwritten letter addressed to this author; tidy and succinct, it documented a mother and daughter's close encounter with a peculiar flying object, piloted by apparently non-human beings.

Many years later, the daughter, Karen – a mere toddler at the time of the incident – solicited from her mother, Brenda, a detailed description of what they had both witnessed that day, making a written record of her response.

Artist impression of this encounter

Brenda had no trouble in recalling the details:
"We were walking through 'The Field' when this aircraft came out of nowhere and stopped nearby. There were two beings inside, sat facing one another. The aircraft was like a boat with a see-though cover. The two beings inside were neat and compact; they were dressed in grey and had helmets with a sort of crest on top. They were looking towards us, then one of them raised a hand as if he were waving. Then the aircraft just went."

Through further conversation with her mother, Karen was able to establish that: "there was no accompanying sound or scent with the aircraft; that it was in view for no more than three minutes; it was about nine feet long and stopped approximately fifteen yards away at bungalow-roof height; there were no trains on the track nearby at the time; and that the area was otherwise deserted." Their dog, incidentally, "was interested in the aircraft, but was not alarmed."

Regarding her nondescript recounting of the object's departure, beyond stating that "it just went," Brenda had difficulty expressing the character of its movement: "She said that it didn't exactly vanish instantly, it just 'went' very rapidly," Karen related.

After examining the details of this previously undocumented report, I was keen to establish the accuracy of its content, and to gauge the sincerity of its writer. Speaking with her by telephone, I found Karen to be charming and genuine – an intelligent and well-spoken woman whose bewilderment at the event described was evident nearly sixty years on. What, then, to make of her story?

It was obvious that Karen had no prior interest in UFOs, and no ufological knowledge of which to speak, and at no time had she or her mother sought to publicise their experience. Indeed, the witnesses' names as written here – 'Brenda' and 'Karen' – are pseudonyms, a reflection of Karen's continuing desire for anonymity (their real names and backgrounds are known to me). The event, as recalled by Brenda, was described in considerable detail; the shape and dimensions of the object, as well as its aerial position in relation to the witnesses all were clearly recalled, so too the basic physical appearance of its occupants (including their attire). Incidental information such as nearby rail traffic (or lack thereof), and the reactions of their dog, was similarly noted.

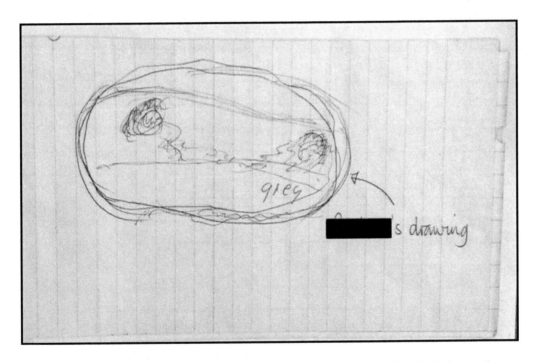

During our telephone conversation, Karen told me that her mother had always been a 'no nonsense' sort of lady and had been reluctant to speculate about the precise nature of the 'aircraft,' or about the possible origin of its occupants. Sadly, Brenda passed away a few years ago, but despite her apparent nonchalance at what she and her daughter had witnessed, she had always acknowledged the high strangeness of the event: "She said that she realised that what she was seeing was 'something very different,'" Karen wrote in her letter, "but that she wasn't alarmed or afraid. She felt the beings were friendly."

Unbeknownst to her, what Karen had reported was a typical close encounter of the third kind, (CE3 – which refers to any sighting of a UFO at close quarters (within 500 feet of the witness/s), during which accompanying occupants are also observed.

Though many thousands of such encounters have been reported over the decades, Karen's has considerable Ufological significance in that it stands as one of the earliest CE3s on record in the modern (post-1947) UFO era, not only in the United Kingdom, but anywhere in the world. (Article by Robbie Graham.)

Mr. Trevor Coombes
1948/49
Wales

Trevor Coombes was contacted by UFO researchers in 1987. His handwritten letter went on to detail his account of a UFO landing and although the details are a little sketchy in places it is nonetheless fascinating.

The following is from his handwritten letter dates 9/6/87:

"My main and most unusual experience with a UFO took place around 1948/49. To the best of my memory, so it may not be of use to you, I am bow 68, so cannot give you anything like exact dates. I'm not too sure of the sequence of events. It is really too much to put in a letter so if you really want to know you can phone me on Treforest 3192, any night at 00.30, if this is too late for you then Sundays at 6,.40 pm. I have good reasons for preferring a call at around half past midnight, we can talk as long as you like without interruption at that late hour.

Other reasons for not wanting to write, except to my friend in Poland, others including a couple of times to newspapers have brought no response. I've had a few other 'unbelievable' things happen to me in my life apart from the UFO CE (close encounter), a few things in my childhood and one around 1960. So, if you phone you will have to be very open minded. After no spaceships or strange events for many years I've almost lost interest. I dare say it's a sign of old age coming on.

Yours Truly, Trevor Coombes."

In the file I have on this case is a copy of a letter to Mr. Coombes requesting further details but there is no name on the letter, so I have no way of knowing who wrote it. Mr. Coombes handwritten letter looks like it was in reply. There is also a copy of further details of his account. They are as follows:

" Sighting in the sky. Silent, appeared very large, like an old airship, grey, multi-colour radiations at front and back. Sky fairly clear – but came out from one blackish cloud and disappeared into another approximately a mile away, stayed in the cloud which drifted out of sight. During the approximate one minute in view. I saw human-type figures at the window, mainly like head and shoulders, bending over, looking out."

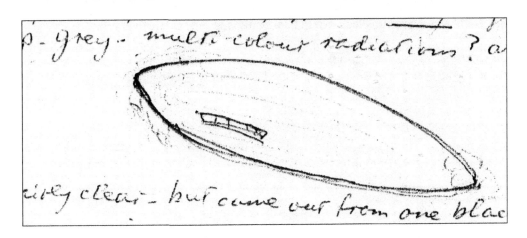

The first sighting related by Mr. Trevor Coombes

Mr. Coombes went on to detail another encounter:

"First airship on the ground, I thought it was an old anti-tank concrete/stone type from the war, then I realised this was impossible as it is isolated, too far inland and I looked into the deep open squarish holes, and it was just black inside, but I sensed something awesome, and I walked around it. At the sides and back it appeared like this (see picture), green/grey metallic. I tried to climb o top (as no door) but it was too smooth and steep, I could only get about half was to the top. On returning to the 'front' I shouted 'hello' through one of the 'windows' and a loud noise like a factory siren started up and almost scared me. I then saw to human-like figures about 70 meters away dressed like frogmen or similar, examining bushes and plants. One was kneeling and produced a white rod which he extended to about 10 feet and pointed it diagonally at the sky. The other figure then caught sight of me and made threatening gestures, lifting what appeared to be a small black box and pointing it at me. At this point I jumped on my bicycle and drove away as fast as possible, through the grass, into the trees and didn't stop until out of sight about a mile away."

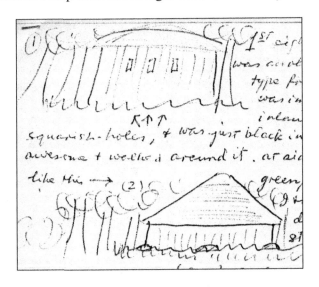

The first UFO landing account by Mr. Trevor Coombes

Mr. Coombes wasn't finished with his encounters and he relates yet more:

"On returning to the site the next day about half a mile from the original place I saw two cone-shaped, grey-coloured objects. They took off seemingly hurried and with difficulty giving off a high-pitched noise.

Going up breaking tree branches, steadying as it went up fast at about a 45-degree angle and out of sight in a few seconds. On the next day I saw circular burnt black areas in the grass and a number of destroyed tree and bushes at this location."

The second UFO landing as reported by Mr. Trevor Coombes

Mr. Coombes was right when he said if you phone be prepared to be open minded. He is one of the first if not the few that claim to have witnessed more than one UFO landing. Again, it is almost impossible to draw any conclusions from these accounts. All you can say is that they are extremely bizarre and definitely not the result of misidentification. The 'high strangeness; factor on these accounts by Mr. Coombes must be almost off the scale.

******

CHAPTER TWO

POST WAR UFO LANDINGS – THE 1950's

By now Kenneth Arnold's sighting had firmly put the tern 'flying saucer' into the public domain and it was completely embedded in popular culture. There was turning back. The second world was now behind us but this had now been overtaken by the cold war. The world's two new superpowers, the USA and the USSR, faced off and the threat of nuclear war was an ever-present danger. But when it came to the UFO phenomenon it certainly wasn't cooing down but quite the opposite. The 1950's in the UK finally saw an end to rationing after WWII and things were looking rosy despite the cold war. High strangeness accounts of UFO landings in the UK continued unabated as we will see.

Farnborough
Hampshire
England
1951

The young witness, (involved in other encounters) was riding his bicycle by a field next to his school which was only over the road from his home. There were several entrances to this land and on one occasion he was going through the Cody Road path to it when he saw a large, illuminated disc sitting in a depression in the ground where an old WWII bomb had exploded years ago.

The grass was very high in the field so he thought that if he got right down into it, he wouldn't be seen. There he splayed his arms and legs out and shuffled forward to see what was happening, when suddenly standing before him was a five-foot-tall figure. Looking up at the being, the only way he could explain how this odd creature looked was like a 'funny tortoise' having never seen any other reptile other than a tortoise at that age. It had scaly skin, brown/green in colour, two black eyes, two slits for a nose and a slit for a mouth, but he couldn't remember seeing it wearing any clothes. Suddenly he was grabbed tightly by his arms and dragged across the bumpy field and underneath this disc, then into a cylinder where the door closed behind them. They were then in complete darkness, and he felt himself rising upwards until they were in a round room which was also dark; the only illumination was from glowing lights and switches on consoles. He found himself thrown on to some kind of bed, stripped of his clothes and invaded in places of his body with a sharp, pointed probe that dug and hurt him from his toes to his head; at this point he lost all further recollection of the event. (HC addendum Source: Hilary Potter, BEAMS, in FSR).

Sheila Burton
Withdean
Sussex
England
September 4 or 5 1951

Sheila Burton, in her late teens at the time, was staying with her parents when she woke up at about 6:30 a.m. got out of bed and walked over to the window that overlooked the long tree bordered garden from a height of perhaps 15 ft. Suddenly she saw something large and flashing descend at incredible speed onto the lawn, a large dome-shaped object settled down, panels like large doors opened and "men" got out from the fluorescent silvery craft. There were three "men" in all, and each moved in a straight line across the lawn away from the vertical, central axis of the craft. They were 5 to 6 feet in height and had bald "Kojak style" heads. Each wore a dark green or khaki one-piece garment and held a "machine gun like device". These men continued walking for perhaps 30 feet, then stopped simultaneously and began walking backwards towards the craft in synchronization re-entering their respective panels and disappearing inside. The panels slid across the openings, red flashing lights re-started, and the mass shot upwards vertically and was lost from sight. The whole incident lasted some 40-50 seconds and had been in total silence. It had occurred so quickly that the witness had not even thought of calling her parents. The object was described as dome-shaped and fitted well into the large garden, accordingly an estimate of its diameter as about 40 ft and height about 25ft can be made. Its color was silvery green, light green or lime. As the "men" walked in their respective directions they seemed completely oblivious of their surroundings and of the witness.

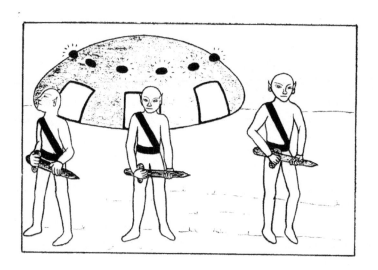

Object and 'men' witnessed by Sheila Burton (Source BUFORA Journal Volume 8 No.1 Jan/Feb 1979)

These "men" had appeared identical in every respect, their one-piece suits included their feet, but ended tightly at the wrists, and at the neck in a "mandarin collar." Their bodies were rather thin in proportion to their size and their legs seemed thick but short. Their arms were long, with hands and fingers apparently similar to humans. Their faces were expressionless and "odd". The nose was small and pointed, the mouth was small with no lips, eyes were small and deep set, ears also were pointed. Their heads were bald, and skin was similar in complexion to humans. From their right shoulders, down to the left-hand side were thick, black bands which joined onto a stomach belt, also black, of the same thickness. Each held a device described as "like a machine gun" in shape. This consisted of a black cylinder some 20 inches long and 3 inches in diameter, rounded off at the rear end and pointed at the front.

The devices were carried with both hands, but they appeared to do nothing with them. Their movements away from the object were as though they were mindless robots carrying out a pointless duty, this impression being strengthened as they all stopped and retraced their steps like a film played backwards. Immediately they re-entered the craft, the panels shut, then the red lights started flashing and pulsating brightly and the vehicle ascended vertically. No physical evidence or traces was subsequently found.
HC addition # 182. Source: Norman Oliver, Quest UFO Magazine and BUFORA Journal Vol. 8 # 1Jan/Feb 1979.

Mr. Nellie Thomas
Near Castlemartin
Dyfed
Wales
1952

Mr. Nellie Thomas was taking an after-lunch stroll among the sand dunes encountered a shiny metallic object partially concealed among the dunes. He went nearer to investigate and saw several men standing on top of the now discernible disc shaped object, one of the men who was apparently the leader or captain told him not to get any closer that he could be injured by the strong rays emitted by the craft, since he wasn't wearing any protective clothing which was recharging itself with the rays of the sun. They also told the witness that they were concerned that the earth was on a self-destructive path. The men looked very similar to humans and told Thomas that they had been visiting the earth for hundreds of years. They told him the name of their planet, but he could not remember.
HC addition # 385 Source: Janet & Colin Bord, Modern Mysteries of Britain.

Isle of Scalpay
Outer Hebrides
Cumbria
England
Winter 1953

A couple had been driving their car along a country road when suddenly they were both astonished to see several "small men" dressed in green, crossing the road. The couple described the small men, "They looked just like dwarfs" they said. The couple also noticed that "tubes of some kind protruded from their heads." The couple quickly swerved to avoid the strange figures around them.

The car then appeared to have stopped as these little figures were then seen to enter a saucer-shaped craft, mounted on three legs standing at the side of a field. The couple watched in shock, as the craft ascended with flames shooting out of the bottom as it rapidly vanished into the night sky. HC addendum. Source: Melanie Cunningham, "Ovni" May-June 2007 page 10.

Gerry Armstrong
Home Counties
England
July 1953

Twelve years old Gerry Armstrong looked over his shoulder to make sure the coast was clear, and then dug into his trouser pocket for the new pack of five Woodbine. Sitting in the shadow of a tree which gave him some welcome shade from the fierce afternoon sun, he fished out his matches, drew out a cigarette and lit-up, his first of the day. "Who wants to play hide and seek with old Rice anyway," he said to himself smiling. He thought it was quite smart of him to sneak away the way he did, right under his teacher's nose.

Gerry was one of a party of London school kids on a summer camp just outside the capital. His teacher, Mr. Rice, had made sure he and his chums were kept fully occupied but the game of hide and seek was just too much for the independent minded Gerry. When his teacher had been looking the other way, he simply sidled off in the direction of a wooded area. Now he was far enough away he couldn't hear the shouts of his school pals, so he stretched out on the grass, eyes fixed on the clear blue sky and enjoyed his smoke. The heat of the day had taken its toll and Gerry was beginning to feel drowsy. He tried to stop himself nodding off, and then suddenly he was in darkness.

"Get up Armstrong, where do you think you've been boy," Gerry opened his eyes with a start. A furious, red-faced Mr. Rice was bellowing in his face. Why was he so angry, he'd only been away a few minutes? Then he followed his teacher's gaze. He was staring at the half-smoked fag which was still stuck between two fingers in his right hand. "Get yourself up lad," screamed the teacher. "I want to know what you've been up to. We've been searching for you all afternoon and I want some answers." Gerry was astonished to learn it was now after 8 pm. Mr. Rice and parties of his school pals had been scouring the countryside for him for hours. They had even searched the spot where he was now, but there had been no sign of him a little while ago. Gerry tried to get up, but his legs gave way under him. Helped by some of his classmates he managed to hobble back to camp where he was checked over by a doctor. The back of his neck was red and sore, his pupils were dilated, and he was exhausted. Prognosis? Possible sunstroke.

The youngster was packed off to bed. Gerry Armstrong completely forgot about the fuss surrounding his mystery disappearance during that school camp until ten years later when he and his wife sited a UFO near London. The event triggered his memory of the seven hours that went missing from his life on that day, but he still couldn't recall where he was or what he had been doing for that period. Gerry's UFO encounters continued and became more frequent after he immigrated to the Lake Simcoe area of Ontario, Canada.

And it was a hypnotherapist from Toronto who enabled him to recover the lost memories from that summer's day in 1953. The fully qualified psychiatrist decided to put Gerry into regressive hypnosis in a series of sessions through 1978.

The following account is a compilation of the memories that came back to him:
As he sat under the tree, enjoying his cigarette, Gerry's attention was caught by a bright light in the sky that seemed descend to a point beyond a nearby clump of trees. Within minutes the lad thought he could detect some movement through the foliage and glancing in the direction the bright light had appeared to land, he could make out two figures walking in his direction. For some reason he could not explain, Gerry was

30

frightened. The fear grew into terror when he discovered that he could not move. Time and again he tried to move his legs, to put out his arm, but his limbs just would not respond to the messages his brain was sending out to them. Gerry began to cry. He didn't understand what was going on, but he was very frightened. The figures were now very close. As they closed on him the youngster was aware of voices in his head. Voices that were telling him not to be afraid, that no harm would come to him. Now the strangers were with him, one positioned on either side of him. They picked him up and began carrying him away. "It was like floating through the air" thought the child, trying to laugh out loud to show he wasn't scared. As he floated through the trees he could see a bright light in a clearing ahead of him, so bright it hurt his eyes. The object took on a vaguely rounded shape as he neared it although the intensity of the light made it difficult to work out what it was. To rest his eyes from the assault of light Gerry turned to his captors. They were small, one was smaller than the boy who was probably about four and a half feet, and they had white-grey skins, small mouths and prominent eyes. At last, they reached the object. Gerry, who had now regained the use of his limbs, was instructed to climb the ladder which seemed to lead up to an entrance.

As he began to do so felt a momentary severe pressure on the back of his neck, caused, he assumed, by something the strangers did. Once inside the strange object he found himself alone and in a brightly lit room with no apparent source for the light. As he explored the chamber, he felt a strange sensation and accompanying noise and seemed to know that the object, or craft, was now moving. After a while the beings returned and led Gerry along a semi -circular corridor to another room where he met a being dressed in red.

The youngster thought this person seemed older than the other two, and he was amused by the way the being addressed him as "My son." Gerry was instructed to look at a screen on the wall. He saw what he at first described as a "little ball." But on closer examination he could see it was a planet. "This is your home," said a voice in his head. The sudden realisation that he was looking back at earth was too much for young Gerry. Once again, he was gripped by fear at the thought of being so far from home. The being in red, seemingly realising the boy's distress, reached over and touched Gerry's forehead. Immediately the fear was replaced by calmness.

At that point he realised the noise had started soon after entering the object had stopped. Had the craft landed somewhere? The two strangers who had brought him on board and the being in red indicated that Gerry should accompany them as they began to walk down a ramp. An automatic door opened at the end of the ramp at which point the boy found himself looking out at the inside of a giant dome. "It's full of children," said Gerry as he saw many youngsters walking this way and that before him.

The voice in his head told him to be calm and to follow the being in red. At which point the being put something into Gerry's hand. "It's like a ball," said the youngster. But it was much more than a ball. On instruction from his captors Gerry looked at the spherical gadget and saw his life flash before him. "Understand, be taught," said the voices in his head. The lad now seemed to be alone, so set off to explore his new surroundings. He studied the building itself and noticed the dome was mauve, and transparent. Through it he could see strange craft traveling through the dark sky, craft that he thought might not be unlike the object he had traveled here in.

A woman approached him, breaking his reverie, and took hold of the silver cross that hung round his neck on a chain. He had taken it from his mother's jewellery box before leaving home for summer camp. The woman passed the cross to the being in red and both studied it.

Their words formed in Gerry's brain: "It is not right to worship." They indicated he should study his screen, the ball like device, once more. The being in red touched boy's head and he slept. Gerry awoke to find himself being carried through the woodland area where he had first seen the strangers. He was frightened again, but not of the strangers, of the reaction he would get from Mr. Rice. The beings set him down in the spot where they had found him. Gerry was surprised to see his cigarette was still there, burning although the sky was now getting dark. The strangers said farewell leaving Gerry alone, once again. Still tired Gerry drifted off to sleep again.... until.
"Get up Armstrong" roared Mr. Rice.

Alien abduction had now firmly become part of the 'high strangeness' category of UFO close encounters cases. As we have seen with Gerry Armstrong, there are cases where 'missing time' plays a major part of the case and that the witness remembers later what has happened or has these 'memories' released via the use of regressive hypnosis. There are of course arguments for and against the use of regressive hypnosis in such cases, an argument that lasts to this very day. Of course, there are cases where there is no missing time and that the witness remembers everything that happened, even the part where they claim to have gone (willingly or unwillingly) onto the landed UFO. One such event from 1956 involves Mrs. June Rice. The author interviewed the witness along with UFO investigator Clive Potter.

June Rice
Filey
North Yorkshire
England
August 1956

Jovial grand mother June Rice dropped her paper in shock as she listened to the radio programme. It was a discussion about UFOs and alien abductions. They were talking about people who had claimed to have been abducted by strange beings who had taken them off. June thought she was the only woman in the world to have been inside a spaceship. The only woman to have met visitors from other worlds.

She scurried off into the kitchen of her neat-as-a-pin home in Wallasey, Merseyside and busied herself by making a cup of tea. Her head was spinning. Could there really be other people who had seen what she had seen? She had always been too afraid to talk openly about what happened to her all those years ago, afraid of the ridicule. But if other people had experienced what she had seen then maybe she could find out more about those strange visitors. Maybe there was an organisation which could help. Without revealing her reasons, June made inquiries about UFO organisations and soon got hold of the number for the British UFO Research Association. She picked up her phone and dialled the number. The voice at the other end seemed friendly so she just blurted it out:" I was abducted by aliens in 1956......"

When two researchers, including (the author and Clive Potter), visited June a few days later, they were struck by her friendly, bubbly nature. A doting mum and grandmother, her living room was full of family photographs, and she was eager to point out the youngsters she was so proud of. At first, she seemed a little embarrassed about what she had experienced all those years ago when she was a young mum with an 18-month-old son, but after some encouragement she agreed to tell her story. It was during the warm summer of 1956 and June was staying at her mum's house in Filey, North Yorkshire. "It must have been that August," she remembered. "A friend and I went out to the pictures one night and when we came out we decided to take the easy way home, which was across the fields." We walked together for some distance until we got near to where she lived. Her house was on one side of the fields and my mums was on the other. We parted company and I set off for home on my own. "It was quiet, unusually quiet that night. You would normally see lots of bats in those fields, but not that night. "I was walking along, and it was quite dark by now, and these two men seemed to appear from nowhere. One minute there was nothing and the next these two men were there. They seemed to come towards me, stop and then stand there. "They didn't say anything, and I didn't. I wasn't frightened. I wasn't scared at all.

"They were quite tall and had whitish or silver suits on, like an all-in-one suit. It was a long time ago, but I remember thinking they were very pale. They had lovely eyes, beautiful eyes and white hair "I don't know if they had any beards or anything, but I'll always remember the white hair and the beautiful eyes." Then they just turned, and I knew they wanted me to go with them, so I just followed them and then I don't remember anything." June can't explain the gap in her memory, but it is a classic case of entry amnesia, a condition reported by many abductees who rarely remember actually entering the UFO they see. June found herself in a round room, again this ties in with many later accounts where witnesses often report alien rooms as rounded, seamless and without corners.

Although June never saw a UFO throughout her experience, she is convinced she was inside a craft belonging to the strangers she met. "The room was completely circular with seats all around and there were people sitting on the seats. They sat me down on one and I remember that by that time I was getting a bit agitated. I had the baby at home, you see, and I said 'No I'm not staying, I want to go home. "They never spoke at all, and I was saying 'No, no, no'. Then I realised I wasn't using my mouth to speak. It seemed as if we were communicating through our brains, you know, and I was upset about this. "One of the people then just came up to me and put his hand on my head and I seemed to go backwards, the seat seemed to come upwards.

All I remember from that part of things was a pain in my side. "I cried out with the pain when this, this whatever it was did something to me. I don't know if something was piercing my skin or what, but I was suddenly in my bed back at home. "I just grabbed hold of my baby and hugged him, and I thought 'where have I been, where have I been?' "I couldn't remember coming home or coming into the house and I had no idea what time it was."

The next morning June's mother pointed out that she had been out late the previous night. June didn't say anything. She couldn't. She didn't have a clue of the time when she came in and climbed into bed. But she clearly remembered leaving the cinema at a reasonable time.

June put the incident at the back of her mind and got on with her life, what seemed to be her very normal life. But when carefully questioned by the author and Clive Potter it appeared that June may have had several sightings after that first incident.

Her recollections were often vague and therefore difficult to check, but it appeared she had experienced further missing time episodes. June had not recorded dates or times in connection with the follow up episodes and although the investigators were convinced of her genuine sincerity there was insufficient data on them for any meaningful investigation} Going back to that first experience we asked June if the events of that night felt physically real. "Oh yes, yes, it was real," she replied. What did she think happened to her? "I don't know. I think they examined me, but I don't know what they did. I know when he put his hand on my head, I felt very calm." Taking her back to the room inside the craft, we asked if June could describe any of the other people she said she had seen sitting in the seats around the room. "I remember seeing a nurse sitting there and I remember an airman but there were four or five people in all," she said. "They were human beings, yes. They were just sitting there in a daze. They didn't speak to me at all. "The ones in the nurse's uniform and the RAF uniform stood out."

How had that event in the summer of 1956 affected her life?" "I believe in UFOs," said June. "I believe there's somewhere they're coming from, where I don't know. I never even thought about UFOs in those days. I don't think there were any then, were there?" In the days after her encounter June became ill. Lethargy and nausea seemed to make her life a misery, so she decided to see a doctor. "I discovered I was pregnant," she said. "The whole pregnancy was a nightmare too. I felt terrible throughout and after giving birth I lost a lot of weight and continued to feel ill for some time. "I used to think why me? I didn't know anyone else had been aboard a UFO." It was nine months after her meeting with the strangers in the field that June gave birth to her daughter. She often jokes:" I don't know whether I was pregnant then or whether they impregnated me. "My daughter says she always knew she didn't belong to this earth."

When Clive Potter and I interviewed Mrs. Rice (full transcript on file) I can confirm that this was no dotty old lady telling tall tales. She was vague at times but at no time did she appear to be filling in the vague parts of her narrative. I have no doubt that this was a genuine experience. What lies behind the experience is of course a different matter. Although Mrs. Rice didn't see a UFO on the ground, I have included it here to give a further example of what I have been trying to point out, tat is the 'high strangeness' factor. Mrs. Rice' account has all the hallmarks. As far as I am aware she is the first person in the UK to claim that she saw other human beings on board the UFO. The beings she witnessed were typical of other similar accounts in the 1950's, tall with white hair and beautiful blue eyes. What some might find to be a surprise is that up unto she heard the radio show she was of the opinion that she was the only person in the world that this had happened to. I had the feeling that when talking to her this was a momentous part of her life. I can't be sure, but I felt she was relieved to know that others had experienced the very same thing. Little did she know.

Next on my list of UFO landings is a controversial one. It involves a member of the British aristocracy. That person is the late Lord Mountbatten. He was not directly involved; instead, it was a member of his staff at his estate Broadlands in Hampshire.

Mrs. June Rice (photo copyright the author)

Frederick Briggs,
Broadlands
Hampshire
England
February 25, 1955

The late Earl Mountbatten, Prince Philip's uncle, who served as Supreme Allied Commander in Southeast Asia during World War II, also held a deep interest in the UFO topic. Louis Mountbatten had allegedly seen UFOs up close. The encounter goes like this.

On February 25th, 1955, Frederick Briggs, a retired Sergeant from the British Army, was working as a maintenance man at Broadlands, the Hampshire home of Mountbatten. Briggs was either riding or wheeling his bicycle in the grounds covered in a light dusting of snow, when he reportedly saw a large craft that looked like a child's top hovering over a field. He saw a column descend from the middle of the object with what appeared to be a small (5' 6") fair haired, humanoid wearing overalls and a helmet. On reaching close ground level the humanoid noticed Briggs observing his descent. Briggs was paralysed by a strange light beam whilst the humanoid retreated back into the craft.

As he arrived at the house, Mountbatten's chauffeur noted Briggs, looked noticeably shocked. Being a good friend Briggs confided his amazing story to the chauffeur who concluded "You must tell the boss." After some deliberation Briggs relented and met with his employer. Mountbatten produced a number of UFO photographs and asked Briggs if he could identify the craft he'd seen. Briggs recalls the Earl saying to him "we know about these things and are very interested in them".

They then went to site where a perfect circle of snow had melted in the ground underneath where the craft had been hovering. There were also markings in the snow where Briggs had slipped with his bike. Mountbatten took Briggs back to the house and asked him to write out a statement which both men signed along with a drawing of the craft by Briggs' (reproduced below).

Mountbatten states in his report that he personally interviewed Mr. Briggs. He reported that Briggs "…did not give the impression of being the sort of man who would be subject to hallucinations, or would in any way invent such a story……I have personally investigated the above claim by Mr Briggs, and I believe it to be true and correct "
Signed: Mountbatten of Burma

The story was almost printed by the Sunday Graphic newspaper but pulled at the last moment when the editor changed his mind so as not to embarrass the Mountbatten family.

However, this was not the end of the tale. In a discussion with UFO researcher and author Desmond Leslie something stranger happened to Briggs on the following day. Briggs was cycling to work up the same road to Broadlands when he encountered the blue uniformed humanoid, standing in the middle of the road, ahead of him. He stopped, shook the hand of the humanoid, he winced and explained, telepathically, that his race was not as strong as humans. Briggs was then invited into the spacecraft and sat down alone in a small compartment with a triangular window. He was then allegedly transported to his chosen destination of the Pyramids of Giza in Egypt. Briggs recalled the flight took all of about 10 minutes and he could see both above and the sides of the pyramid from the window. This somewhat confused him along with the whole experience only lasting around 30 minutes at most. Before he was returned Briggs stated the alien said: "If Lord Mountbatten met us he could change the world."

A rather bizarre statement when had they really wanted to contact the Earl they almost certainly could have done. It is odd that Mountbatten never admitted to seeing the craft or the humanoid(s) Briggs encountered on his grounds. Subsequently when Mountbatten was later told this second tale via a letter from Desmond Leslie to the Queen's Private Secretary, he dismissed it all as nonsense.

There is little more I can do with this incident as it is very well known. There are those researchers who dismiss it. In a recent discussion with UFO research Dr. David Clarke of Hallam University, Sheffield, he had interviewed a number of those at Broadlands who dismissed the story completely stating that they believed Mr. Briggs was just looking for an excuse to get the afternoon off of work.

Personally, I can think of better excuses to get an afternoon off work and I'm sure you can as well. True or false it still does have all the hallmarks of a 'high strangeness' incident.

The attached statement was dictated by Mr. Briggs to Mrs. Travis on the morning of the 23rd February 1955 at my request.

My own electrician, Heath, reported his conversation and I subsequently interviewed Mr. Briggs, with my wife and younger daughter, and as a result of his account, Heath and I accompanied him to the place from which he saw the Flying Saucer.

We followed the marks of his bicycle in the snow very easily, and exactly at the spot which he described the tracks came to an end, and foot marks appeared beside it. Next to the foot marks there were the marks of a body having fallen in the snow, and then the marks of a bicycle having been picked up again, there being a clear gap of 3ft. between where the front wheel marks originally ended and then started again. The rear wheel marks were continuous but blurred. From then on the bicycle tracks led back to the drive.

The bicycle tracks absolutely confirm Mr. Briggs' story, so far as his own movements are concerned.

He, Heath and I searched the area over the spot where the Flying Saucer was estimated to have been, but candidly we could see no unusual signs.

The snow at the bottom of the meadow had melted much more than that at the top, and it would have been difficult to see any marks.

This statement has been dictated in the presence of Heath and Mr. Briggs, and Heath and I have carefully read Mr. Briggs' statement, and we both attest that this is the exact story which he told us.

Mr. Briggs was still dazed when I first saw him, and was worried that no one would believe his story. Indeed, he made a point of saying that he had never believed in Flying Saucer stories before, and had been absolutely amazed at what he had seen.

He did not give me the impression of being the sort of man who would be subject to hallucinations, or would in any way invent such a story. I am sure from the sincere way he gave his account that he, himself, is completely convinced of the truth of his own statement.

He has offered to swear to the truth of this statement on oath on the Bible if needed, but I saw no point in asking him to do this.

I confirm that I have read and agree with the above statement.

Part one of Frederick Briggs handwritten statement

Statement by Frederick S. Briggs, 8, Chambers Avenue, Romsey, Hants.

I am at present employed at Broadlands as a bricklayer and was cycling to my work from Romsey on the morning of Wednesday, the 23rd February 1955. When I was about half way between the Palmerston or Romsey Lodge and the house, just by where the drive forks off to the Middlebridge Lodge, I suddenly saw an object hovering stationary over the field between the end of the gardens and Middlebridge drive, and just on the house side of the little stream.

The object was shaped like a child's huge humming-top and half way between 20ft. or 30ft. in diameter.

Its colour was like dull aluminium, rather like a kitchen saucepan. It was shaped like the sketch which I have endeavoured to make, and had portholes all round the middle, rather like a steamer has.

The time was just after 8.30 a.m. with an overcast sky and light snow on the ground.

I turned off the drive at the fork and rode over the grass for rather less than 100 yards. I then dismounted, and holding my bicycle in my right hand, watched.

While I was watching a column, about the thickness of a man, descended from the centre of the Saucer and I suddenly noticed on it, what appeared to be a man, presumably standing on a small platform on the end. He did not appear to be holding on to anything. He seemed to be dressed in a dark suit of overalls, and was wearing a close fitting hat or helmet.

At the time the Saucer was certainly less than 100 yards from me, and not more than 60ft. over the level where I was standing, although the meadow has a steep bank at this point, so that the Saucer would have been about 80ft. over the lower level of the meadow.

As I stood there watching, I suddenly saw a curious light come on in one of the portholes. It was a bluish light, rather like a mercury vapour light. Although it was quite bright, it did not appear to be directed straight at me, nor did it dazzle me, but simultaneously with the light coming on I suddenly seemed to be pushed over, and I fell down in the snow with my bicycle on top of me. What is more, I could not get up again. Although the bicycle only weighs a few lbs. it seemed as though an unseen force was holding me down.

Whilst lying on the ground I could see the tube withdrawn quickly into the Saucer, which then rose vertically, quite as fast as the fastest Jet aircraft I have seen, or faster.

There had been no noise whatever until the Saucer started to move, and even then the noise was no louder than that of an ordinary small rocket let off by a child on Guy Fawkes Night.

It disappeared out of sight into the clouds almost instantaneously, and as it went, I found myself able to get up. Although I seemed to be lying a long time on the ground I do not suppose, in reality, it was more than a few seconds.

Part two of Frederick Briggs handwritten statement

2.

I felt rather dizzy, as though I had received a near knockout blow on the point of the chin, but of course there was no physical hurt of any sort, merely a feeling of dizziness.

I picked up my bicycle, mounted it and rode straight on to Broadlands where I met Heath standing by the garage.

I was feeling very shaky and felt I must regain my confidence by discussing what I had seen. I said to him: "Look, Ron, have you known me long enough to know that I am sane and sober at this hour of the morning?" He laughed and made some remark like, "Well, of course." Then I told him what I had seen.

Heath and I went back along the road where I showed him the tracks of my bicycle. I then went back to work, where I saw my foreman, Mr. Hudson, and told him what I had seen.

Frederick S. Briggs

Part three of Frederick Briggs handwritten statement

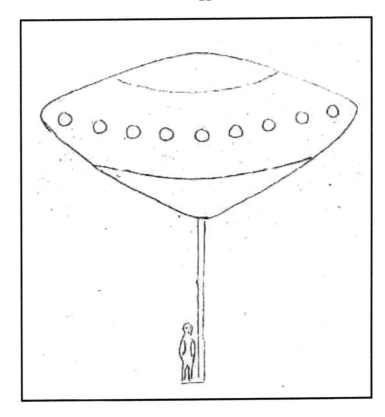

Drawing of the UFO and occupant by Frederick Briggs

It is rare that several witnesses that are unrelated to each other actually observe the same thing. The following UFO landing account was one such incident. The main witness is a Mrs. Margaret Fry. I have personally met Mrs. Fry on several occasions and discussed this incident with her.

Margaret Fry
Bexley
Kent
England
July 17, 1955

It was July 17, 1955, when Margaret Fry spotted the object as she was making her way to her GP's surgery in King Harold's Way from her home in Hythe Avenue. Both she Dr Thukarta, and around a dozen children playing in the street, saw the strange craft. Mrs Fry described it as saucer shaped with a "blue/silver/grey/pewter texture, yet none of those colours."

She said it had three spheres set into its base, one of which "flopped out", landing on the ground at the junction of nearby Ashbourne and Whitfield roads. The children went over for a closer look before it rose into the sky and disappeared from view after a few minutes. The News Shopper newspaper ran an appeal in 2002 for any of the children to come forward.

Rodney Maynard, who was in his 60s and living in Belvedere, remembered the incident vividly. He was 15 at the time and working as a labourer on the building site in nearby Streamway. Mr Maynard said: "We were on our lunch break when we heard something was happening in King Harold's Way. So, we went up there to have a look. "This thing had landed in the road." He added: "It took up the whole width of the road and overlapped onto the pavements. It wasn't on the ground. It had about eight massive suckers. The centre was still, but the outer rim was spinning slowly, and it had white lights flashing, like a camera flash." He said there were about 30 people watching it and they could hear it humming. Mr Maynard recalled: "It had what looked like windows, but the glass was concave and moulded together so you could not see in. "A couple of us went forward to try and touch it, and it began to spin faster." He said the craft then lifted slowly, tilting lightly and hovered above their heads. Then it moved slowly until it was over Bedonwell Primary School, where it hovered again for about a minute. Mr Maynard said: "It shot up into the sky and disappeared." He says his brother, who was 16 at the time, also saw it. Mr Maynard says the craft was "black, sleek and streamlined, with a surface like polished metal." He added: "It was very fine and beautiful. It wasn't a prank." Mr Maynard said he had never forgotten the experience but did not talk about it because "people would think you were barmy". He said he and his friends used to talk about it among themselves, "but our mums kept telling us we had not seen anything". Mrs Fry, now in her late 80s, now lives in Abergele in north Wales. She relives the experience in her book entitled 'Who Are They?' and gives details of other UFO sightings in the Bexley and Kent areas.

I have met Margaret Fry on several occasions both at UFO conferences and at her home in North Wales.

It may well be that this UFO landing led to her lifelong interest in UFO research and investigation. Mrs. Fry became an active UFO investigator and still to this day has an avid interest in the subject.

Margaret Fry on the scene of her UFO landing encounter (photo courtesy of John Hanson)

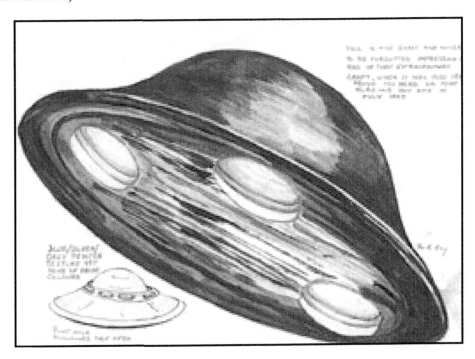

Artist impression of the UFO seen by Margaret Fry

The 1950's saw yet more landing accounts in the UK. There seemed to be no let up. We have to remember that there was no digital network, no computers or mobile phones and no home computers in the 1950's unlike today's modern UK. The main way that news spread was in the newspapers or on TV. It therefore made it far more difficult then than now to obtain information on any subject and UFOs were not an exception. It therefore made it much more difficult for anyone to confabulate or simply lie about these close encounters.

UFO landing accounts were still very rarely reported but they were as we see with this next account. The following account is courtesy of John Hanson and Haunted Skies.

Nigel Frapple
Wincanton
Somerset
England
May 20, 1954

Nigel Frapple was walking home from a dance in Wincanton in Somerset at around 2.00 am. The date was 20th march, 1954 and this was a regular journey for Mr. Frapple. While walking home he noticed an orange glow low down in the sky, which he at first thought was a farmhouse or a house on fire. Being curious he stopped near a farm gate just near Redlynch crossroads and he crouched down to take a closer look at this peculiar sight.

"I was curious to see this dome-shaped object hovering approximately 490 feet off the ground in one of the nearby fields just a few hundred yards away. It had a cockpit in the centre wit three portholes and was glowing with violet light. The outside of the 'craft' consisted of what looked like glass panelling, gun-metal grey in colour. At one end I could see an orange 'ball', cascading with light, like the disco lights you now see. The curious thing was that it didn't appear to be attached to anything, just suspended in the air. Inside the cockpit were shadowy movements indicating the presence of something or someone, moving behind the light, spilling out of the portholes. After five minutes or so, it moved as if it sensed me watching it. I stood up and took a couple of steps forward. To my surprise it tiled and shot across the sky. When I arrived home in an extremely agitated state and told my brother what had happened, and later reported the incident to the police at Bruton, 'all hell then let loose'. I was besieged by reporters from local and national newspapers and the BBC, who asked me to show them the field. When we arrived there, we saw a blackened circle in the grass which was still there 12 months later. I was bombarded with questions; somebody even asked me if I was drunk at the time! I told them that I had been drinking but had only consumed a couple of pints over the evening."

Mr. Frapple made his own enquiries in the area and spoke to Mr. Henry Toogood who lived in a cottage lower down the hill from where he had seen the UFO. Mr. Toogood confirmed to also seeing the 'craft' on the same evening but from underneath: "It looked like a huge dinner plate with something resembling metal balls set into the underside." About a week later Mr. Frapple received a visit from two smartly dressed men.

"They didn't show any ID but said they were from London. One of them was in his late fifties and wore a grey suit and he did all the talking. His companion was dressed in a dark pinstripe suit and a bowler hat. He never said a word to me but kept his horrible 'black eyes' focussed on me in a most disconcerting was after I told them what had happened. Presuming they were from the Air Ministry, or some other branch of the government, the elder of the two said, 'If you persist in telling these silly stories we'll have to take you somewhere where you can't tell them anymore.' They say time is a great healer and that as you get older you forget many things in life. My recollection of what those two said to me will forever remain crystal clear in my memory."

Nigel Frapple (photo courtesy John Hanson)

As a result of the newspaper publicity a Mrs. Doreen Heffer from Five Oaks, Shobley, Ringwood in Hampshire, wrote to the Western Gazette newspaper on June 4th, 1954:
"Sir, with reference to your account of the 'Mystery in the Air', I should like to confirm that I saw exactly the same thing here, although not at such close range, about 11 o'clock at night. At first a huge glow appeared, which I thought must be a forest fire. When it topped the crest of a hill, I could see it was something moving forward. I thought a huge plane was on fire and expected something to drop off, but as it moved along, perfectly evenly on a straight course and did not lose height in any way, it left me baffled.

It was exactly as your Somerset reader described-a yellow/orange glow, with a deeper shade which I imagine was the think itself. Behind it, apparently following, was a sort of tall 'thing' of orange fire colour moving perfectly evenly, not very fast and travelling towards Ringwood."

Although the witness Me. Frapple said that the UFO was some 40 feet above the ground I have classed it as a UFO landing case because of the blackened circle discovered at the location a day later. Sadly, there are no photographs to support this, or at least none that I am aware of. And who were the two mystery men that paid Mr. Frapple a visit? Where they really men from the Ministry? If they were would they really make such a statement to Mr. Frapple? It sounds ludicrous to some especially as the account of Mr. Frapple's had already had quite a lot of coverage in the news media. Could they have instead been two flying saucer enthusiasts who simply wanted to add a bit of spice to the story? Who knows? It is however another good example of the types of encounter cases that have a degree of 'high strangeness' about them.

Another brief account of a peculiar landing case this time comes from Kent:

Harold Carpenter
Dover
Kent
England
July 1954

Sometime in July 1954, after hearing a strange, deep, loud humming noise which lasted for two or three minutes over several weeks, Dover resident Harold Carpenter had had enough and decided to investigate. He set off into a wooded area known by local residents as 'Sunny-Calvert'. He was determined to find the source of this humming noise once and for all.

With the humming noise still audible apparently emanating from the south-west, Harold Carpenter climbed down a deep slope where the sound seemed to be coming from and peered down. He was astonished to see a strange grey device resembling a mushroom without a stem hovering about eight to ten feet off the ground.

After making his way to a vantage point up among the trees, he was able to see the underside of the 'craft' which was definitely hovering above the ground. Harold estimated the object to be approximately twenty feet in diameter across the base which housed what looked like a lip on the inside bottom part of this object.

Even more astonishing was the sight of up to five 'peculiar-looking beings' gathered underneath the 'craft' on the ground below. These 'beings' were about four to five feet tall and were carrying what looked like 'pound jam-jars', with a handle in one hand and an implement resembling a pair of tweezers in the other. The 'beings' used these to pick up twigs and leaves before placing them in the clear jars. They wandered around picking various samples while keeping close to the 'craft' which hovered silently above them, the humming sound having now ceased. All of the 'beings' wore the same one-piece grey, flexible-looking suits, which stretched over their feet and covered their heads, much like a balaclava, leaving their faces exposed allowing Harold to: "See they were human in appearance, totally devoid of expression and normal human-like eyes, but the facial resemblance to humans ended with a snout-like nose resembling that of a pig. Their mouths were similar to humans and so were their hands until I noticed they didn't appear to have thumbs. No ears could be seen owing to the nature of the one-piece suit, which hid them from view".

While taking in all this detail Harold suddenly realised, he was only within ten feet of the 'craft'. At this point on of the 'beings' suddenly looked up with the same expressionless face and stared directly at him.

Without so much as a sound or movement, it somehow, in some way, alerted the others to Harold's presence, for all suddenly stopped what they were doing and slowly began to retreat to the 'craft' which by now had descended, hovering barely two feet off of the ground.

One by one the 'beings' disappeared underneath the 'craft' by means of its 'lip'. The 'craft' then began to rise, at which point Harold saw one of the 'beings' climb through a type of 'gate', housed o the inside of the 'lip', which then closed. The 'craft' slowly continued to climb, moving slightly to one side, towards a clearing in the trees.

It gradually gained altitude and speed before suddenly emitting a flash of light and departing at an incredible speed. (Source, Chris Rolfe, UFOMEK).

You must admit that this is truly a bizarre case. It never ceases to amaze me how many different descriptions there are of both the UFO and the 'beings' associated with them. Some may argue that the above case is not a landing account as it apparently never touched the ground, but as it was reported as bring just two feet above the ground that is close enough for me.

There are debunkers out there that will dismiss such cases as they take place in isolated locations but what would they say if one such incident was reported to have taken place on an abandoned Royal Air Force base runway? Well, the following account details just such an event.

Mrs. Jessie Roestenburg
Stafford
Staffordshire
England
October 21, 1954

Extracts from a newspaper interview: 'In 1954, a Ranton woman, near Stafford, told the Express & Star that she and her two children had been terrified by a flying saucer, carrying 'two long-haired human-like creatures'.

The machine landed in the garden, she stated "when she heard a noise like a crashing aircraft, yesterday, Mrs. Jessie Roestenburg, of isolated Vicarage Farm, ran out into the garden.

She found her two children lying prostrate and terrified. Above the children was a huge, saucer-like object with a dome, the front part of which was transparent, she stated. Staring at the children from the machine were two 'unsmiling, human-like creatures, with long faces and long hair'.

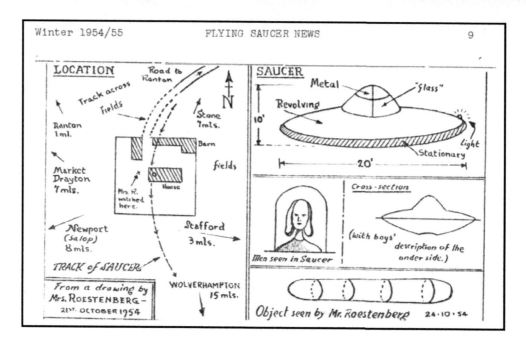

Map and drawing of what Mrs. Roestenburg saw

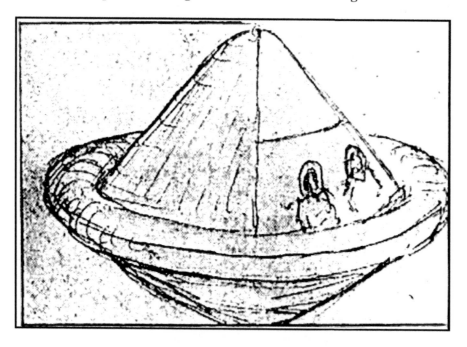

Mrs. Roestenburg's drawing of what she saw

She told our reporter that she ran to the back of the house in fright. The objected moved over the house, hovered for about 15 seconds, and then shot off at high speed. "The boys were so terrified that they would not go out again last night," she said. "The dog was no-where to be seen. I think it must have bolted." Incredibly, "in June of this year, the vicar of nearby Seighford, the Rev Cedric Wright, also reported seeing a flying saucer over the vicarage at about midnight." End quotes.

Midland woman says flying saucer men terrified her

A RANTON, near Stafford, woman today told the "Express and Star" that she and her two children had been terrified by a flying saucer, carrying "two long-haired, human-like creatures in tight-fitting jerseys."

The machine landed in the garden, she stated.

When she heard a noise like a crashing aircraft, yesterday, Mrs. Jessie Roestenburg, of isolated Vicarage Farm, Ranton, ran out into the garden. She found her two children lying prostrate and terrified.

The next house to Vicarage Farm is about two miles away.

Above the children was a huge, saucer-like object with a dome, the front part of which was transparent, stated Mrs. Roestenburg.

Staring at the children from the machine were two "unsmiling, human-like creatures, with long faces and long hair."

Mrs. Roestenburg told our reporter that she ran to the back of the house in fright. The object then moved over the house, hovered there for about 15 seconds, and then shot off at high speed.

In June of this year, the vicar of nearby Seighford, the Rev. Cedric Wright, reported seeing a flying saucer over the vicarage at about midnight.

He said it was like a "giant illuminated spider," and estimated it to be about 25ft. in diameter.

Today, Mr. Wright said: "I was not lucky enough to get such a close up view, as was Mrs. Roestenburg.

"This seems much more exciting and seems to confirm very much the sort of thing that I saw.

"It seems to me that these things are in the habit of frequenting our district. It cannot have been more than a couple of miles away from where I saw mine."

When her husband, an architect's assistant employed by Staffordshire

Mrs. Roestenburg, with her two sons keeping close beside her, points to the place where, she says, she saw the flying saucer hovering near her home.

This is a sketch, made today by Mrs. Roestenburg, of the strange object that she states she saw in her garden. It appeared to be of "a dull silver metal," and the outer rim seemed to be revolving

Above: Incomplete newspaper cutting from 1959

Above: An artist's rendition of the beings Jessie saw was later created -and here is the witness herself holding the picture up during an interview (copyright John Hanson)

Researcher Gavin Gibbons wrote that one October evening in 1954, a Dutchman living in England named Tony Roestenberg returned home to find his wife, Jessie, "in a terrified state." According to Jessie: earlier that day nothing less than a flying saucer hovered over their isolated farmhouse in Ranton. In addition, Jessie could see peering down from the craft two very "Nordic"-like men that could have stepped right out of the pages of the controversial Desmond Leslie-George Adamski tome, Flying Saucers Have Landed.

Their foreheads were high, their hair was long and fair, and they seemed to have 'pitiful' looks on their faces. The strange craft reportedly circled the family's home twice, before streaking away. Curiously, on the following Sunday, Tony Roestenberg had a "hunch" that if he climbed on the roof of his house "he would see something unusual," which he most certainly did. It was a high-flying, cigar-shaped object that vanished into the clouds.

Gavin Gibbons, who investigated the case personally, stated: "When I visited the Roestenberg's house almost three weeks after the sighting…Jessie Roestenberg appeared.

She seemed highly strained and nervous and her husband, coming in later, was also very strained. It was evident that something most unusual had occurred." Source: 'The Coming of the Spaceships' by Gavin Gibbons – 1956.

John Hutchinson
Moneymore
Republic of Ireland
September 7, 1956

At around noon on September 7th, Mr and Mrs. Hutchinson were in their farmhouse when both noticed an object descending rapidly into a field some fifty yards away. The object fell into a small valley on the far side of a hedge and stream. It remained there completely motionless, so Mr. Hutchinson pulled on his boots and went to investigate. It was a very wet day so the witness took a detour round the lanes coming upon the object some ten minutes later. It still had not moved from its original position.

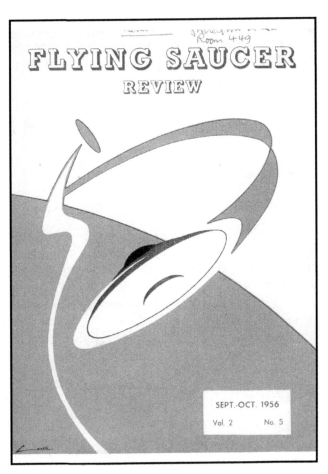

Mr. Hutchinson found the object sitting on a tuft of grass, the only dry bit in this muddy field and about six feet away from the stream. The UFO was an elongated, pointed sphere about three feet six inches on its major diameter and two feet at its minor diameter. It was red in colour and had a 'rubbery' appearance. There was a small red knob or point on top, and the bottom was gathered rather like the neck of a bag, but more regular. Round the middle were four thinnish irregular white stripes.

Mr. Hutchinson found the object sitting upright on this gathered base. Gingerly, he kicked it over and it promptly righted itself.

Then, seeing that it didn't move, and no Martians came out, he reached down and picked it up by the gathered base. The object felt like canvas on the outside with a slippery rubber inside. The moment he picked it up it began to spin. It first spun a few times in an anti-clockwise direction, then it spun in a clockwise direction. He carried this object to a point where he could climb through the hedge and cross the stream, intending to take it to his house as a souvenir. On the way he tried to turn it over (still holding it at arm's length) but was unable to do so. The object weighed somewhere around two pounds and as soon as Mr. Hutchinson put it down near the stream it shot off up into the clouds and was gone in a matter of seconds. The clouds were low and it was raining hard and the object was gone. The area was searched by Mr. Hutchinson and the local police, but nothing could be found.

Mr. Hutchinson was interviewed by Desmond Leslie, and he informed him that the spinning lasted for about three minutes and that he only put it down in order was so he could make a hole in the hedge to get through. Desmond Leslie quizzed the witness asking if he thought the object might have been a balloon. Mr. Hutchinson said he thought it might have been until it took off at such speed. He said "Frankly, I don't know what it was, but it was NOT a balloon. (Source: FSR, 1956, Sep-Oct, V 2, N 5 (1).

Mr. Venerables
Aveley
Essex
England
1956

The witness, Mr. Venerables was a teenager at the time of this event. He woke up at around 00:15 and 00:30 and saw an orangey-yellowing flashing light in the corner of the ceiling. He slipped out of bed and went to the window from which, not one hundred yards away, he could see lights of various colours rotating around a dark form. On top of this form was an orangey-yellowish light turning around rather like the light on a police car. Underneath it more lights of the same colour could be seen spinning in the opposite direction, and through these lights, horizontal oval windows in a line could be seen emitting a bright yellow-white luminescence. Inside these windows several 'people' dressed in 'frogmen suits' were casually strolling around continuing their work or whatever it was they were doing.

Behind the row of lights was another much wider circumference of colour coming from what could have been a rim-type base. This (from the position of the witness) looked as if flames were swirling around the circumference of the object at the sides, and where the flame should have continued around the front, was what was described as 'gas fire blue flames' spewing out towards the ground almost like a gas jet in appearance. Although no real shape could be discerned, due to the mass of intense coloured lights, the witness was sure that the object was either hemispherical or a rim-type base with a dome on top.

No noise was being emitted either. In order to get a better view, he opened the bedroom window but in doing so made a noise after which the object suddenly shot off into the sky at a tremendous speed, being seen as only a silver pencil line' moving away into the heavens. The whole episode had only lasted about two to three minutes.

The entities had been silhouetted against the intense yellow glow from inside the object. There appeared to be at least three or four of them and each appeared to be 'going about their business' in a leisurely manner. Their height and appearance was difficult to describe due to their distance from the witness but their heads seemed to have 'little or no hair 'and was in proportion with the rest of their body. The witness could not make out exactly what the 'frogmen' were doing but one appeared to be holding an 'instrument' of some kind. The object's size was uncertain but was described as 'considerable.'

No check was subsequently made for any traces on the ground. On the same night the witnesses mother got up in the early hours and as she glanced outside saw a red orb (through the living room window) which moved so close she thought it was going to hit the house.

Amazed and frightened she fetched her husband, but by the time they returned to the living room the object had gone.

British UFO Research Association

1956 " Frogmen." See Report-Extra !

bufora journal

Vol 8 No I   Jan/Feb 1979

John Payne
RAF Winkleigh
Devon
England
May 1957

RAF Winkleigh lies twenty-three miles from Exeter in Devon. In early May 1957, John Payne, a milk tanker driver for Wincanton Transport of Yeovil was driving from Weston-Super-Mare to Torrington in Devon. It was a regular journey when he decided to pull into the abandoned airfield to have a drink of coffee and take a short break just before sunrise.

"On the morning in question it was a fine, dry day with good visibility. I pulled onto the perimeter track at about 4.50am at RAF Winkleigh Aerodrome in North Devon to have a drink. After a few minutes I noticed what appeared to be a submarine at the end of the runway. My first thoughts were, how did it get up there? Also, it looked very new. I watched for some minutes and then thought I would take a closer look and got out of the cab and walked towards it.

After getting within some 200 yards of it I found it impossible to get any closer. It was like walking into sunshine. This was the very first intimation of anything out of the ordinary. It then went straight up, like an elevator, for about 1,200 feet, and it headed towards the North Devon coast. The speed was terrific. There were no windows, exhaust, movement, that I could see. Possibly the tail fins were just a little more fluorescent when in motion. No 'green men'-nothing. Please, I am not a crank-just a lorry driver. I make no claims as to its identity. More information on this account came via Mr. Ronald Toft the editor of Pegasus, the magazine of the Surrey Investigation Group on Aerial Phenomena. Mr. Toft stated that Mt Payne had provided further details:

"John (Payne) wrote of a 'force field' which seemed to completely surround the object. When he approached to within 90 yards away, it was like walking into an invisible air cushion that you could actually lean on. After the object took off, Payne (was able to walk without any difficulties) discovered a feint black powdered circle on the ground, approximately 50 feet in diameter, like black carbon in appearance, which he didn't touch. "

In communication with Mr. Toft John Payne wrote:

"My personal feelings were one of intense relief at its departure. Mentally, it felt as if a weight had been lifted from me but physically, I felt no pain, shock, tingling, loss of memory, or any other ill effects, but discovered when I arrived at the Torrington factory, that my watch was 20 minutes slow. I believe that many other people also witnessed the passage of this object through the air and saw one other person on the runway who didn't want to get involved, believing people would call him a crank and subject him to ridicule."

John Payne (photo courtesy John Hanson)

No strange 'beings' this time and could John Payne's report be the first to describe a 'force field' of some kind? It is fair to say yet again that the witness here got up close and personal with something truly bizarre and there is little chance that he could have misidentified a common object on a disused airfield. An object that Mr. Payne described as looking like a 'submarine'. In UFO-lore the 1950's was famous for its contactees, people who claimed to have met aliens and were taken in a spaceship to visit their home planet. The most famous of these cases comes from the USA with a gentleman by the name of George Adamski. Most UFO researchers today dismiss Adamski and his claims but by no means do all. The UK did however have its own contactees one of which we will look at here.

James Cook
Runcorn
Cheshire
England
September 7, 1957

This encounter is best described as a typical contactee account from the 1950's. It involves James Cook from Runcorn in Cheshire. Mr. Cook described a close encounter with the occupants of a 'flying saucer' which landed at 2.15am on Frodsham Hill, after receiving 'telepathic' messages at 2.00am on September 7th, 1957. Mr. Cook was interviewed by UFO researcher Thelma Roberts from St Albans. Mr. Cook told his story thus:

"I was instructed to jump onto the rail leading into the spacecraft from the ground-not to step onto it, or I would be hurt. After putting on a tight-fitting suit I found on board the spacecraft, I was directed to descend from the ship into a larger one below, where I was met by twenty people, tall by Earth standards, who didn't speak but made gestures, placing their left hands over their eyes and they right hands over their hearts.

They had no problem reading my mind. I was taken to a planet called 'ZOMDIC', which had a road network-a relic of a bygone age.

The inhabitants used small ships, which moved over the ground, operated by the pilot striking what looked like metal strips protruding like organ stops, producing musical notes.

While in flight, the ship is controlled by a small black ball on which the pilot's left hand rested. I was taken to meet one of the wise men on the planet was told; 'Inhabitants of your planet will upset the balance if they persist in using force instead of harmony. Warn them of the danger, but they won't listen to me or anyone."

Mr. Cook was returned home back to planet Earth. In the process he had to remove the tight-fitting suit with a razor blade in his pocket and arrived home at 10.50pm on Sunday, September 8th, to be met by his mother and four friends – Mr. and Mrs. Hocknell, Mr Thomas and Mrs. King.

Mr. Cook showed them a burn on his hand, which had been caused by him forgetting to let go of the rail on the stairs leading off of the UFO and touching the ground with his feet. After his contact on Frodsham Hill, James Cook started a UFO cult - the Church of Aquarius.

It became so popular a second 'church' was opened where James Cook 'channelled' information from the elders of 'ZOMDIC' for ten years before he eventually disappeared from public view in 1969.

What happened to James Cook, his churches and parishioners are unknown from then on. UFO researcher Thelma Roberts believes, from her interviews with James Cook, that he was a sincere and kind man, devoid of vanity and with a good sense of humour. According to Thelma Roberts:

"There was no question of any fabrication at all. He (James Cook) firmly believed what he experienced did actually happen. I seem to remember speaking with the other people, who witnessed his return home. One of them confirmed that he had a burn mark on his hands."

The encounter of James Cook does indeed have all of the hallmarks of a typical contactee case of the 1950's. You must admit that his account does sound more like science fiction than science fact.

The small ships on the planet 'ZOMDIC' even gave off musical notes when their operating mechanism was used, and the pilots hit small metal strips. We may well snigger, but did not movie director Steven Spielberg have his UFOs emit musical notes as a way of communication in the film Close Encounters of the Third Kind?

Thelma Roberts (right) photo courtesy John Hanson

Stratford-upon-Avon is known world-wide as the birthplace of William Shakespeare, and it is visited by millions of tourists ever year. In 1959 in was the scene of another drama the likes of which Shakespeare could only dream of.

Two un-named Army Reserves
Tarland
Scotland
November 1958

During a Territorial Army (Army Reserves) weekend exercise a few miles outside of the village of Tarland (about 60 miles from Aberdeen in Scotland), two your men were left guarding a small hilltop for several hours. At sunrise they heard a strange gurgling sound coming from some nearby trees. Both men went to investigate, and they came across two large figures stumbling towards them. These figures were very tall, some 7-8 feet, and the gurgling noise was apparently the sound of them both talking to each other. They were dressed in a very peculiar way, and they seemed to have difficulty in walking across the rough ground. The two men turned around and ran away down the hillside, taking refuge in a small hut. As they were running towards the hut, they heard a swishing noise behind them and, tuning around, they saw a huge, brilliant disc-shaped object coming down the road, only a few feet off the ground. The object swooped up and over their heads pulsating and leaving a shower of sparks in its wake. (Source: Janet Bord- FSR 1972 V 18 N 5).

Leonard Hewins
Stratford-upon-Avon
Warwickshire
England
January 1959

In January 1959, Leonard Hewins, employed by Stratford-upon-Avon council, was walking home towards the car park in Arden Street, to collect his bicycle at 5.15pm, when he noticed a fiery red object about the size of the setting sun, approaching his position from out of the dark sky.

"It then came to a stop above the ground, about a hundred yards away from where I was stood, next to the fence of a nearby tennis court. As the glare dimmed, I was able to make out what looked like three human figures inside a blue haze, twelve feet or so off of the ground. In a clumsy, bulky, movement, one of the figures lifted itself and sat down again, joined by a fourth occupant-now seated two behind each other, in what looked like an invisible craft. At this stage I became very frightened and found I was unable to move any of my limbs. The object then rose swiftly upwards, increasing in luminosity to that when first seen, leaving a trail of multi-coloured stars, accompanied by the sound of rushing water."

A short account here at the end of the 1950's. I have included it as it was a mere few feet off the ground, and it was entirely different from the account of James Cook and his visit to the planet 'ZOMDIC'. I have, however, included it to give an example of the type of landing accounts that were being reported in the UK in the 1950's. We have no 'telepathic' messages here and no invisible force-field; instead, we have an invisible craft. How many such accounts are reported today? None would be my guess. What not? You might ask. Well. That is a question that I cannot yet answer. What this chapter does how is that these landing accounts are full of 'high strangeness' and it will be interesting to see how things progress when we look at the 1960's.

******

CHAPTER THREE

UFO LANDINGS IN THE SWINGING SIXTIES

The 1960's are universally known as the swinging sixties. Britain had at last shrugged of the baggage from the Second World War and British music, fashion and culture ruled the roost. The Beatles ruled the pop music world, and the England football team won the world cup in 1966. Things were definitely looking up in Britain in the 1960's and when it comes to high strangeness and UFO landings in the swinging sixties they certainly had not disappeared.

Mr. Ronald Wildman
Dunstable
Bedfordshire
England
February 9, 1962

Mr. Ronald Wildman wrote to the UK magazine Flying Saucer Review (FSR) to inform them of his own encounter in 1962. The witness lived in Luton, Bedfordshire and was delivering a brand-new Vauxhall car on February 9th. This is what he has to tell the FSR: "I left home at 3.00 am to proceed to Swansea with a new estate car from the factory. I had driven through Dunstable and was approaching the cross-roads at the end of the deserted Irvinghoe road at Aston Clinton and the time was now around 3.30 am. Then I saw something – it was oval-shaped with black and white marks at regular intervals around it, which could have been portholes or air vents.

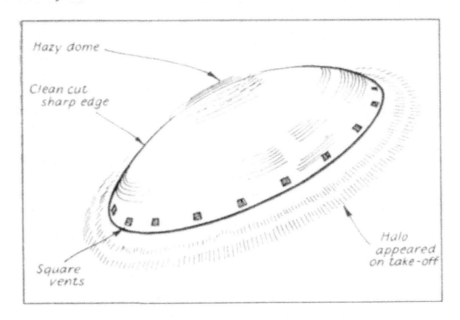

UFO as witnessed by Mr. Ronald Wildman (Courtesy FSR)

It was about twenty to thirty feet above the ground and at least forty feet wide which in my estimation was fantastic. As soon as I came within twenty yards of it the power of my car changed, it dropped right down to twenty mile per hour. I changed down into second (gear) and put my foot flat on the accelerator-nothing happened. I had my headlights full on and although the engine lost revs, the lights did not fade. The object, which was silent kept ahead of me by approximately twenty feet to two hundred yards, then started to come lower-it continued like this till it came to the end of the stretch (landed?)-then a white haze appeared around it, like a halo around the moon. It veered off to the right at a terrific speed and vanished as it did, so it brushed particles of frost from the tree tops on to my windscreen.

It was definitely a solid object because the reflection of my headlights was thrown back from it." In his letter Mr. Wildman makes the point that prior to this experience he was a sceptic on such matters, "but this encounter of mine has completely changed my outlook." On behalf of the FSR three investigators went to interview the witness.

He was found to be an honest, reliable man who had no prior interest in this subject. Enquiries were made locally but no other witnesses to these events were uncovered. Mr. Wildman had also reported this event to the local police and from them in went to the Air Ministry (now the Ministry of Defence). (Source: FSR, 1962, Mar-Apr, V 8, N 2 (1). UK author and UFO researcher Nick Redfern sound more information on this case in the released Air Ministry UFO files. In an article he wrote for Mysterious Universe on April 23, 2019 he had this to say:

"Just five months after Betty and Barney Hill's late night encounter in September 1961, a similar incident occurred in the U.K. In this case, the witness was a man named Ronald Wildman. It was in the early hours of February 9, 1962, that Wildman had an extraordinary experience, one which led him to fully believe he had seen a UFO at very close quarters. So amazed, and even slightly unsettled, by what occurred, Wildman contacted the local police. It was via the police that the U.K.'s Air Ministry (today, called the Ministry of Defence) came to hear about the story. The press, who were tipped off by someone in the police, gave the story more than a bit of coverage, which led the U.K.'s UFO research community to descend on Wildman and pick his brains about what he saw, too.

Behind the scenes, the military was taking a very close watch of Wildman and his experience. That much can be proved: the old Air Ministry file on the man and his encounter has been released into the public domain and can be accessed in person at the National Archives, Kew, England. The Wildman file runs from 1962 to 1964 and is predominantly comprised of clippings taken from newspapers, from various issues of *Flying Saucer Review* magazine – which was a highly popular publication for UFO enthusiasts, particularly so in the 1960s and 1970s – and from other newsletters and journals on the issue of Flying Saucers. The file contains something else too, as you will now learn.

Exactly one week after the furore concerning Ronald Wildman's encounter calmed down, an employee of the British Royal Air Force's Provost and Security Services paid a quiet visit to the local police, to get all of the data they had in-hand. It should be noted that the P&SS was an elite arm of the Royal Air Force. Its employees typically got involved in the investigation of terrorist threats against the military.

They were experts in the fields of disinformation and espionage and are skilled in the domain of counterintelligence. That the Air Ministry felt it was important for Wildman's case to be investigated by the P&SS speaks volumes for its credibility. With that all said, let's take a look at the initial report prepared by P&SS officer Sergeant C.J. Perry. He wrote:

"At Aylesbury on 16th February 1962, at 1530 hrs. I visited the Civil Police and requested information on an alleged 'Flying Saucer' incident. I was afforded every facility by the Civil Police authorities and although no official report had been made, details of the incident were recorded in the Station Occurrence book. The details are as follows:

Mr. Ronald Wildman of Luton, a car collection driver, was travelling along the Aston Clinton Road at about 0330 hrs. on 9th February 1962 when he came upon an object like a hovercraft flying approximately 30 feet above the road surface.

As he approached, he was travelling at 40 mph but an unknown force slowed him down to 20 mph over a distance of 400 yards, then the object suddenly flew off. He described the object as being about 40 feet wide, oval in shape with a number of small portholes around the bottom edge. It emitted a fluorescent glow but was otherwise not illuminated.

Mr. Wildman reported the incident to a police patrol who notified the Duty Sergeant, Sergeant Schofield. A radio patrol car was dispatched to the area but no further trace of the 'Flying Saucer' was seen. It was the opinion of the local police that the report by Mr. Wildman was perfectly genuine, and the experience was not a figment of imagination. They saw that he was obviously shaken. I spoke to Sergeant Schofield and one of the Constables to whom the incident was reported. Both were convinced that Mr. Wildman was genuinely upset by his experience."

As interesting as the above report certainly is, a follow-up report from Sergeant Perry reveals something more. It's something that is presented only as a passing reference, but which – from the perspective of the story you are reading – is incredibly important. Following a return visit to see Sergeant Schofield, Sergeant Perry wrote in his report that the police had failed to mention one particular thing in the initial discussion.

At the time, the police didn't feel it was too important. Namely, that when he spoke with the police, Ronald Wildman was *"muddled about the time."* Regrettably, these four words are not expanded on, but as brief as they are, they suggest there was some degree of missing hours; that Wildman believed the timeframe of the encounter was very different to what it *really* was.

An interesting account that does have its own degree of high strangeness, on this occasion that being the effect on the car. Such cases have become known as 'vehicle interference' cases. It is highly unlikely that a brand-new car fresh from the factory would suffer such a loss of power on its way to being delivered.

Although the object may have briefly touched the ground it is not your typical UFO landing case either, however, I think there is enough to this case for it to be included in this book.

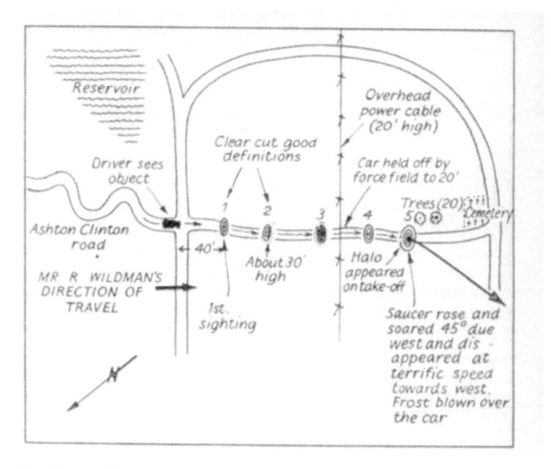

Sketch map of the area and key points of the encounter (Courtesy FSR)

Paula Mandham
Reigate
Surrey
England
August 1962

Paula Mandham was walking down a lance close to the main A25 road near Reigate in Surrey. She was accompanied by her friend Bruce. Paula described what they saw:

"It was getting dark at the time was around 8.45pm, when I noticed come colourful lights in a field, just a short distance away. 'Look, it's a fair', I shouted to Bruce. I ran along the lane and eventually reached a hedgerow which bordered the field. On the ground was what I can only describe as a very large 'flying saucer', with a flashing red light on its dome. Running down its sides were these flickering-coloured lights, like the ones you see at a fairground. It also had a single light which flickered around the widest part of its body. At this point out attention was caught by movement in the sky above us. When we looked up, we saw at least six other similar 'craft', shining gigantic spotlights downwards. I looked back into the field. The first 'flying saucer' was still there, now apparently a hundred feet above us, but a section of it, which I hadn't noticed, was now closing. I heard the sound of rushing air, and then it shot away so fast for the eyes to register it properly and it was gone.

When we arrived home, I thought it was about 9.30pm. Imagine our shock when we saw that it was now 3.30am!"

There is a hint here of things to come in the realms of UFO research. It is a puzzling aspect of such encounters simply known as 'missing time'. Paula Mandham was sure it would be around 9.30pm when they arrived home, but it was six hours later. What had happened to this period of 'missing time?"

This next case is a rather contentious one, but I have decided to feature it regardless. It involves two Royal Air Force trainees at RAF Cosford. You can make up your own mind once you've had the opportunity to digest the following information.

Robert Hirst and Mrs. Margaret McCuthcheon
Liverpool
Merseyside
England
May 1963

Thirteen-year-old Robert Hirst let out a yell as he looked through his kitchen window. There was a flying saucer in the back garden. His mother rushed to his side, and she too saw it. So reported the Daily Express newspaper on May 8th, 1963.

According to the press report Robert Hirst and his mum and reported the incident the day before to the local police. "People may laugh at us, but we definitely saw something that looked like a flying saucer" said thirty-four-year-old Mrs. Margaret McCutcheon of Kirby near Liverpool. "We were watching the television when the electricity went off and Bob (Robert) went to put a shilling in the meter. He shouted out, and when to him he pointed through the window. It was about sixteen feet in diameter and was hovering just above the garden-it to have two aerials and a red light fixed to it. There was a low buzz coming from the flying saucer, and the light kept flashing on and off." Added twice married Mrs. McCutcheon: "It stayed for nearly a minute and then went off over the rooftops. Robert, the eldest if five said: "I have seen pictures of flying saucers on the television and in books. It was just like one of them." Then Robert drew a picture of what it looked like: "It doesn't appear to be a police matter, so we are not concerned about the report." (Source: FSR, 1963, Jul-Aug, V 9, N 4 (1).

Drawing made by Robert Hirst (Courtesy FSR)

This is only a brief report and I know from my own experience that newspapers are not always the most accurate source of information. However, there seems enough high strangeness involved for the two witnesses to report the event to their local police. Not something you might think of doing if you were playing a prank of course but there is no hint of this in the newspaper article.

John Flaxton, Mervyn Hutchinson (and two others)
Sandling Park
Kent
England
November 16, 1963

In 1963, four British teens saw a UFO land in a nearby forest, but what would haunt them for the rest of their lives was the bizarre bat-like beast that apparently came out of it! On the chilly autumn evening of November 16, 1963, 17-year-old John Flaxton, 18-year-old Mervyn Hutchinson and two other youthful friends were walking home from a party on Sandling Road in the county of Kent — a region apparently rife with cryptozoological and paranormal activity — when they saw a silent, glowing, orb-like object descending from the heavens.

The unusual, self illuminated, ovoid object, which was described as being just a few meters in diameter, hovered above a field. It eventually made its way behind the trees and settled into the shadow infested foliage of the woods at Sandling Park. While the teenagers were still reeling from their astonishing sighting, something even more inconceivable would soon grab their attention. Moments after the extraordinary craft apparently landed behind the trees, the teens noticed a shaking in the brush and what emerged was one of the most unique "creatures" ever to be chronicled in ufology.

Later the four horrified eyewitnesses would explain that an erratic, shambling, quasi-humanoid figure emerged from the woods and waddled towards them. The beast apparently looked like a headless bat that was approximately 5-feet tall, with large, webbed feet and wings protruding from its back. In Hutchinson's own words: "It didn't seem to have any head. There were huge wings on its back... like bat wings." The group of friends, understandably overwhelmed with terror and adrenaline, sprinted away from the freakish bat-thing and made their way to the nearest police station. Once there they related their tale to what one must assume were highly sceptical officers. Flaxton would later state that he had "felt cold all over" during the episode.

Less than a week later, on the 21st of November, a young man named Keith Croucher seemed to confirm the teens claim of an unusual object soaring over Kent, when he announced that he too had seen an oddly shaped craft hovering over the local soccer field, not far from where Flaxton and his crew had claimed to have their curious encounter with a UFO and its bizarre occupant.

On November 23rd, John McGoldrick decided that the reports coming from Sandling Park were simply too outrageous to be ignored. So, after soliciting the help of an unnamed (yet clearly intrepid) friend, McGoldrick and his cohort made their way to the site of all the unusual goings on, hoping perchance to have a face-to-face encounter with the strange alien creature.

Artist impression of the creature seen in Sandling Park

Once inside the wooded area, McGoldrick claimed that he and his companion discovered no less than three "footprints" — each 24-inches long and nine inches across. He also stated that they had stumbled across an area where the foliage bracken had been flattened, as if by some tremendous weight. McGoldrick's claims caught the ear of the local press, who were no doubt eager to feed the public's ever-growing appetite for new information regarding this strange phenomenon. To that end, the newsmen accompanied McGoldrick back to the scene of the "weirdness" on December 11th.

While the reporters did not manage to turn up any new evidence, it was stated that thickets were still bathed in an eerie glow, which continued for some days before subsiding. The case was reported in scads of newspapers as well as a 1971 issue of "Flying Saucer Review," under the title the "Saltwood Mystery," due to its proximity to the area. In the 1970s, ufologist Chris Wolfe also re-opened the case of this almost avian anomaly. According to records, he interviewed Flaxton and also inspected the scene of the unearthly encounter. Following his investigation, Wolfe came to the dubious conclusion that what Flaxton, Hutchinson and their chums actually saw was an ordinary crow oddly illuminated by the flashing of an electric train passing not far away in the chilled autumnal air.

He apparently did not attempt to explain, however, how the crow managed to appear to be nearly 5-feet in height, web footed or headless. Other sceptics have even more dubiously suggested that the quartet saw nothing more than a scarecrow.

Thus ends the apparent saga of the Bat Beast of Kent, but it has been pointed out by numerous investigators that — as unusual as this creature's description was — it bears an uncanny resemblance to its British crypto-cousin (and Cornwall's most famous monster) the Owlman. The headless, bat-like description also begs comparison to a bizarre, yet eerily common, breed of cryptid that includes West Virginia's Mothman, Germany's Freiburg Shreiker, China's Man-Dragon and the former Soviet Union's Black Bird of Chernobyl — just to name a few.

Most of the aforementioned creatures are considered by many Fortean researchers to be "paranormal" entities, essentially oracles of doom, but what makes the Kent case so intriguing is that it marks the first reported association between these bizarre beings and the UFO phenomenon.

While, admittedly, none of the young eyewitnesses saw the thing actually exit the UFO, one would be hard pressed to deny at least some tenuous connection between the unusual aircraft seen landing in the woods at Sandling Park and the monster that soon thereafter emerged from the thicket… and ever after into the lore of both ufology and cryptozoology. It would seem that the high strangeness cases were getting even stranger.

While this creature is unique and does have overlaps into other field such as the paranormal and cryptozoology it cannot be ruled out as fitting into the types of cases we are examining in this book. I would ask myself this: "could four witnesses mistake something ordinary and conventional for that of this strange looking creature?" I leave you to decide.

Ray Wardle and Ian Jones
RAF Cosford
Shropshire
England
December 1963

A report of a landed UFO at RAF Cosford was initially brought to the attention of Leslie Otley of the Tyneside UFO Society, on the 10th of December 1963, by a colleague who told him of an incident which had taken place at an RAF base at least ten days earlier, indicating a time period towards the end of November/very early part of December 1963, although, at this stage, the location was not given. This means the 'universally accepted date', the 10th of December 1963, is wrong: Leslie "The details were exactly the same as our typed-up report of the 14th of December 1963. His information related to a matter at least ten days earlier."

The information was passed onto Harry Bunting - President of 'DIGAP', who contacted Staffordshire based investigator Mr. Wilfred Daniels, who in turn wrote a letter to the local newspaper the Express and Star, which was published on the 7th of January 1964: quote- "Reports of a flying saucer having landed at RAF Cosford have been discounted after an investigation.

Two boy entrants and a signalman were thought to have seen an unidentified object on the station two weeks before Christmas. A report in the Tyneside Unidentified Flying Objects Journal claims that it was seen by several RAF men, and after flashing green lights around the airport, took off again. Mr. Wilfred Daniels of 134, Weston Road, Stafford, a member of the British Flying Saucer movement and the British Unidentified Flying Objects Association, has been seeking the help of airmen and civilians in the Cosford area about the report."

Wilfred Daniels received a letter from a Stockport colleague (Harry) saying there were two RAF witnesses and a British Railways signalman near to the spot where the 'saucer' was said to have landed, and contacted Flight Lt. Stevens' station officer, at RAF Cosford, who told him that Wing Commander Wolsey, in charge of boy entrants, had investigated this matter and found no substance to it.

According to the newspaper: "Mr. Cecil Evans, the signalman concerned, laughed at his home today when asked about the report of a flying saucer. 'An RAF Flight Lt. called to see me the day after the object was supposed to have been seen. He said that two boy entrants had seen a blue flashing light on the end of the clothing stores at the station, opposite my signal box, at 11.45pm, the previous night. At that time, I had been looking out of the signal box and saw nothing unusual. Later, it occurred to me that what the boys might have seen were the reflections in the clothing store windows of lights on the Air Ministry estate at the bottom of Elm Lane - the reflections seemed to be dancing in the windows. Had a flying saucer landed, I would have certainly known about it. It is just another case of mistaken identity; we had a good laugh about it.'

On 9th January, retired British Army Royal Electrical and Mechanical Engineers (REME) Captain Wilfred Daniels, drove to Albrighton, close to the RAF Technical Training Establishment, (RAF Cosford), on the west side of the A41 Wolverhampton to Salop Road. First, he made some enquiries at Cosford Road Garage, about whether they had heard any rumors of any UFO landing at the Camp. He was told they had no such knowledge.

While walking along the High Street, he came face-to-face with a young man in clerical garb. It was the Chaplain at the RAF Station, (Flt. Lt. Reverend Brian George Henry, Service number 507521, discharged 26th June 1981 with rank of Wing Commander). After identifying himself, Wilfred asked him a number of questions about the incident, including his personal knowledge of the two boys involved, and received the following reply, "Oh yes I've talked about it to them, and they really believe they saw it."

When asked how they described it, and about their reactions, he answered:" They said it looked like what you would take for a flying saucer down on the ground as they watched a trap door in the upper part slowly open. Frightened, they ran away, and after telling someone what they had seen, they were told to sober up. But they were not drunk -quite sane and sensible."

Wilfred asked him if he was willing to arrange an interview with the two boys. The Chaplain refused and asked that his name be withheld.

Wilfred then went to see the signalman Mr. Evans, but - although spending over an hour with him - learnt nothing of any value. Interestingly, Leslie Otley discovered that one of the boy entrants came from the Newcastle-on-Tyne area, and pondered whether he was responsible for leaking the information relating to the UFO landing in the first place? On 14th January 1964, Leslie Otley wrote to Wilfred Daniels, suggesting the real date of the landing was between 17th November and 1st December 1963. Wilfred contacted the RAF Station, and spoke to the Station adjutant, who said: "The story had come out on the 14th of December 1963, but it did not really happen - several of the trainees conspired together to 'cook up 'the yarn of the flying saucer, but what started as a joke, got out of hand. It was the 14th of December 1963, when it emerged."

A letter from Flying Officer Robert Alan Roberts, (service number 2201456 D, discharged 29th April1964) at Cosford, to the Air Ministry, at Whitehall, stated that Flight Lieutenant Henry "categorically denies all statements attributed to him". Flying Officer Roberts further added the chaplain was seriously considering taking legal action. In a letter sent to Waveney Girvan, editor of Flying Saucer Review magazine, on 13th April 1964, Wilfred Daniels reported: "Flight Lieutenant Henry said that publication of his name would cause him trouble; that it was 'more than his job was worth' to arrange a meeting between me and the two RAF apprentices; he really ought not to be talking to me about it at all; that security had dropped right down on the whole thing."

Waveney Girvan resolved to get to the bottom of the mystery, and wrote a number of letters to both RAF Cosford and the Air Ministry, following the disclosure of several contradictory explanations offered by the authorities to explain the encounter: including, *"Nothing at all"*, *"two drunk apprentices"*, *"a hoax"*, and - somewhat amusingly - *"a British Railways steam train"*, were the various theories offered by the Air Ministry in its attempts to kill interest in the case. He also wrote an article in *Flying Saucer Review,* the *Kensington News* and *West London Times* about the incident, 'AFFAIR AT COSFORD', in which he challenged (on behalf of the *Kensington News* and *West London Times*) Flt. Lt. Henry to:*" come forward and swear an affidavit that he did not say what Mr. Daniels swears he did when they met in Albrighton last February."* Waveney identified one of the RAF trainees as Ian Jones and commented on the Government's self-contradictory explanations. *"What is it that the Air Ministry is trying so desperately to hide?"* Later, following further enquiries into the incident, he established the identities of both of the witnesses as being Ian Jones and Ray Wardle.

In 1997, UK UFO research and author Nick Redfern received a telephone call from Graham Birdsall, the editor and publisher of *UFO Magazine*, who told him he had been contacted by a chap called Ray Wardle. Ray Wardle was one of the eyewitnesses to the events at RAF Cosford back in 1963. As a result of this Nick Redfern conducted an interview with Mr. Wardle." My friend and I went out for the evening. We had passes that covered us until 9.00pm. But, by the time we got back to Cosford, it was 9.15pm, so I said, 'the best thing we can do is to climb the fence'.

We walked alongside the chain link fence, near the hangars, close to a railroad track outside the Camp site, and climbed over the fence, took a few steps, and there was this object. I'm not going to say it was a 'flying saucer' because it wasn't.

It wasn't shaped like one - it didn't look like one. It was very bright, mainly orange, with white lights, and reminded me of a church organ. It appeared to have pipes on it, things like that in the centre of it, but there was no distinct outline to the object at all, and I couldn't tell if it was on the ground or just above it.

" During further conversation, Ray told Nick he estimated the size of the object as being:" twenty feet across, by thirty feet high, and that he and his companion were probably a hundred yards away from it." Although Ray wanted to investigate further, Ian ran away. Ray deliberated what to do and then caught up with Ian, between two hangars, where they discussed what they should do about the sighting, and after some conversation, decided to report it. Ray:" What bothered me was that they refused to come back with us. Nobody would go to the spot that we were telling them about. It was frustrating. I suppose we were humoured. I really don't know. Nobody said, 'Oh, you're lying'. They just wanted the facts and that was it. It was quite strange."

Ray confirmed he had made a written statement to the officer in charge but couldn't recall having signed it. (There was no sign of this document in the MoD file.)

Ray Wardle (courtesy John Hanson)

This report is in Air Ministry files stored at the National Archives in Kew. Unfortunately, Nick Redfern was unable to keep his copies of the files when he moved to live in the USA and at this moment in time the National Archives are closed due to the Coranavirus crisis.

I asked Nick Redfern via email what his thoughts were on this case. "The Air Ministry file is pretty lengthy at 61 pages. Something may have happened, but there's definitely nothing in the file at all that was seen as important to the old Air Ministry." (Source: FSR, 1964, Mar-Apr, V 10, N 2) John Hanson and Nick Redfern.

Pauline Abbott
Buckhirst Hill
Epping
Essex
England
December 27, 1963

Pauline Hill was seventeen and was a trainee riding instructor at the Ivy Chimneys Riding School in Epping. It was around 4.00pm and Pauline was exercising her horse in the yard of the riding school. Pauline heard a 'squelching' noise coming from a nearby field which she thought was a duck making a noise and she wondered if there was someone in the field that had disturbed the duck. Pauline shouted out "who's there" but received no reply. Looking over towards the field Pauline reported the following: "I saw this thing on the ground. It was about three feet high and eight feet wide, greyish in colour, with a glow coming from one end. I sat on my horse, too frightened to move. Whatever it was it took off slowly and disappeared into the distance. When I later went to have a look in the field I found a number of deep indented marks in the ground, approximately 8 feet across, by one and a half feet deep, with four lines radiating outwards from the circular marls, with 'cup' marks at the end of each line."

After the case featured in the local media (The Times and Wessex Star) two girls contacted the newspaper to report to also having seen a dome-shaped shiny object in the sky. One of the tow girls mentioned that it was common knowledge locally that other 'strange marks' and ground traces had been found in the locality 'where something had crash landed' in 1958. Fortunately, a Dr D.G.Doel, who had become involved in a number of investigations during this period, heard about this matter and paid a visit to the area accompanied by his daughter Diana. They were directed to the riding stables where they would meet Carol Foster aged 18, Robert Ewing aged 13 and Pauline Abbot aged 17.

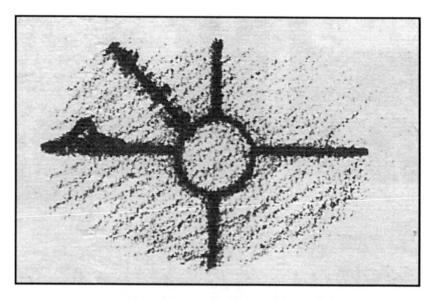

UFO 'landing mark' as drawn by Pauline Abbott

A statement was obtained which told of the couple arriving at the stables at around 8.00am on December 26th. It was an overcast day when they observed an unusual object crossing the sky. They described it as being long and flat, with a dome-like protuberance, with no visible windows and it was a slivery-white colour. When they took their eyes off the object to look around for any other witnesses and looked back again, it had gone. Dr. Doel then interviewed Pauline Abbott. She told him of arriving at the stables at 4.00pm on the 27th of December and riding the horse to the field concerned where she heard the squelching noise. Thinking the noise was made by a man walking in mud, she looked around and saw the peculiar object on the ground in front of her and shouted out, "Mr Banks, there is a UFO in the field", describing this thing as looking like: "It was eight feet long, three feet high in the middle, tapering down to a point at each end, bright and white in appearance, despite localised misty weather conditions. Towards the left of the object was a feature that looked like a car windscreen, or panel, glowing much brighter than the rest. After calling out the object took off in a shallow climb, where she lost sight of it as it passed behind a haystack. The next morning some of the occupants of the riding stables went to the scene and examined it, finding the previously described 'marks' as if a blunt knife had been dragged across the grass."

Mr. Banks was also interview. He informed Dr. Doel that by the time he arrived at the scene there was no sign of the UFO, although he did see some vague marks in the ground. However, he did tell them of an earlier incident which took place in 1958 bright to his attention by a Major Frank Collins.

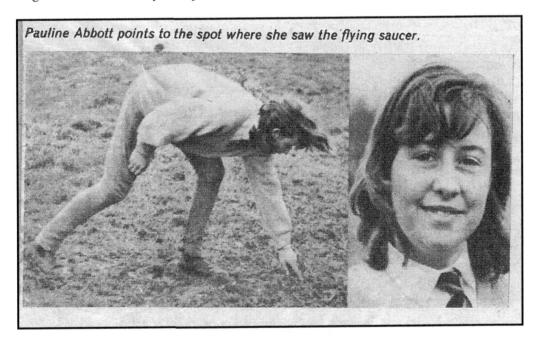

Pauline Abbott points to the spot where she saw the flying saucer.

Pauline Abbott went public with her account and sadly was subjected to a great deal of ridicule as a result. It is highly unlikely that Pauline Abbott misidentified some natural occurrence. She was close to the unidentified object, and it left behind indentations in the ground. For this reason, I think this case has its fair share of data to label it as 'high strangeness'.

Harold South
Penkridge
Staffordshire
England
February 1964

This case is slightly different as it is an alleged UFO crash landing which also allegedly involved H.M Armed Forces. Originally this report was sent to UFO investigator and author Nick Redfern by the late Leonard Stringfield. Stringfield specialised in cased of alleged UFO crashes Just before his death Stringfield wrote: "Having learnt from an informant of a decoded report revealing a UFO had crashed in two parts: the main section was in Penkridge, Staffordshire, the remainder in West Germany, and the artefacts had been recovered with three dead alien personnel. The top-secret decoded radio message stated that wreckage and the bodies were shipped to Wright-Patterson Air Force Base in the USA."

After discussions with Nick Redfern Staffordshire UFO researchers Irene Bott and Graham Allen contacted the local newspaper the Burntwood Post and placed an appeal in the newspaper looking for any information about this alleged incident. As a result, Irene Bott received a letter from a Mr Harold South who had this to say:

"I had been driving across the Chase when I came across a military cordon and was ordered to turn my vehicle around and find an alternative route. I did as I was told, however, when out of sight of the military, I parked my van on the side of the road and stealthily crept through the forest on foot back to the area that had been cordoned off, when I was shocked and fascinated to see some form of small triangular-shaped object that did not look man-made, being loaded onto a military transport vehicle. As I always carry my camera with me, I took a couple of photographs of the object."

When Harold South arrived home his mother told him that the local police had been looking for his. After attending the local police station, he was interviewed by police officers who informed him that he had been seen taking photographs and they demanded from him both the camera and the film. Harold South never saw these officers or his camera again. Nick Redfern and Irene Bott considered Mr South to be a credible witness and during an interview with him in 1996 he told them that only minutes after speaking with them on the telephone to arrange the interview, he received a strange and disconcerting telephone call from the Ministry of Defence Police warning him not to speak with the UFO investigators.

Nick Redfern and Irene Bott had to be sure that this witness was not lying or fantasising but by utilising the telephone 'ring back' system they confirmed that the call had indeed originated at the office of the Ministry of Defence Guards Service the nearby Whittington Army Barracks in Lichfield. This would appear to prove that a phone call was made from someone there, but there was no way of knowing the content of that call. UFO investigator Graham Allen of the Staffordshire UFO Group confirmed to Researcher and author John Hanson that a number of other people had come forward to confirm the account of Mr Harold South these included a fireman and a police officer. UFO crash cases or UFO crash landing cases in the UK are extremely rare and just by their very nature are very bizarre.

With only one eyewitness to this event, it is very hard to categorize it but I have included it in this book simply because such incidents are so rare. The very nature of this event must put it into the 'high strangeness' bracket but with a hint of scepticism thrown in just for good measure.

Dennis Bills
Cannock Chase
Staffordshire
England
1964

Dennis Bills from Huntington in Staffordshire reported the following event to UFO researchers Irene Bott and Graham Allen of the Staffordshire UFO Group in 1978. The incident to which he had been witness took place in 1964 while walking through Cannock Chase: "It was an overcast night and I had trouble keeping to the trail which led to a clearing near my home in Stanley Croft, when I noticed a neon green and red light about 200 yards away which I took to be someone using a child's multi-coloured torch which were quite popular then. As I approached, now some fifty yards away from the clearing known as Cavans Wood, I saw what looked like a board lit up with luminous paint standing on the edge of the clearing. I thought, why would someone put that up? And carried on walking towards it. When I was about ten to fifteen yards away, I realised that it was reflecting some sort of colour, rather than being self-luminous and began to feel frightened but plucked up the courage to walk closer when I saw it was, in fact, circular, about fifteen feet in diameter and just less than six feet high."

Mr. Bills decided not to walk past the object, fearing what might happen, and took a different path home. Despite a large amount of 'leg-pulling' from those in whom he confided, he is adamant that there was no mistake in what he saw, and it remains perfectly clear in his mind to this very day. He told John Hanson and Dawn Holloway is 2010:

"I don't know if it is of relevance, but the streetlights and house light were all out because of a power cut. For some years after the grass would not grow over the area in the field where I had seen the object."

Mr. Bills went on to say: "I was about fifteen feet away from it. There was no mistake about what I saw. It had pointed ends and was saucer shaped. When I reached home, I told my dad, who was a coal miner at Littlehampton Pit, about what I had seen. He told me not to be so daft and thought I had been reading a Dan Dare comic book.

At the time I was working as an apprentice lathe engineer and decided to approach one of the typists there, Laverne Newall from Great Whorley and ask her if she would type out what I had seen, which she did. I fully intended to write a letter to the Daily Mail or Daily Express and explain what I had witnessed, but then decided against it thinking that no one would have believed me. Although the area was a grassy clearing bat the back of the houses where we played football it is now covered in trees and undergrowth.

About a year later I went back to have a look and discovered a 15-foot circle with a ragged left-hand edge, resembling the continent of Africa, inside of which was devoid of any plant growth which outside was normal. This was in the same place where I had seen the UFO."

Although only a one witness event surely it is almost impossible for the witness to misidentify a conventional object from such close quarters. Added to that we have to ask what type of illuminated object could he have misidentified and what such a thing would also disturb the normal growing of the plant life in the area? Personally, I can't think of anything that would fit the bill. Mr Bills was adamant that he saw this object at close range and that there was no way he could have been mistaken. I tend to agree with him.

Joan and Roy Vincent
Karslake
Cornwall
England
1965

Another lesser-known UFO classic is that of a dome-shaped UFO in Cornwall in 1965. Joan Vincent, County and Restormel Borough Councillor, revealed that she and her husband Roy had observed a mystery craft late at night during 1965 in a then rural area.

The matter remained "virtually a family secret" over the years because the couple feared that they would be ridiculed if they told their story. The UFO was "a large, dome-shaped object that looked as if it were made of glass," estimated to be 50-70 feet across and 30-40 feet high.

Mrs. Vincent's drawing of the unidentified object. (Cornish Guardian)

Joan and Roy Vincent at the site of their close encounter. (Cornish Guardian)

"Councillor reveals 30-year secret of a 'close encounter'" by IAN SHEPHERD

A 33-year silence was broken this week when a leading figure in Cornwall spoke publicly about a close encounter with what she and her husband firmly believe was a flying saucer. Joan Vincent, chairman of the County Planning Committee for nine years until last May and now a long-serving County and Restormel Borough Councillor, revealed that she and her husband Roy had observed the mystery craft late at night during 1965 in a then rural area between St Dennis and Carthew.

Both remain convinced that what they saw, in considerable detail, was from another world. The matter remained "virtually a family secret" over the years because the couple feared that they would be ridiculed if they told their story. "But it is now a much less taboo subject because of the number of such sightings," said Mrs. Vincent.

"There is now no reason for it to remain a secret." She said that late one night in 1965, she and her husband Roy were driving past the hamlet of Karslake, deep in the china clay country, on their way home to Stenalees. "We knew that students at Fowey College used to spend night-time vigils at what is now Caerloggas Downs and that they had reported seeing flying saucers there several times," said Mrs. Vincent.

"We stopped to have a look at the sky ourselves. We had been sitting in the car for about 15 minutes when suddenly it was as if a light had been switched on outside. One minute it was dark, the next we could see for miles over the surrounding countryside. The light was brilliant, and it was constant, not like lightning. "About 50 yards away, in a field behind a hedge, we could see where it appeared to be coming from. It was a large, dome-shaped object that looked as if it were made of glass. "Because of the hedge, we could not see all of its lower section closer to the ground, so neither of us know if it was hovering or resting on the grass." We could see inside the dome, where the light was coming from. There were big cabinets with dials on them. Below the dome, where the object was solid and a grey-green colour, there were portholes.

"We later estimated that what we could see must have been about 50 to 70 feet across and between 30 and 40 feet high, although we couldn't see the base because of the hedge." After about 30 seconds, I said to Roy, my husband 'My God, let's get out of here,' because I was quite shocked.

We drove off and went straight home. "As soon as we arrived, we agreed to go into separate rooms and draw what we had seen. When we compared the drawings, they were virtually identical. "We never told anyone apart from my mother and later my son, David, who was aged four at the time.

"My husband was an absolute sceptic about such things as flying saucers, but we know both know that there really is something out there. We are glad we saw what we did together, because I don't think either of us would have believed the story if we hadn't been there." The couple returned to the scene the following day but could find no clues to the sighting.

The field where Mr. and Mrs. Vincent saw the craft ceased to exist years ago when it became a spoil tip for nearby clay workings. And the road where they had stopped their car, prior to the strange encounter, has also been re-routed.
Source: Ian Shepherd, Cornish Guardian (Bodmin, England), Nov. 26, 1998

Mr. G.M.
Epping
Essex
England
January 4, 1965

Mr G.M. was driving along the road to Theydon Bois and was accompanied by a lady friend. Nearing a bridge, he turned off the road onto a 'green' lined by trees. He parked the car under the trees and got out to take off his raincoat.

He noticed a bright spot of light flying across the sky towards him high up and concluded that it must be a 'shooting star' although it was moving more slowly than he expected a conventional shooting star to travel. Dismissing this phenomenon from his mind he got back into the car. The time was now around 9.15 pm. At around 9.45 pm he stopped the car again this time to put his coat back on.

Looking around he was shocked to see just a matter of yards away tucked under a hedge, an extremely bright object shaped 'like an igloo'. It was about the same length of his car but higher and was des cribbed as being of a uniform brilliant whiteness.

Mr. G.M. did not hang around or try to take in any further details but instead jumped back into the car. He started the engine and with the headlights blazing turned onto the green in a wide circle which would bring his headlights to bear on the strange object. The car headlights swept across the place where a moment before he had seen the igloo-shaped object but it was nowhere to be seen. As they drove home somewhat shaken by the incident, they saw a bright object flying away beyond some houses in the direction of Walthamstow.

Vol. 1 No. 3 WINTER 1964

BUFORA

JOURNAL

AND BULLETIN

Published by the
BRITISH U.F.O. RESEARCH ASSOCIATION

The incident was originally reported to BUFORA member Paul Webb. Mr. Webb along with the witness re-visited the area but nothing out of the ordinary as located at the scene. Mr. Webb was convinced that the witness was telling the truth and there had been other sightings in the area as well.

BUFORA's research officer Mr. G. Stephenson carried on where Paul Webb had left off. He paid a visit to the witness's parents who informed him that they believed their son was telling the truth as when he returned home that night, he was very excited. One curious aspect of this incident was that the witness's mother informed BUFORA that the other person in the car that night, Mr.G.M's fiancé, did not see the object. The mother seemed very agitated by the whole event and felt that there must be a logical explanation to it all. (Source: BUFORA Journal Volume 1 No.3 Winter 1964 Epping 1965).

Geoffrey Maskey
Felixstowe
Suffolk
England
September 20, 1965

This encounter has a very large amount of 'high strangeness' as it includes a UFO landing and occupants and a whole lot more as you will see. The case in question has featured in numerous publications but the following account comes from UFO investigators and authors John Hanson and Dawn Holloway (Haunted Skies volume 2). John and Dawn took it upon themselves to interview Mr. Maskey in person:

"I was with my girlfriend, Mavis Forsyth, driving along Walton Avenue in Felixstowe, at around 10.30pm, with my friend Michael Johnson.' Mick' asked me to stop the car because he needed to attend a call of nature. After a few minutes had elapsed I began to wonder what had happened to him, especially when we heard what sounded like a mixture of very weird noises and a high-pitched humming noise, followed by the appearance of orange, glowing, object lighting up part of the road as it headed off eastwards, over Walton Avenue towards the coast. Now worried I reversed the card up and down the road with the window open calling out his name. About fifteen minutes Mick staggered out of the hedge at the side of the road, clutching the back of his neck, and fell onto the ground, apparently unconscious. We managed to put Mick, who had a noticeable burn mark on the back of his neck, into the Vanguard car and rushed him to Felixstowe Hospital. After arriving at the hospital and explaining to the casualty staff what had happened, he became the butt of much humour, being referred to as the 'Martian' by his friends. Mick, who seemed completely oblivious to what was going on, seemed to have some sort of 'fit' and tried to take his clothes off, flaying his arms about. It required the strength of three or four members of staff to restrain him before he was taken for treatment."

When Mr. Maskey telephoned the hospital the next morning, enquiring about his friend's condition, he was told that Mick was being treated for severe shock and that nobody was allowed to visit him. Following his discharge from hospital, five days later, Mr. Maskey spoke to Geoff and asked him what had happened. This is what Mick had to say:

"I remember seeing a glowing silver/orange object descending next to where I was stood, about twelve feet above me. Standing on the side of this 'craft' were two humanoid figures wearing steel-coloured suits with arms outstretched at chest height, showing long pointed fingers. I saw them go back into the 'craft' and the next thing I remember was waking up in hospital."

Mr. Maskey discovered that the burn mark had now disappeared from the back of Mick's neck and that the police had found nothing at the scene of the incident.

Again, there is simply no way that the witnesses involved here could have misidentified a conventional object. One of those involved, Mick, even ended up in hospital as a result of his close encounter. Mr. Maskey has stuck to his story down the years and this incident must surely be labelled as yet another 'high strangeness' incident.

Glowing Object Mystery

STAR 21/9/65

The story was told late last night by Mr. Maskey who, looking shaken, told an "Evening Star" reporter that neither he nor his friend had been drinking.

Here is the story in Mr. Maskey's words: "At about half past ten I drove my car down Walton Avenue, Felixstowe, and stopped about 50 yards past the last street-lamp.

"My girl-friend, Mavis Forsyth, who lives in Granville Road, Felixstowe, was also with me. Mick got out and went for a walk, leaving Mavis and myself in the car.

"After about five minutes, there was a noise. It was just like something out of a space fiction film—a high-pitched humming sound. A few seconds later we saw a long oval object in the sky. It was glowing a dull orange colour, and the light from it lit up quite a large part of Walton Avenue. It was in view for about half a minute and moved across the sky from west to east.

"Nothing happened to us, but I was worried about Mick. Mavis was petrified and grabbed hold of my arm. We called Mick from the car, but there was no answer. After a few minutes, I reversed the car, and we called again.

Ian Hahn
Bath Road
Warminster
Wiltshire
England
December 8, 1965

Ian Hahn went on the record in 2004 when he told the curious story of him being overtaken by a UFO. Mr. Hahn told investigators John Hanson and Dawn Holloway the following:

"I was driving along the Bath Road some ten miles from Warminster when this vehicle overtook me. I thought it was a Land Rover without any lights on apart from two green flashing lights on its roof.

I switched on my main beam (headlights) and was astounded to see the absence of any lights, reflectors or number plate. I gave chase for about two miles. Suddenly, I heard this high-pitched whine, so deafening that I was obliged to stick my fingers in my ears and steer with my elbows. It then became enveloped in yellow smoke and disappeared.

I stopped the car, feeling anger rather than fear and rushed over to where I had last seen it land. There was nothing to be seen. I reported the matter to the police and returned to the scene the next day and examined the ground in daylight but saw nothing unusual."

Although there is not a great deal of information in this report it surely must come under the heading of 'high strangeness'. How many other reports are there where a motorist has been overtaken by a UFO?

Dame Rebecca West
Ibstone House
Hertfordshire
England
January 7, 1966

At 2.45pm on January 7th, 1966, the well-known author Dame Rebecca West, residing at Ibstone House in Hertfordshire, was in the grounds of her home when she noticed a man walking on her property some distance to the right on the path she was walking on. Her curiosity aroused she watched as the man reached a point where the wood ended, near a hedge running down the valley along a sharp ridge and stopped just past a gap in the hedge, allowing her to see what appeared to be some form of strange aerial contraption. Dame Rebecca west added: "It seemed to descend quite rapidly on the other side of the hedge from the man, but close to it. It consisted of something like a metal band, grey-blue in colour, flattened at one point, so as to seem almost leaf-like, and crossed with a herringbone system of metal strips. There was also, somehow attached to these, an odd object-like a bag, with an opening that had points of yellowish material. As I looked the whole thing collapsed to the ground. I saw it crumple, but crumpling is not the right word. The metal band seemed to curl backwards and disappear, while the curious 'bag' about six feet tall looked as if someone was squeezing the air out of the lower portion, so that all points stood up and fell back."

The mystery man was then seen to turn around and follow the hedge track down the valley, looking once or twice to his left, as if he was scrutinizing the valley, seemingly unaware of her presence, but at the bottom of the track he stopped again and looked around the slope where she was standing, this time as if he had suddenly become aware of her presence. Dame Rebecca West added further details:

Dame Rebecca West circa 1971

78

"We stood and looked at each other for quite a long time and I had an uncomfortable feeling. I felt uneasy and decided to head home. Later that day I spoke to one of the farm workers who told me that he had seen what he believed to be a helicopter flying in the vicinity earlier.

Dame Rebecca West wrote to the Ministry of Defence explaining what had happened and what she had observed and she received a reply from a Mr.L.K.Akhurst suggesting she "......may have seen a helicopter, possibly a Bell 47 or similar type, which in conditions of poor visibility, appears to have some unusual characteristics."

Dame Rebecca West, unhappy with the Ministry of Defence' explanation wrote back to them denying that what she saw was a helicopter: "...to have appeared where I saw it, a helicopter would have had to fly twenty to thirty yards with its lower half deeply embedded in the earth and of the fact that there was, at the time, complete silence and that visibility seemed, to me, not poor at all, for I spotted several birds at a considerable distance. I do not expect an answer to this letter.

I reported this incident partly because I feared the object might be a parachute, or some such construction, which was being used to drop somebody, or something, for criminal purposes and partly because the construction I saw, or thought I saw, puzzled me, as I could not conceive how it could have got into the air, could stay in the air, or could be brought down out of the air."

The MoD response to this letter was short and sharp:

"No further evidence has become available concerning this particular sighting, so there is nothing to add.

Signed

L.K.Akhurst"

A most bizarre close encounter and a curious response from the UK's Ministry of Defence. However, it is clear that Dame Rebecca West was not going to fall for the MoD's brush off letter. Normally the MoD's response was a standard letter and rarely did the offer an explanation for UFO sightings.

If, as they say it was a helicopter then surely the helicopter in question could have been traced? This was, after all, an unscheduled landing or private property. The one fact of course that completely rules out the helicopter theory is the lack of noise. Could it have been something to do with the MoD hence the cover story or was it yet another 'high strangeness' UFO landing. I support the latter of these two explanations.

Bridget Kelly
Shropshire
England
August 1967

Bridget Kelly was on her way home with her husband and three children late one evening in August 1967. Mrs Kelly recounted their remarkable encounter:

"We were driving along the road when we saw what we took to be a shooting star but realised it wasn't falling. It then hurtled towards the ground as if about to crash, stopped, and hovered right in front of us, allowing us to see a glistening silver metallic object, with a bright light flashing on top and an illuminated window to one side.

The next thing I became aware of was standing outside the front door. We looked up and saw the 'craft' taking off across the rooftops. I had this feeling of sadness that whoever, or whatever, was on it was saying goodbye. The following day I discovered a curious circle of dead skin on my stomach. If I had told anyone what had happened to us they would have thought us mad."

In 1992 Mrs Kelly had a 'flashback' of the experience and decided to contact the British UFO Research Association, who arranged for her to undergo regressive hypnosis. After just one session of regressive hypnosis, she became aware of having been the subject of some form of medical examination performed on her which she was on the craft in 1967. She added:

"I could see faces around me, while something was done to my stomach. There was no pain, just faces with large eyes. They looked like ordinary people, rather than anything alien looking."

Bridget Kelly passed away in 2006 and is on the record as one of the UK's earliest alien abduction cases. The most famous of such cases was the 1961 encounter in the USA involving Betty and Barney Hill. The UK has its own fair share of such encounters of which Mrs Kelly in one. By their very nature they are cram-packed with different levels of 'high strangeness'.

Whether or not such encounters are some kind of psychological experience or are in fact real, physical abductions by beings not of this Earth is still a matter of great debate. I will include a few such cases in this book, but I will stick to pure UFO landing cases wherever I can.

Arthur Shuttlewood
Warminster
Wiltshire
England
August 27, 1967

Arthur Shuttlewood was a local journalist in Warminster, Wiltshire who made the UFO subject popular in 1960's due to a 'flap' of sightings in and around the town of Warminster. Shuttlewood went on to author a number of books on the subject.

In the late evening of August 29th, 1967, Arthur Shuttlewood and a number of other people were on the slopes of Cradle Hill just outside of the town of Warminster. Cradle Hill has been a regular vantage point for 'sky-watching' for UFOs since the 1960's. Shuttlewood and the others observed a cone-shaped object which descended through the sky and land in a clump of trees, about a thousand yards away.

In an interview by the late Ken Rogers Arthur Shuttlewood had this to say about the evening's event:

"I advised onlookers to stay at a safe distance while I explored the area. The landed UFO was shooting out beams of bright light from a conical and revolving rim. It will tax the reader too harshly if I recount exactly what happened some three hundred yards away from the glowing UFO and whom I spoke to. Near a rustic gate, separating two large fields, I became terrified, soon afterwards, in spite of being with other people. The UFO blacked out after about six minutes, and I went along a hedgerow skirting the edge of the copses. Walking back, I was struck by the utter silence, night birds ceased to make a noise around me. I passed a second copse and for a few seconds stopped to glance up at the stars. I placed a hand on the hedge to steady myself.

Arthur Shuttlewood (photographer unknown)

My thoughts were widely disturbed, shattered by what happened, then, in no more than ten seconds, right above my head, came the sound of a gigantic bird, flapping its leaden wings. It was a heavy thumping noise, so ponderous the whole hedge trembled under my palm and my hands were lifted by the sheer variation of power pulsing through them. Imagine the down beating thrust of the wings of a swan in flight. This aerial intruder was a thousand times larger and disquieting. The phenomenon passed my eyes. I saw nothing to mark the winged monster's flight."

Cradle Hill, Warminster, Wiltshire. (Photo by the author)

What had become known as the Warminster 'thing' became a regular phenomenon in the town and it would seem that on this occasion Arthur Shuttlewood had experienced it first-hand. The 'thing' was not so much as a UFO sighting but a series of strange noises in and around the town. Although an Army Garrison town the locals were used to the noises that the military made, and this 'thing' was nothing like them. Even today UFO researchers and enthusiasts travel to Warminster and make their way to Cradle Hill to try and encounter the 'thing' or see a UFO for themselves. This author has done this once or twice himself

Paul Quick
Storrington
West Sussex
October 29, 1967

The Sun newspaper of October 31, 1967 featured the following account of a UFO encounter made by Paul quick just two days earlier. At around 6.45 pm on Sunday October 29, he was riding his motorcycle home when it broke down. He was just two miles from his home in Storrington when this happened. As he was pushing his motorcycle along through a thickly wooded area he happened to look up and "there is the sky above me was an object like a rugby ball floating towards me. It was one and half times the size of a double-decker bus and made no noise. It was about two hundred and fifty up.

I was scared." Mr. Quick continued to push his broken-down motorcycle and now headed towards his mother's home in nearby Longberry Hill. He told his story upon arrival and his mother, and two sisters looked out of the window with him. They all saw the object, which had now landed on the crest of a hill about two miles from their house.

Mrs. Quick is quoted as saying: "There is no question of a mistake or imagination. We called the police." Despite a thorough search, says the newspaper account, the police, who combed the area, found nothing and no sign of anything that had landed. Questioned later Mr. Quick stated that it was a clear and starry evening. The object seen by him was luminous, with a kind of bright white light, but not dazzling. It seemed to be coming straight towards him, but then it disappeared behind a clump of trees. The whole sighting lasted about fifteen seconds. After he reached home, his sister Leone who with her mother and sister had been watching TV, all at once looked out of a large French window in their living room and called the rest of the family to come and see a large bright-coloured ball which was slowly floating downwards on to Chanctonbury Downs, about two miles from their house. They all rushed out to the veranda and climbed on chairs to get a better view. The object had now stopped floating and had seemed to have landed. It also stared to change colour.

Mrs. Quick described it as looking like a horseshoe upside down, and said its colour changed from white to a deep ruby-red, extremely glowing. Then the object began to "flutter and flicker about". Suddenly, it broke into what seemed to be three separate parts. The ted part remained stationary while the other two parts moved towards the left. One of them was green and the other blue. For a while she thought she was experiencing some sort of optical illusion but found that her son and two daughters were seeing exactly the same thing. The three parts of the object remained separate for what seemed to be about one minute, and then joined up again to form an "upside-down horseshoe" as before. Mrs Quick went on to add: "It was all red.....but behind the object there seemed to be a sort of yellow glow which appeared to go off and on....this yellow faded into the red glow."

Although it was very cold outside on the veranda, Paul Quick, his sister Michele and Mrs. Quick ran over to a clearing some five hundred yards away from their house in order to get a better view.

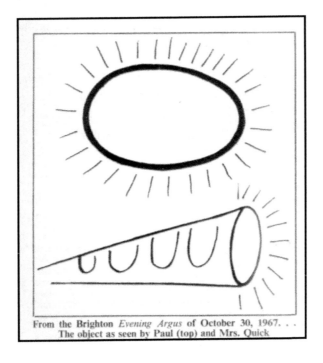

From the Brighton *Evening Argus* of October 30, 1967. . .
The object as seen by Paul (top) and Mrs. Quick

Arriving there, they now perceived that the object looked like "a huge ice-cream cornet. The part where the ice cream would be, was bigger than a lorry and was bright red in colour. This apparently was the part we had seen from the veranda. From where we were looking at it, it appeared to be resting on the Downs (hills). It looked like nothing we had ever seen....I was of course frightened and we didn't have the courage to walk towards the object....I've always been sort of sceptical when I've read about people spotting these flying saucers in the past, but now that I've seen what appears to be one.....We watched it from our veranda for about fifteen minutes, and now a further twenty minutes from the field. It was dreadfully cold.

When we were watching it from the veranda, the way it fluttered and changed colours seemed to me as if it was wanting to attract attention.....Suddenly; it seemed as if it was sliding down. It began to move, and then we lost sight of it. We didn't see it go back into the sky.

We them immediately phoned the police (Steyning Police Station). They searched part of the Downs with some dogs but didn't find anything. The area where we had seen the object is quite desolate, with no roads through it, so I don't know if the police actually hunted through the area. The next day a journalist the Evening Argus interviewed us, and I drew a sketch of the object for the newspaper."

Corroborating what her mother had said, Leone Quick added that she estimated the cone-shaped object might have been one hundred feet long.

A few days later the family received a letter from a Mr. N.E. Satterly from Patcham near Brighton, which is about ten miles from the Quick's home. Mr. Satterly said that at the time in question, 6.50 pm, on October 29, he had watched the object through binoculars.

The object seemed to be about half a mile from him, and he estimated it to be between fifty and seventy-five feet in diameter. This object was blood-red in colour and seemed to be following the powerlines across the Downs.

He watched the object for about three minutes before it vanished. The speed was estimated at around thirty miles per hours. He stated that it "didn't look like anything he had ever seen....certainly not of this world...." Mrs. Quick was later interviewed by UFO researcher Omar Fowler and she reported a second sighting to him that took place on November 16, 1967, although it was not a UFO landing event. (Source: FSR 1968 V 14 N 2).

This case surely has its fare share of high strangeness. It was observed from several different locations by multiple witnesses. It is highly unlikely that the Quick family could misidentify it as something conventional as this was seen from their family home and they were therefore very familiar with the location.

We also should not forget the witness that wrote to them as well. The police obviously took it serious enough to attend the scene and even search the area with dogs. I wonder if the police would do that today?

The Moody Blues
A6
England
Autumn 1967

The Moody Blues are an English rock band formed in Birmingham in 1964, initially consisting of keyboardist Mike Pinder, multi-instrumentalist Ray Thomas, guitarist Denny Laine, drummer Graeme Edge, and bassist Clint Warwick. The group came to prominence playing rhythm and blues music.

They made some changes in musicians but settled on a line-up of Pinder, Thomas, Edge, guitarist Justin Hayward, and bassist John Lodge, who stayed together for most of the band's "classic era" into the early 1970s. They are perhaps best known for their international hit song 'Knights in White Satin'. In 1967 the band is said to have their own close encounter. Graeme Edge, drummer with the band spoke with Peter Wilshire who wrote this account up for the Flying Saucer Review. "We (the band) were returning to London from a convert in Carlisle. I'd like to point out straight away, that given the reputation of musicians consuming alcohol and other substances after a show all of the 'Moody Blues' personnel were completely sober and straight.

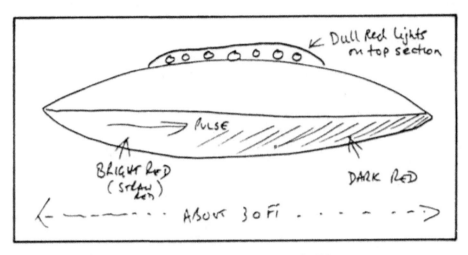

Landed UFO as witnessed by the Moody Blues pop group

The road crew, as usual, had taken the equipment in a truck, and the band members were following along behind in a car. Apart from myself in the car there was Denny Laine, Mike Pinder, Ray Thomas and Clint Warwick.

At around 1.30 to 2.00 am we were driving south on the A6, when a bright light appeared and flashed past us. Everyone became highly excited as to what the light might be, with the usual nervous jokes about UFOs.

Personally, I was convinced it was probably and aircraft warning light on the top of a radio-mast, apparently moving because of the motion of the car. However, the light returned from the opposite direction, and I suggested stopping the car for a proper look. I was still convinced of a logical terrestrial explanation.

As the car stopped, we all saw the light again on the left-hand side of us, it went backwards and forwards, and then actually over the car before settling in a field near the road, but on the opposite side of the dual carriageway. As we scrambled out of the car, part scared and part fascinated, we all noted an odd stillness around us. No other cars were on the road in either direction, and there was none of the usual nocturnal animal noises either. We could see the object in the opposite field; it was shaped like a fat cigar with a low protrusion on top, with several dull-red lights on it. The upper half of the object appeared metallic, whereas the lower half was red, and pulsed from left to right. The lower half was a bright red on the left and a duller red to the right and did not seem to be metallic like the upper half. *Suddenly, all five of us were simultaneously gripped with dread and panic.* We rushed back into the car, which started perfectly, and drove off. As we looked back, we could still see the object pulsing away in the field." Paul Wilshire went on to add that Graeme Edge was a very likeable, friendly outgoing man, with a warm and generous personality, remaining totally unaffected by decades of international pop stardom. He was pretty well-off and has undoubtedly had all the publicity he could ever wish for. Therefore, he has no motives to make up such a story simply for publicity purposes. He is also not concerned about being labelled a crank. What happened, happened. And they all remember it. (Source: FSR 1991 V 36 N 2).

Andrew Perry
Bideford
Devon
England
February 27, 1968

Lorry driver Andrew Perry arrived at a Police Station on the night of February 27, 1968, to report his own very close encounter. Ina police statement Mr. Perry stared how he was driving his lorry on the road from Bideford to Cullompton at 6.55 pm when he saw a bright light appear at the top of a hill. AS he got closer, he could see the light came from a mushroom-shaped object.

"I drove a bit further down the road until I was abreast of the object, and I would think by then it was about three hundred yards distant. I stopped the lorry and climbed out of my cab, leaving the engine running. I climbed onto the trailer to get a better view and saw also what appeared to be five or six figures about four feet in height, they were a dozen or so yards from the object and were spread out around it...."

Suddenly these figures scrambled towards the UFO and disappeared inside. Then it climbed vertically and emitted a very high-pitched whirring noise that caused his lorry to vibrate. By this time, fear had replaced curiosity and he jumped back into the cab. Then: "I put the engine in gear and started to go down the road as fast as I could go.

The object had risen to about two hundred feet, and I travelled about a dozen yards, the noise from the object was so intense I couldn't hear my engine running-as it passed overhead. Suddenly, for no apparent reason, my engine cut out. I braked, stopped and cradled my head in my arms as I thought this object was coming right down on top of me.

A few seconds passed, the noise went and when I looked up it was about the size of a football and was going away into the sun at a really fantastic speed. I pulled myself together after a moment or so and automatically pressed the started button. The engine started and I went as fast as ever I could to the nearest police station."

Mr. Perry's report was located in the UK's Ministry of Defence UFO files by Dr. David Clarke. Dr. Clarke featured this account in his book 'The UFO Files' and added that Mr. Perry's report was distributed to a number of Mod branches and that checks were made on air defence radar without any success. Officials attempted to apply a sensible explanation and suspected that a low-flying helicopter was involved but checks with the Royal Air Force and nearby naval based ruled out this possibility. Unable to reach a conventional explanation, the MoD categorised Mr. Perry's report under 'miscellaneous' and decided to take no further action.

It would seem that the police once again took this matter seriously in passing on the report to the Ministry of Defence (MoD0. It made me smile and I'm sure it did you as well when the MoD files this as 'miscellaneous'. Although this is a single witness observation it has without doubt a good degree of high strangeness to it. Again, the witness was so troubled by what he had experienced that he felt in necessary to report it to his local police. We also have Mr. Perry's vehicle possibly being affected by the close approach of the UFO and we can't of course ignore the five or six figures observed as well.

Reverend Anthony G. Millican (and wife)
Arnos Park
Brislington
Bristol
Avon
England
April 27, 1968

At 9.20 pm on April 27, 1968, the Reverend Anthony Millican was taking an evening walk with his wife in Arnos Park. The park is on the Brislington side of Bristol. It was a fairly warm evening after a day of continuous rainfall. Visibility was good; there was no wind and a clear sky with only a small amount of light clouds cover.

 Suddenly, and without any warning, the couple saw a 'glowing' object which appeared to hover (or even be on the ground) some six feet off the ground at an estimated distance of seventy-five to one hundred yards away.

This single dome-shaped object was estimated to be twelve to fifteen feet in height and some ten to twelve feet in circumference. It was complete symmetrical, it neither increased nor decreased in size and its overall size remained constant. The colour of the outer rim was a dull yellow and the inside of the rim was an off-white colour, and the inner light was subject to irregular variations of size.

The whole thing was transparent, for the skyline at the crest of a slope beyond its position could be seen through the object. No sound was heard throughout the duration of the sighting.

A curious feature was mentioned by Reverend Millican, he stated that there was curious feature to the object this being a central pillar about four to five feet in height, but he did not say if this looked solid or was a different area of intense light. After about twenty seconds the object simply disappeared by just fading away.

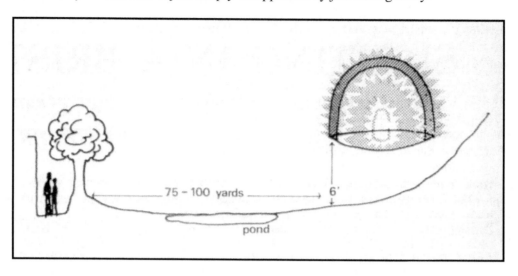

Layout of the sighting in Arnos Park

The witnesses reported the incident to the police at 10.00 pm that evening. The Chief Constable of Bristol was later supplied with a full report and the Bishop of Bristol was also informed.

This event was investigated (in writing, not in person) by Squadron Leader Alastair Provost. He asked the witnesses a number of questions:

Q: Did you feel a desire to attract anyone else's attention?

A: No, we were too awestruck.

Q: The sighting then appeared to be unusual to you. Could you later explain it in conventional terms?

A: Yes, very unusual. I could not explain it in conventional terms.

Q: Did you suffer from any physical effects during or after the sighting?

A: A chilling sensation. My wife felt chilled for three hours and vomited. My wife also slept badly that night and had dreams about it. I was all right.

Q: Are you knowledgeable about UFOs?

A: No, only from what I have read in newspaper articles.

Q: Looking back on your experience, can you now describe them any differently?

A: No.

Q: Has this sighting affected your outlook in relation to this phenomenon generally?

A: Yes, in the sense that I have seen 'something', but I am still not sure what it was. It may have been psychic (Mathew 24:24) or a materialisation of a 'fallen being' (Ephesians 6: 12-Heanenly places, upper atmosphere?). A chemist thinks it might have been Will 'o the Wisp.

Q: What was the immediate reaction of the police?

A: Serious, but they found nothing.

Like Paul Quick and family, the witnesses reported the incident to the police and according to the witnesses they treated it in a serious manner. Perhaps we could say that the sighting has a low degree of high strangeness, but it is peculiar to say the least. There seems nothing that immediately springs to mind that two witnesses would misidentify while walking through their local park. (Source: FSR 1968 V 14 N 4).

George Graham
Woodmansterne
Surrey
England
Summer 1968

Farmer George Graham stood quietly at the edge of a copse, shotgun in hand, waiting to eliminate any foxes as they emerged from their dens for another night of plunder. Suddenly his attention was drawn to a strange glow around one hundred yards away in the field which opened out in front of him. "At first I thought it was my neighbour tending to his lorry," said Mr, Graham, who runs a farm in the village of Woodmansterne, near Banstead, Surrey. After coming to this conclusion Mr. Graham paid no more attention to it and resumed his search for the foxes.

Then he heard what could only be described as a loud "whoosh" and, instinctively looking in the direction of the glow, Mr. Graham could just about make out a dark circular shape rising silently into the air. It gathered momentum and, in a matter of seconds, was lost to view in the night sky. Next day, Mr. Graham found evidence in the field that something out of the ordinary may have rested there the night before.

This incident took place in the summer of 1968, one night in either the last week of August of the first week of September, Mr. Graham cannot remember which. Details of this sighting did not come to light at the time simply because Mr. Graham did not report it to either the press or the police. He was afraid, as many witnesses are, of being ridiculed. UFO investigators Ron Toft and Dick Beet interviewed the witness at his farm. Elaborating further, Mr. Graham, of Hilltop Farm, said that he had seen the object between 10.00 and 10.30 pm. He was standing on the edge of the copse which crowns the summit of a small hill. The hill is surrounded on three sides by open grazing land. The field from which the UFO took off is bounded on three sides by a thin row of trees. On the fourth side is a fence which marks the boundary of Mr. Graham's farm. On the other side of this fence is more grazing land, belonging to Mr. Graham's neighbour.

View from the spot where Mr. Graham was standing

Photo courtesy of the Flying Saucer Review

Mr. Graham said he had been looking for foxes "quite a little while" prior to seeing the glow, which he described as being dark-blue and "acetylene-like". The glow was under the base of the UFO. The UFO took off "ten to fifteen minutes" after Mr. Graham saw the glow. He added that there was no sign life or other activity in the vicinity of the craft and there was no noise at any time.

Mr. Graham went on to add that when the UFO rose into the sky "I heard only a rush of air. It went straight up. It didn't go one way or the other. The glow went out after it went up." The UFO, which was not illuminated in any way, rose slowly at first increasing its speed as it got higher. Mr. Graham could only make out the spherical shape against the background of the night sky. He could not see any details on the craft.

The next day Mr. Graham returned to the field. He was surprised to find on the ground, a huge keyhole-shaped marking. Mr. Graham described it as being like "a big horseshoe with a heel on it." Mr. Graham estimated the length of the marking was about forty feet and the width twenty feet.

The width of the band as shown in the sketch was about eight inches. Inside this band it was discovered that all the grass, both blades and roots had neatly been plucked or sucked out of the ground "by a giant vacuum cleaner." Mr. Graham said that the UFO had been a "good deal higher than a double-decker bus." He had heard the "whoosh" only after the craft had attained an altitude of about one hundred feet. In the field at the same time as the UFO were twenty horses and an equal number of cattle. None of the animals showed any sign of distress during the sighting. Mr. Graham was adamant that the UFO was not an aircraft. "I came home straight away. I was frightened. I didn't know what it was at the time. I never heard it coming and I never heard it go. There was a rush of air, and it was gone. I think it was somebody from other countries, experimenting. They say it's from outer space, but I can't see it myself. I think it's a foreign power. I've never seen anything like it before or since."

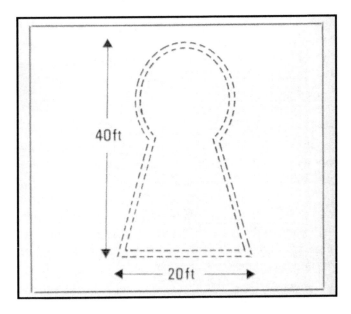

Sketch of the mark found in the field (courtesy the FSR)

Mr. Graham continued: "It was bloody big thing. How did they lift it without making any noise? I admit I got the wind up." Mr. Graham often returns to the copse at night-time looking for foxes and that he had heard of other sightings in the area before his. (Source: FSR-CH 1971 N 3).

The Milakovic family
Hanbury
Staffordshire
England
November 20, 1968

On the evening of November 20, 1968, many parts of England saw the re-entry of the Russian satellite Cosmos 253. This happened at around 7.00 pm. At around 5.30 pm that same evening a family from Hedensford had an encounter with a UFO near Hanbury in Staffordshire.

Mr and Mrs Milakovic and their eleven children lived in Hedensford which is not far from the southern edge of Cannock Chase in Staffordshire. That afternoon Mr and Mrs Milakovic and their son Slavic went on a house hunting trip which took them through Rugeley, Abbots Bromley and finally Hanbury.

After viewing Hanbury Hall they started on their homeward journey, stopping just outside of the village to look at another old house that was up for sale and, when they finally resumed their journey, the light was fading rapidly.

Soon after leaving Hanbury, they saw a rabbit run across the road and commented on their chances of catching it. They were soon amazed to see a large number of other rabbits following the first one from under a hedge on the left-hand side of the road. Suddenly, so much so that it must have been in darkness an instant before, they noticed a brilliantly lit object in the field on their left.

Rising slowly from the field the object then proceeded to pass over the car, which had been stopped by Mr. Milakovic, towards a solitary house standing approximate one hundred yards inside a field on the right-hand side of the road. Now out of the car, the witnesses were able to watch the progress of the object towards the house, over the top of which it stopped and hovered.

The sky was overcast, and it had started to rain. Mrs. Milakovic mentioned that when she first got out of the car but as the object moved away the temperature seemed to drop. All of the witnesses stared that they heard no noise from the object and that it appeared to 'wobble like jelly' as it hovered over the house.

The object was said to be much larger than the house and there were no lights on in the house as the UFO hovered over it. For about five minutes the witnesses were able to watch several figures, which they described in human from the form of silhouettes, walking backwards and forwards across the brilliantly lit top portion.

Occasionally some of the figures were seen to bend down as though looking at something in the part of the object below the rim, although nothing except the three lights and the figures was visible in the top part.

Once again, the object started to move away from the witnesses, only this time, instead of moving in a continuous motion, its progress was more of a pulsating or jerky nature. As it moved it climbed and the lights became very intense, so much so that Mr. Milakovic commented that it felt as though his eyes were burning with the brilliance.

Totally alarmed by now, Mr. Milakovic insisted that they leave the area as soon as possible and as they drove away the object was still visible over the fields.

Mrs. Milakovic explained that the feelings of both her and their son Slavic had been a mixture of excitement, curiosity and apprehension and at no time was there any malfunctioning of their car.

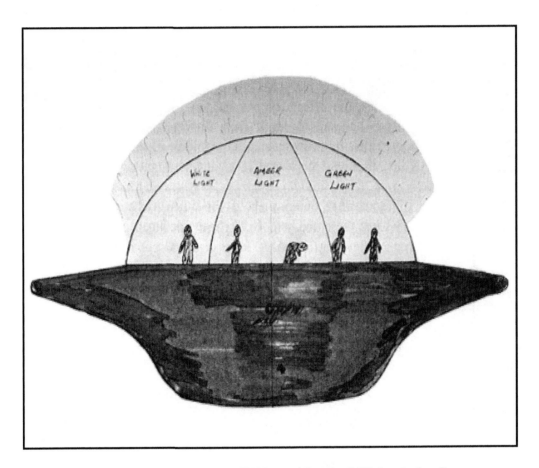

Artist impression of the UFO seen by the Milakovic family

This case was investigated by the British UFO Research Association, and they visited the witnesses and tried to find the location of the sighting. Unfortunately, they didn't come across the exact spot probably due to the fact that the witnesses were not familiar with the area and did not know the exact route they took.
(Source: BUFORA Journal Volume 2 No.7 Winter 1968(9) Hanbury 1968).

I think it is fare to say that this incident does have a fairly high degree of high strangeness. The close proximity of the UFO to the witnesses, three witnesses, effects on the temperature, the 'figures' seen in the UFO and so on. Surely with such a high degree of high strangeness this case can't be written off as a misidentification of something ordinary?

Miss Helen Carr
Bangor
County Down
Northern Ireland
August 11, 1969

At Groomsport near Bangor in Northern Ireland the witness's attention was first drawn to something unusual at 1.00 am on August 11, 1969. Helen Carr was awoken by a bright light. This light was coming from behind a small hill opposite her bedroom. After watching the light for a short while she observed a disc rise up over the top of the hill. She described the object as being oval-shaped with a large bright light at the front.

She could not see the outline of the object but presumed it to be oval because she saw what she thought was a row of lights around the rim. The object made no noise and appeared to be higher in position above the ground when it came over the hill than it was when it began to descend the hill towards the by-pass which runs in front of the Carr family home.

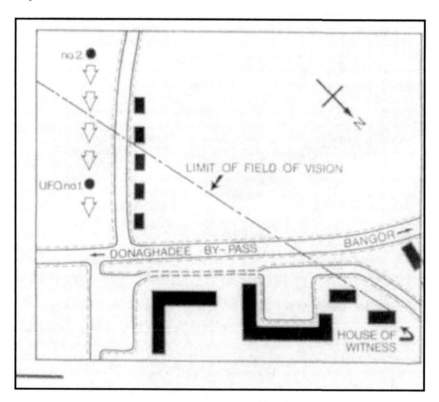

Map of the UFO sighting by Helen Carr

Miss Carr's description of the behaviour of the light is extremely interesting. According to her, the light appeared to be operating the same way as searchlight but although she could see the light moving around the houses on the estate, she could see no beam connecting it to the bright like on the vehicle.

At one stage the light crossed her bedroom illuminating part of the walls. Miss Carr was unable to describe the exact nature of the light but was quite definite that it was not a spot like that created by a torch or searchlight. The beam never stopped but kept moving, apparently shining on the upstairs rooms of all the houses. Miss Carr remarked that she could not look away from this object in spite of the fact that she felt rather cold, and that the entire affair lasted about an hour.

When the first object was about halfway down the field it was followed by a second object which appeared to be in similar appearance to the first. Eventually Miss Carr's view of the objects was obstructed by the next-door house.

Sat this point a car came along the by-pass in front of her house and she heard it apply the brakes although she was unable to see if it had stopped since both it and the two objects were by now out of view. Miss Carr watched to see if the objects would reappear but when they did not, she got back in bed and went to sleep.

The following morning Miss Carr discovered that her father had been awakened during the night by bright lights but did not get up to investigate. Her next-door neighbour had also noticed something peculiar but she too had decided to stay in bed. Miss Carr when to have a look in the field where the object had been observed but nothing unusual was found.

There is a lighthouse in the area, but it cannot be seen from the witness's house. Miss Carr was quite emphatic about what she had seen and had not seen anything like it since. (Source: FSR-CH 1971 N 5).

We could argue with this case that there isn't a lot of high strangeness involved, however, the fact that two objects were observed and that there were other witnesses to the 'lights' does give it a fare degree of possibility that it was not anything conventional. For example, if this was a conventional aircraft of some kind then why would they be flying around a housing estate at one in the morning shining a bright light onto the local resident's houses?

The 1960's in the UK saw many political, musical and cultural changes to the country. Changes that would last forever and many of which, like music, would still have an influence on the world today.

Interest in UFO research was growing, and we can see by the sample of cases featured in this chapter that more often than not if you reported your sighting to the police then they would deal with it in a serious manner. The high strangeness factor in the close encounter reports has not diminished and despite the fact that UFOs were not being taken serious by the mainstream scientific establishments the general public still continued to report them. Again, just from the sample of cases in this chapter it is easy to see as far as I'm concerned that the close encounter cases seem to happen at random.

There is no one geographical area where they are more prevalent, no age group, social standing, religion, race or cultural background of individuals that would suggest they are more susceptible to these experiences. Sceptics will inform you that such encounters always happen in out of the way locations and are only witnessed by one witness. Well, again from this chapter we can see that this is simply not true. The high strangeness factor increases in fact when we have multiple witnesses to such events.

Whatever UFOs may or not may be and whatever is their nature and origin, the swinging sixties in Britain had its fair share of UFO close encounters around the nation and as the sixties faded into history the UFO phenomenon continued onwards and possibly came to a peak in the next decade, the 1970's.

*****

CHAPTER FOUR

CHANGING TIMES – THE 1970's

If the 1960's in Britain had been a time of The Beatles and flower power, then the 1970's could not have been more different. On the music scene the early 1970's saw the rise of 'glam-rock' out of which global superstars Elton John and David Bowie emerged. As the decade changed so did the music first with punk rock scaring the living daylights out of parents and then disco seeing the nightclub dance floors fill with would-be John Travolta's. Economically Britain was not in a good place with high inflation, unemployment and strikes bringing the government of Edward Heath to its knees. The major political change came in 1979 when Britain's first ever woman Prime Minster, Margaret Thatcher was elected. Of course, it was in 1978 (1977 in the USA) that UK cinema goers flocked to see Start Wars and of course Steven Spielberg's epic Close Encounters of the Third Kind. Not only were UFOs the stuff of science fiction movies but more and more high strangeness cases were reported. Was this just a coincidence?

Barry Canner
Warminster
Wiltshire
England
September 28, 1971

The following case was investigated by Eileen Buckle, Charles Bowen and Bryan Winder. They were all connected to the Flying Saucer Review magazine and were alerted to this case by local journalist and author Arthur Shuttlewood.

Barry Canner on site in his car (photo courtesy FSR)

The witness was Barry Canner who is described as mild-mannered Yorkshireman. Mr. Canner was said to be an enthusiastic runner and it was whilst on a training run that he spotted an unusual looking object in a field. Barry Canner described the incident carefully, perhaps a little bit hesitantly, as follows. It took place on September 28. That evening he left his carat the side of a trackway at Lord's hill. He knows this path well and often uses it for running practice as it is quiet, and he is bothered by no-one. He began his run at about 8.00 pm and returned to his car at about 9.30 pm. By this time, it was quite dark. A few stars were out, but there was no moon that night.

As he was nearing the car, he noticed a weird looking object some ten yards away to his left in a field alongside the lane, and which had not been there when he set out. He claimed that despite the darkness he had been able to make out the details of the object quite clearly. This was due, he said, to a faint pinkish glow it emitted, rather like that given out by a luminous watch dial at night. The shape was like a bio-convex oval, rising up to a projection at the rear which looked rather like an exhaust pipe. At what could have been the forward end was a dome-shaped window, and at one side were three triangular markings which might have been 'portholes'; these, evidently, gave out more light than the rest of the object and the light was more of a whitish hue. The length of the object was about fourteen feet, and its diameter was twelve feet. Three legs supported the structure from underneath, the ground clearance being six feet and the total height above the ground being eleven feet. There was also a cylindrical hatch projecting from the underneath and reaching to with two feet of the ground.

Illustration courtesy of the Flying Saucer Review. Barry Canner's UFO based on his sketches.

Bryan Winder, a design engineer, was particularly in the structure of the legs which were said to taper from a diameter of about two feet at the top to about three inches at the extremity. He asked if the legs would be in the same relation-were the structure an aircraft-as that between the nosewheel and the two wheels behind it.

The reply was in the affirmative, but Barry added that there were no wheels; instead, each leg terminated in a foot or a pad in the shape of an equilateral triangle of side one and a half feet. These, he said, had made a two-inch-deep impression in the dry, chalky soil. He was asked if he went back to look at these impressions. His reply was that he returned to the site with local UFO researcher Bob Long who took some photos but whether they came out or not was not known.

The three investigators asked if there was any movement of the object, or any sign of life seen. Barry said there was none whatsoever, and because of this he had become growlingly uneasy. He was sure that it was a machine from outer space, and he felt he was being watched. He theorised that 'they' had been attracted to his 'streamlined' car, a Singer Chamois Coupe. After eyeing the strange contraption for an estimated five to ten minutes, he jumped into the car and fled homewards, covering the distance from Lord's Hill to Warminster in 'record time'.

Later the three investigators went to the scene of the incident at Lord's Hill. They followed Barry Canner up the trackway and parked by a gate that which marked the spot where he claimed he had stood at closest proximity to the object. This had apparently been resting in a slight hollow in the field adjacent to the lane, which was lined by a wire fence. The field, which sloped downwards into a valley, was now freshly ploughed. It was a very open kind of terrain with rolling downs (hills), and the few scrubby bushes alongside the lane would have afforded little cover for any person. The investigators didn't stay long as it was a cold and wet day. On the way back to Warminster Barry collected his friend Andrew Pritchard. Mr, Pritchard was somewhat sceptical about the large amounts of UFO sightings in Warminster (Warminster was a hotbed of UFO sightings in the 1960's and 1970's) but he did say that Barry did look a little unwell for a few days after the encounter.

The three investigators questioned Barry about his background and discovered that he had reported a previous UFO sighting back in 1967 and that he was very much a UFO enthusiast. They were convinced that Barry was not lying but could not be certain about what he had seen. Various ideas were dreamt up, even the possibility that Barry had failed to recognise some farm machinery and had been scared of it, fleeing the scene believing he had seen a UFO. However, the three investigators did go on to discus other ideas of why a lone runner might be the witness to such an event. They wondered if Barry's 1967 sighting and this one might be connected. (Source: FSR-CH 1971 N 3).

Although the investigators at the time were somewhat biased as they knew full well of Mr. Canner's interest in UFOs this surely cannot be held against him. Mr. Canner watched this object at close range for five to ten minutes. Surely if it had been some kind of farm machinery, he would have easily identified it as such. Mr. Canner's case has its fair share of high strangeness, and he is either lying or telling the truth. You decide.

Mr Sydney W.
Aylesbury
Buckinghamshire
England
December 8, 1971

The following case was originally investigated by Andy Collins and Barry King of the UFO Investigators Network (UFOIN). The incident wasn't reported until 1978 after a feature in the Daily Express newspaper. The witness's real name is on file and the encounter took place in December 1971 near Aylesbury in Buckinghamshire.

Sydney W. was twenty years of age at the time and on the night in question he left his girlfriend's house (later to be his wife) and headed off home on foot along the A418 road towards Aylesbury. As usual he was hitch-hiking, although none of the cars that passed stopped to offer him a lift. He walked about three miles out of the village of Wing towards Aylesbury and was about one and a half miles from the village of Rowsham. Glancing around he caught sight of a "falling star" in the sky to the north-west descending rapidly. Suddenly to his amazement this white "falling star" stopped, then carried on its path of descent, then stopped again. In total it stopped and started three times, during which time it seemed to be getting considerably nearer and was showing a small trail behind it as it moved.

After the third leaping movement it stopped motionless over a clump of trees some four hundred yards away, thirty to forty yards up and almost horizontal in his line of sight. It was at the point that the brightness of the light began diminish and a cigar-shape, with a blue-green hue around it could be observed. Again, the object began to move this time 'gliding' nose first, horizontally across the path of the witness, stopping some thirty to forty yards in front of him above the road. He was now able to see that the object was not a cigar-shape, but was in fact a blunt bullet-shape, or a cylinder rounded at the nose and flat at the rear.

The object was around seven to eight feet above the ground and was silent and motionless apart from a quivering luminescence around it. Although this was strong it cast no light on the ground blow. There were no protuberances noted at all, it appeared perfectly smooth all over, and could only be estimated as "the size of a house." The duration of the sighting so far had been no longer than one minute.

Up until this point Sydney had felt stunned, almost frozen to the spot, but once the object took up this close position, he felt warm, relaxed and calm. He had no desire to leave; in fact, he could not recall ever thinking about leaving.

Suddenly, midway along the underside of the object a dark circular shadow appeared, suggesting that "something had opened", and from which, a bright white glowing parallel shaft or tube of light quickly extended towards the ground. This shaft of light had an estimated diameter of around three to four feet and could what some researchers call 'sold light', for as it descended a definite base to the 'shaft of light' could be observed. AS it touched the ground, the shaft of light seemingly started to glow red, and a tall figure descended down inside it. Once the entity had reached the ground, the shaft of light quickly returned up into the object, leaving the entity standing directly below it.

Within a few seconds the entity started moving at a fast pace along the road towards the witness in a shuffling movement, yet also, as Sydney tried to explain, in a gliding movement, all the time keeping his arms down by his sides.

The entity was a lot taller than Sydney, approximately seven feet tall. It had very broad shoulders with a large chest, large arms, although in proportion with the body, and oddly enough "spindly" thin legs and small feet. He was wearing a shiny silver one-piece, tight fitting suit, made of what appeared to be a thin material.

This suit covered the entire body including his feet, excluding his hands, and covering the side and back of his cranium in what he described as a "balaclava", which extended around level over his forehead, coming down in front of his ears, then down the side of the neck and under his jaw. Bumps wear the ears would have been were noted on each side of the head. The face was perfectly human-like with two eyes, a nose and a mouth all well proportioned. Eyebrows were also visible which appeared to be a "bleach-blonde" colour. Across the whole of the face was a very fine, closely knit, silver mesh, likened to the wearing of a woman's stocking, which seemed to be joined onto the one-piece suit. The skin appeared to be smooth and light in colour, although as can be imagined it was hard to see under the mesh. The hands were likewise covered in a similar type of silver mesh, modelled into mittens separating the thumb from the other four fingers on each hand. The one-piece suit ended in a 'V' shape over the top of each hand, from which, extending up each arm, over the shoulder to the base of the neck was a black line. A similar line ran from the side of the hip diagonally up over the abdomen then back down to the other hip. In the region of the lower abdomen there appeared to be a large protrusion, as if the entity was wearing a jockstrap. Around the whole outline of the body appeared a fluorescent glow, extending some half an inch and a radiant heat was felt "as if he were hot."

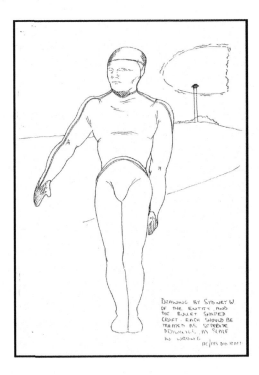

Illustration courtesy of UFOIN

The entity stopped at an arm's length away from Sydney and stood with its feet together and arms by its sides. After a few seconds the entity moved its head down to look at the witness, and then raised its right arm, keeping it perfectly straight with the palm facing downwards, and the fingers together with hand open, up until the arm was level with Sydney's head, then dropping it down almost to its original position. This exercise went on for around two minutes with each movement taking approximately twelve seconds, with the hand passing within one inch at the closest point.

While this was happening Sydney said that he felt an odd sensation inside him, described variously as nice, soothing, warm, relaxing and tingling, which was aside from the sensation already present since the object had been in close proximity. Alongside these sensations, Sydney felt as if the entity was "drawing something" from him "my life, and things I had done", also that he was being "used as a guinea-pig to find out information." Why he thought this he does not know. He said he "just felt it" at the time.

After the arm returned to its original position, the entity remained motionless, then suddenly a high-pitched hum or buzzing noise was emitted from its head which lasted just a few seconds. It then swivelled around slowly and began to move backwards towards the waiting object in a similar shuffling and gliding manner as that of its approach. Once it had reached the position at which it had originally stepped onto the ground, there was bright flash and once again the tube or shaft of light was surrounding the entity.

Sydney watched the entity ascend quickly up the shaft of light after which it disappeared. After another five or six seconds, the object began gliding away at a leisurely pace, nose first towards the south-east picking up speed as it did. Eventually the object was surrounded by a white glow and a tail behind it. Then, suddenly there was a loud bang along with a bright flash of light, and the object was gone. The whole incident had taken around five or six minutes, although Sydney said it seemed much longer.

Sydney said that once the object had moved away the warm sensation and the tingling sensation dissipated but the warmness he felt when the entity was moving its arm still remained. He said he felt a rush of adrenalin through his body, and he waited a few minutes after the object had gone before deciding what to do. He decided it was time to run which he di until he reached the village of Rowsham around one and a half mile away.

At the point a car passed him, the first one since he's left the village of Wing. Unfortunately, it did not stop. Then a police car came by and stopped and gave Sydney a lift into Aylesbury, leaving him with just a short walk home. Sydney did not mention what he had just witnessed to the police. Sydney thinks he arrived home at two or three in the morning, but he can't be sure. Sydney kept quiet about the whole event for over a year before he decided to tell his close family and friends only.

The investigators of this case came to the conclusion that Sydney's encounter was authentic and objective and it had a great effect on him as a result. (Source: UFOIN_19711200).

The investigators at UFOIN were very experienced and trustworthy and not worried if they found something suspicious during their investigations. Similarly, they were more than prepared to go on the record and state openly that a case was unidentified. This encounter is pretty unique in many ways and is of course very strange. If UFOIN state that it was authentic then who am I to disagree with them?

Anthony Cureton
Barnsley
South Yorkshire
England
January 1972

In January 1972, Mr. Anthony Cureton was out walking the family dog with his two children – Jacqueline and Tony, just around one hundred and fifty yards from their house at Kendray, Barnsley, in South Yorkshire. The time was 7.30 pm. While walking the dog they saw a strange looking torpedo-shaped craft, which appeared to have two or three levels to it, all full of dark lights, with a halo around it, which descended vertically. The object, then about seven hundred feet above them, landed on the other side of a six-foot-high concrete wall (forming the boundary line to a complex of football fields.

Artist impression of the UFO observed by the children. (Artwork by Steve Franklin).

According to the two children: "A pointed face then popped up above the wall, showing pointed ears and large red eyes." Frightened the children ran back to tell their father, who was trailing just a short distance behind. On looking back there was no sign of the craft or the entity.

Mrs. Cureton confirmed that the children had arrived home in a very frightened state and refused to go out in the dark for some time afterwards. Jacqueline, who was apparently the worst affected by the experience, could remember little about what had taken place, whereas Tony (who was older) had no problem remembering, with clarity, what he had witnessed. Mr Cureton said: "I remember Tony mentioning this event, from time to time, and didn't attach much importance to it: besides, there was a story of a UFO landing in the nearby school playing fields back in the 1950's. No details of this earlier event have been located.
(Source: Dan Goring – Earth link and John Hanson – Haunted Skies volume 5).

John and Sandra Taylor
Near Thirsk
North Yorkshire
England
August 17, 1972

It is not always wise to look at such close encounter events when the only source of information is a newspaper. However, we have to realise at times that the newspaper, usually a local one, was the first point of contact for someone wishing to report a UFO sighting. In the 1970's there was of course no such thing as the internet so if you wanted to report anything, not just a UFO encounter, then the local newspaper was always there.

The next encounter that we look at here was featured in the FSR, but the original source of the information was a local newspaper.

The following account is taken from the Stockport Advertiser of August 24, 1972. "Probably the closest ever sighting of an unidentified flying object has been made by a Heald Green couple-in fact the object was not even flying but almost settled in a field on a lonely Yorkshire road.

It fitted the description of a flying saucer, a glowing melon-shaped structure with a tapering base with a 'T'-shaped door. This is about all the couple noticed, for when the door began to open they got back in the car and fled.

Safe at home at Heald Green 30-year-old Mr John Taylor told the Advertiser about his experience. His wife Sandra had left for a holiday in Gibraltar. "I can only describe it as my weird experience" he said. "My wife and I were driving home from Newcastle at about two o'clock in the morning on Thursday (17th August). We were on Ripponden Road, between York and Thirsk, and suddenly Sandra to pull up. The thing was in a field beside the road. We could not see the base properly because of a high edge. It was about twenty feet high and a great deal more than that across, and glowing a weird luminous colour, which I could not possibly describe. At one time I would have laughed at anyone saying things like this, but it was a weird experience, and when that door began to open nothing would have made me stay around. "

Mrs Taylor made a statement to Cheadle Hume police when she arrived home, expecting to meet with scepticism, but their inquiries told them that other people had reported a similar experience, including a man who had stopped his car at the same time as the Taylors. "York police are investigating."
(Source: FSR 1972 V 18 N 5).

Ernest Scott
High Wycombe
Buckinghamshire
England
Winter 1972

Ernest Scott from High Wycombe (owner of a private pilot's license) found himself the witness to a UFO around midnight in the winter of 1972. He was travelling towards Marlow by car on the A4155 road, between Henley-on-Thames.

As he approached a bend at the end of a long, straight part of the road, he noticed some lights by the verge of the dual carriageway ahead of him. When he drew closer, he was astonished to see a strange object in the bushes by the side of the road.

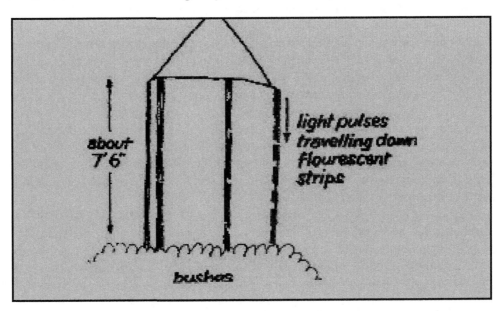

Sketch of the UFO seen by Ernest Scott (courtesy John Hanson)

"It was the size of a telephone kiosk, with a conical top, with four fluorescent strip lights, pulsing with light, that moved slowly from top to bottom, attached to the outside of the object, which I thought would have been hexagonal if you could have looked down from above."

The next thing Ernest remembers he was driving through Marlow, some miles further down the road, and looking at his watch, when he realised it was about one and a half hours later than when he last looked. (Source: John Makin, Police Officer Nicholas Maloret, WATSUP and John Hanson, Haunted Skies volume 5).

105

Andrew Westmorland, William Holt and Kevin Jackson
Eccup
West Yorkshire
England
Jan 4, 1973

Another case from the excellent UFOIN team came to light in 1977 although the UFO sighting in question took place in 1973. Thankfully UFOIN kept the original paperwork for this case which sadly has been lost for a lot of cases. I quote directly from the paperwork on the UFOIN file.

The UFOIN file begins with a handwritten letter direct from the main witness a Mr. Andrew Westmorland:

"Dear Sirs,

I was a member of the now disbanded organisation known as LUFORG and hence I will try to give you a clear as detailed as possible. I have used the old LUFORG (Leeds UFO Research Group) questionnaire for basic information, but the 'sighting' was a rather 'good one' so I feel a much more comprehensive report is necessary.

On the report form you will find an ordinance survey map grid reference. This is a house. We had parked the vehicle (Ford Escort Estate) and were stood beside it. The night was crystal clear, and we were observing stars through binoculars. We were also watching for meteors, because there was a shower on.

One of my companions, Bill Holt, shone his torch off the road into a field, which is a golf course, and at once remarked that he had illuminated something, which had rapidly moved away. He did it again, and we all observed a point of light, similar to a 'cats' eyes' look out of the beam. On further investigation, we realised several in the field. The time was now approximately 21.15 GMT.

We then heard the sound of clanking metal, apparently come from the field. This, however, could have come from a nearby farm although we doubt it as it sounded so close. Nothing 'metallic' could be seen in the field. The farmers dogs were by this time causing quite a racket and were whining as if in pain or fear. Time about 21.20 PMT.

We next observed a stationary single light in the woods surrounding the reservoir. There is nothing down there (i.e., roads, houses, etc) and shortly after its appearance; all the birds which were on the reservoir suddenly took off. This struck us as strange, as the birds are used to ordinary disturbances such as people, sound of cars, aircraft etc. This was at about 21.25 GMT.

I proceeded away from the other two and walked down the road just about one hundred yards, to a gated entrance to the field. I could see nothing. I turned to go back, when I saw, further down the road and on the other side, a faint light. I approached it and found it to be a faintly glowing triangle with sides about two feet long and with a width of about eight feet. This was lying on the grass verge beside the road. I approached within one foot of it and bent down to take a closer look.

I then heard a humming noise, similar to H.T. hum of about 50 Hz (hertz). It ceased after about a second and from above me, as if I was still bent, I heard a voice say the word 'come' as if it were an amplified whisper. Time was 21.30 GMT.

I am afraid to say, this came as rather a shock to me, and I proceeded in considerable haste back to my companions, who immediately drove off. A regretful action, I now, but that's it! As I ran back to the car, Bill said he saw an enlarging black triangle following me. We drove back to Leeds.

Points of interest may be.

Eccup is built on a 2000 feet deep shale Bed. There is a reservoir. We have observed other strange happenings in the area. The weather was cold, clear and dry. I believe both my companions to be trustworthy, and although Bill may exaggerate at times, he would never invent a story for the sake of it.

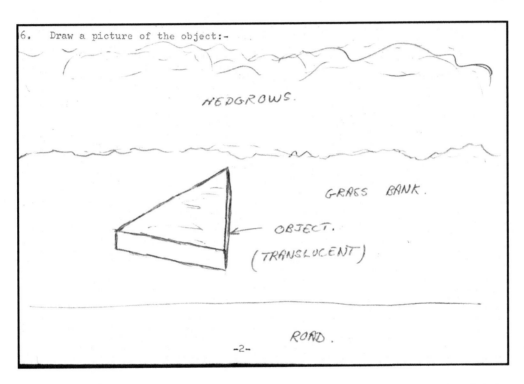

Drawing of the triangle object taken from Andrew Westmorland's sighting report form.

If all this sounds far-fetched, I can only assure you of its truth and of our sincerity. I hope the report is of some use to you; if you require any further information which I may have neglected, I shall be pleased to answer any and all questions, as I am sure my companions will. I must now apologise for the delay in sending this report, but I have been occupied on a different matter.

P.S.

I have deleted the questions on the form which are not applicable.

Yours Sincerely,

A. Westmorland
W. Holt
K. Jackson

P.S.

If you require further information as regards Q.31, please write to me and I will be glad to oblige. "

The report submitted by Andrew Westmorland was accompanied by a typed written and signed statement from one of the other witnesses, Andrew Jackson and a handwritten and signed statement from William Holt. (Source: UFOIN_19730104).

Signed statement from Andrew Jackson from the UFOIN file

There will be those that scoff at the sighting, and I can easily see why but when viewing the full case file like I have it helps you come to a conclusion. All three witnesses provided written and signed statement. I'm sure you have read elsewhere of triangular UFOs been spotted round the world but surely this one is very unique. The triangular object in question is rather small and it's seen lying on the ground next to a hedge. How strange is that?

Mr. Y's daughter & friend
Sandown
Isle of Wight
England
May 1973

Mr. Y's details had been passed to Norman Oliver of the Flying Saucer Review by author Leonard Cramp. Mr. Y had requested anonymity because of his young daughter's involvement. Mr. Y detailed two UFO sightings that he had on the Isle of Wight, one in 1970 and the other in 1972. Interesting although these two sightings maybe it his young daughter and her friends encounter that we will concentrate on.

It was May 1973 that Mr. Y's seven-year-old daughter claimed to have a very bizarre encounter. 'Fay' as we shall call her, was ear Lake Common, Sandown on a Tuesday afternoon with a boy about the same age when they both heard a weird noise not unlike an ambulance siren. They follow it across the golf-links and through a hedge leading to a swampy area adjacent to Sandown Airport. Now the noise disappeared.

Artist impression of the creature seen by Fay and her friend (courtesy BUFORA)

As they were crossing a wooden footbridge over a narrow brook, a blue-gloved hand appeared from under the bridge and a strange figure emerged. The figure fumbled with a book, dropped in into the water, then splashed about to retrieve it. The two youngsters then watched the figure enter a metallic hut similar to those used on building sites except that it had no windows. The figure moved along with a strange hopping motion with knees raised high.

The children walked away and were some around fifty yards away when the figure (which will now be referred to as 'he') reappeared carrying a black-knobbed microphone with a white flex attached. The wailing noise immediately returned, this time being so loud that the boy was scared and began to run away: the noise ceased, and 'he' spoke into the microphone and although he was a good distance from the children they could still hear his voice as clearly as if 'h' was right next to them. "Hello, are you still there?" he asked, and in response to what sounded like a friendly tone they moved back close enough to speak to this oddly attired 'person'.

He was nearly seven feet tall and had no neck-as his head appeared to be wedged straight onto his shoulders. He wore a yellow, pointed hat, which interlocked with a red collar of a green tunic. A round, black knob was fixed to the top of his hat and 'wooden' antennae attached to either side. The face had triangular markings for eyes, a brown square of a nose and motionless yellow lips. Other round markings were on his white-coloured cheeks and a fringe of red hair was across his forehead. 'Wooden slats' protruded from his sleeves and from below his white trousers. His first communication was in writing.

He wrote in a notebook in large print, "Hello and I am all colours, Sam." The boy was hesitant, but Fay read each word as it was pointed to. This was necessary as the words were not laid out in sequence. The children ventured closer and discovered that the creature could talk without the aid of a microphone, though his lips did not move and his speech was unclear, rather like that of a person who does not open his mouth properly. He asked the children about themselves so they in turn decided to ask him some questions. They asked about his clothes, which were all ripped, and he told them he only had one set so he could only wear those. Because of his strange white features, they asked if he really was a man. He answered with a chuckle and said "no".

His vague reply was more of, "Well, not really, but I am in an odd sort of way". What are you then they asked, but he replied "you know" with no further explanation. He also said he had no name. There were others like him, and he drew a rough sketch of them. He also confided that he was frightened of people and was sacred they might hurt him. Apparently if attacked he would not retaliate.

At his invitation the children crawled through a flap into his hut, which contained two levels. The lower, had plenty of headroom and was 'wall-papered' in blue-green and covered in a pattern of dials. It also had an electric heater and simple, wooden furniture. The upper level was less spacious, and the floor was metallic. He told the children that he fed upon berries which he collected in the late afternoon but didn't say where but did indicate that he had a 'camp' on the mainland that he could go to. He also said that water from the river could be drunk once he had cleaned it. Once inside the hut he removed his hat to reveal round, white ears and thin brown hair. Before eating a berry, he performed an odd 'conjuring trick'.

He placed the berry in his ear, thrust his head forward and caused the berry to disappear and reappear in one of his odd eyes: repeating the process, the berry travelled to his mouth.

Artist impression of the hut that the creature lived in (courtesy BUFORA)

The children talked to this strange being for half an hour or more, then after saying 'goodbye' they rushed across the golf-links to tell the first man they met that they had seen a ghost: he merely laughed. But the children were convinced of their experience and that the being was either a ghost or someone dressed up.

Fay told her father (Mr.) of her experience some three weeks later, on June 2nd, 1973. At first, he found the story very hard to believe but was amazed at the detailed account and Fay's certainty that it was true. Mr. Y also spoke to the boy who was with Fay and although he was not as talkative as his daughter, he did confirm their story and that it was indeed true.

Mr. Y added that although bizarre, certain elements of the children's story rang true to him, and he also took account of the possibility of some connection with his own previous UFO sightings. Summing up he said: "I get the impression that Fay was somehow taken into a bubble of alien reality created by this strange personage.....he told then he had just made the hut.

Also, Fay told me that while they were talking to this 'ghost', two workmen nearby were repairing a post. They paid no attention to the weird charade, as though they could not see it."
(Source: BUFORA Journal Volume 6 No.5 Jan-Feb 1978).

Some might say that this is not a UFO related story but what I will say is that it is really bizarre. When it comes to high strangeness this case has it all. Although the witnesses are young there are two of them. The entity observed is like nothing I have seen anywhere else in the UFO literature and the 'UFO' looks like a work-man's tin hut. The most bizarre aspect of the whole incident to me is that there were workman nearby fixing a post of some kind, but they did not observe anything out of the ordinary. This case is like a mixture of folklore, fantasy and ufology all mixed into one.

Peter and Diane Shepherd
Roade
Northamptonshire
England
August 1973

Peter and Diane Shepherd had a close encounter of their own in Roade, Northamptonshire back in August 1973.

Peter and Diane Shepherd with a drawing of the UFO (courtesy John Hanson)

"We were just leaving a friend's house at 3.00 am when we saw a saucer-shaped object about the size of a football pitch in a field," said Mr Shepherd. "I stood on the roof of the car to get a better look and was completely dumbfounded by the sight, because its size was staggering. "The craft was dark grey in colour and perfectly smooth, with seven rectangular, amber-coloured lights or windows on the side facing us. It was beautiful to behold and was as real and as solid as the car I was standing on. We were all sober and fully conscious and saw and experienced the same thing." Mr Shepherd added that the saucer was accompanied by illuminated red spheres in the sky which hovered over the treetops and the road. "I wanted to get a closer look, so my wife and I got in the car and drove a few hundred yards towards them, he said." I thought we would be in a good position when they passed overhead but when I stopped the car one instantly appeared in front of us."

Mr Shepherd said he and his wife then experienced a period of "missing time", with about 40 minutes they couldn't account for. "The next thing I knew I was driving down the road about 300 yards further down and the dawn was already coming up," he said. "It was an incredible experience that has changed the way both of us see the world and our perception of reality forever." We were elated afterwards because we knew we had experienced something amazing." Mr Shepherd, who said he had seen UFOs since he was a child, added that they were well aware that many people would dismiss their experience and refuse to believe it could be possible.

"Even our families won't believe us, he said." We still get people ringing up who just can't tell anyone else because they are worried that people will think they are daft or crazy. "A lot of people are afraid to come forward and say they have seen something, or they can't handle it, because it is a life-changing thing." My wife and I are very fortunate because it's rare for a couple to have the same experiences, and it can drive people apart. "But we are confident that future phenomena will help everyone, who chooses to, to gain a greater understanding of ourselves, the alien intelligence, and the position we share together in the overall scheme of things.

My friend and colleague John Hanson personally interviewed Peter and Diane and he found them to be the most warm, friendly and honest people one could wish to meet: As well as running NUFORUM - the Northamptonshire UFO Forum, (now sadly defunct), they always enjoyed speaking about their strange encounter to other UFO groups and individuals. John met the pair numerous times and interestingly, on one occasion, when I asked Pete to elaborate regarding the makeup of the main object he had seen, (e.g., whether he thought it was metallic etc, etc), he described it as looking rather like a 'glowing jellyfish'! (Source: John Hanson).

Two witnesses here and some may doubt this encounter because of Mr. Shepherd's previous UFO sightings. However, for me the most curious part of this case is the element of 'missing time'. I have come across this in a number of cases down the years and it does give a 'hint' to the authenticity of such events.

Lance Corporal Mike Perrin and Trooper Carvell
Bellerby Moor
Bellerby
North Yorkshire
England
Summer 1973

The following account came to light in 1977 after Jenny Randles had appeared in a magazine article and the case was passed on to Barry King for investigation.

A place caller Bellerby Moor was the setting for the following encounter. It is a lonely and desolate location on the edge of the Yorkshire Dales National Park in North Yorkshire, England. Much of the land is agricultural but certain parts were owned by the Ministry of Defence. The area is dotted with woods and small villages.

The incident took place at a location near a large, wooded area and is divided by a minor road. On either side of the road, before reaching the woods, are larger rolling fields. In the field to the east of the road a herd of cows.

Stationed at Catterick Garrison Lance Corporal Mike Perrin and his colleague Trooper Carvel were taking part on a regular radio exercise out on the moors, several miles west of their camp. On the evening in question more than twenty vehicles were to drive out on to Bellerby Moor. Mr. Perrin was now uncertain of the date but thinks it was May or June 1973. All went well when they separated on the moors; Mike Perrin found a suitable spot for the Land Rover and pulled into the side of a small road while listening to the two-way radio for instructions. It was about 11.00 pm when the radio began to crackle, and the voices began to break up. After a few seconds the radio went completely dead, and at the same time the headlights on their vehicle faded and went out. The engine of the Landrover was not running at the time, as it had been switched off a few seconds before the radio failure.

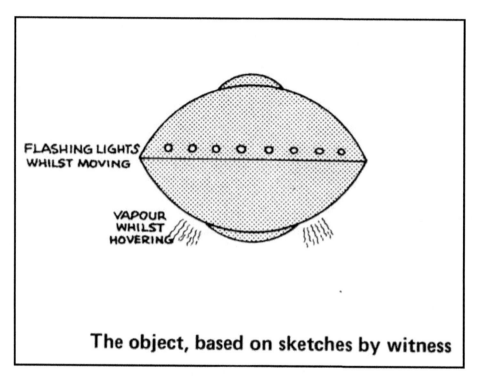

The object, based on sketches by witness

Illustration courtesy the Flying Saucer Review

The two soldiers were a little bit concerned as they were due to report to base and were now unable to do so. Knowing for sure that they would be in trouble they desperately tried to fix the radio; they also tried switching channels, but all to no avail. They could not summon help on foot as the nearest unit was between ten and fifteen miles away, and their base was also around fifteen miles from them.

So, they just sat there hoping that the radio would somehow come back on again. After a while Mike Perrin was about to start the Landrover when he noticed something in the air above them and to the left. He nudged his colleague and they both watched the strange aircraft that was approaching them. Whatever it was, it was about half a mile away when first seen. Silently it flew towards them and stopped at a distance of around one hundred yards, hovering some ten feet above the ground. The Landrover side windows down as it was a very clear and warm evening. The shape of the strange craft was easily discernible against the clear sky. It was shaped like a rugby ball and had a row of small circular windows around its middle section.

Through these windows shone white lights which seemed to flash; the two soldiers also observed what they thought to be some form of vapour coming from the lowest part of the object.

A very slight buzzing sound emanated from the object the whole time it was in view. They sat dumfounded and more than a little nervous, and while looking around for any other possible witnesses who may have arrived, they noticed that the herd of cows in the field to their left, but beyond the craft, were 'frozen' to the spot. Not one of them moved an inch, and their eyes were fixed on the UFO.

After what seemed like an eternity, but in reality, was only five or ten minutes, the craft lifted silently and headed away from the two soldiers and disappeared over the woods. The Landrover lights came back on and the radio came back to life. The soldiers thought of reporting what they had just witnesses but decided it would be better if dome officially upon their return to base. They radioed their position and continued their work on the exercise, arriving back at base at 4.00 am. (Source: FSR 1978 vol 24 no1).

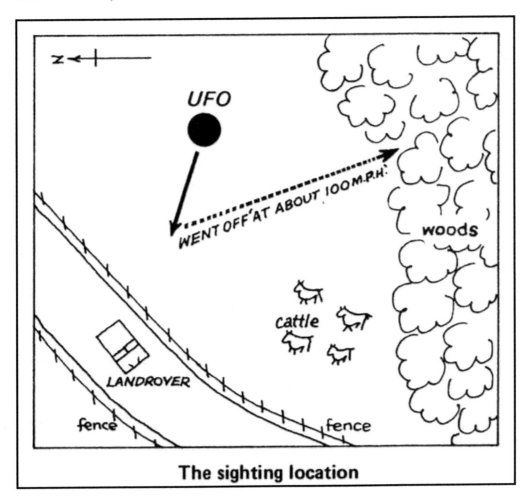

The sighting location

Illustration courtesy the Flying Saucer Review

115

When the two soldiers went to make an official report of their experience they were met with disbelief and ridicule and were actually charged by their superior officer of being drunk on duty and leaving War Department property unattended. Everyone at the camp got to hear of their unusual experience, but no one else had seen the object or had experienced radio or other malfunctions while on the exercise. Yet, interestingly enough, the Landrover was checked the next day. Both soldiers went back to the site the following day and found a large area of burnt grass in a circular shape. Their account of this and the sighting was officially logged, and Lance Corporal Perrin requested that the Ministry of Defence be informed but he was informed that the MoD had no interest in such things.

He was certain that a full investigation did take place behind closed doors but has no evidence to prove this. He left the army in 1974 and was speaking to civilian UFO researchers for the first time in 1977.

These two young soldiers had more to lose than to gain by reporting such an event. They observed this UFO at pretty close quarters, their radio malfunctioned and there even seemed to be an effect on the cows in the field as well. How much more high strangeness would we need?

Mr. Peter Leather
Epsom Downs Racecourse
Surrey
England
September 1973

The following incident took place in September 1973 on Epsom Downs and involved a jockey. His name was Peter Leather, and the case was investigated by Derek James of UFOIN and the FSR.

Peter leather was walking between the road and the Derby starting post on Epsom Downs (horse racing racecourse) in Surrey. He says he was startled by a strange noise. Turning round he saw an object that seemed to be shaped like a disc, engulfed in a blue haze. Shocked, he stood still, watching the thing which hung some twenty feet above the ground, between two clumps of trees.

As the object hovered Mr. Leather said that on the upper part there appeared to be a "flash of yellow sparks" like, he said, that on a burnt-out electric hand drill. This flash appeared in intervals of about five seconds.

Suddenly the disc was seen to descend and as it did, so the frequency of the flash increased. The blue haze may not have been constant in its luminosity; certainly, the yellow flash seemed to become brighter every few seconds. The UFO took an estimated five minutes from the time of first being seen until it 'landed'.

While he was wondering what to do, he says he saw an orange-coloured light coming from the blue haze close to the ground. Slowly he became aware that it was a light held by a human-shaped figure. While the noise from the object remained constant, Mr. Leather observed that the entity was moving towards him; he turned around and fled from the racecourse, back on to the road.

Looking back as he ran, he was surprised to see no sign of the humanoid or the light; only the UFO remained. When he reached the road, he again looked back; now the UFO was gone as well. The interview with Mr. Leather was conducted by telephone simply because as a jockey his work took him all over the country and when the racing season in the UK had finished, he would be riding overseas instead. (Source: FSR 1978 V 23 N 5).

You have to ask yourself this question, would a professional jockey make up such a story or would he mistake a conventional object for a UFO? Mr. Leather had this object in view for a good period of time and as a jockey there is no doubt that he would be familiar with his surroundings. Added to this we have the humanoid figure as well. Although there is not a great deal of information available with this account, I felt that it deserved inclusion in this book simply because it does have an appropriate degree of high strangeness with it.

Mr and Mrs Scothern and father
Rainhill
Liverpool
Merseyside
England
May 18, 1975

It was Sunday May 18, 1975, at 10.00pm that an unusual, illuminated object was seen by three witnesses to fly low over fields in Rainhill near Liverpool. The investigation at the time by the Northern Aerial Phenomena Research Association led to the possibility that this sighting could have been a landing case complete with physical traces.

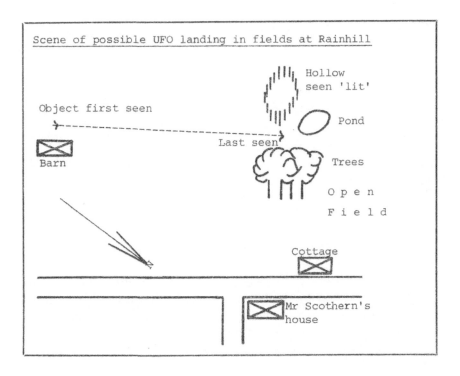

A lady by the name of Mrs. Scothern was the first to spot the object through a window of her house. She called her husband and father who both came and watched for around a minute as the UFO moved slowly over a barn and across fields. It was low down and apparently loosing height all the time. After it was lost from view Mr. Scothern rushed outside and at first saw nothing out of the ordinary.

The description of the object is of three pulsing white, globular lights, each the size of a tennis ball. It had only seemed to be one hundred yards away and was heading to the north- west. Mr. Scothern ventured further into the field over which the object was seen and noted a white glowing illuminating a tree-lined hollow in the middle of the field.

He rushed back to tell the others but when they returned there was nothing to see. However, a faint humming sound was heard just for a short while.

Mrs. Scothern's father brought a torch and went alone to look at the hollow but found nothing. However, the situation was very different the following morning. The area in question contained a small duck pond which was surrounded by mud. Four strange looking footprints were found in the mud leading up to the pond. They were fourteen inches by six inches and of an odd square-shape with no instep. They were also heavily imprinted and gave a suggestion of metal inlays. A small stone found inside one of the prints was heavily 'scuffed'. Perhaps the most interesting feature of the prints was that there were only four. The only other feature of the area were some dog tracks.

Veteran UFO author Jenny Randles, the author of this report goes on to add: One might speculate that the markings and the UFO report are connected and that the object hovered just above the area lowering an occupant who then walked to take a sample from the pond before ascending back into the craft. This possibility is yet unsubstantiated.
(Source: BUFORA Journal Volume 4 No.9 September October 1975).

Although Jenny Randles speculates about the way the 'footprints' were made it does give you food for thought. Such cases rarely have more than one witness, but this is not the case here. The more witnesses the better when it comes to dealing with high strangeness events.

Trevor P.
Cambrian Mountains
Machynlleth
Powys
Wales
July 22, 1975

Veteran UFO author and researcher Jenny Randles was featured in the in the Daily Express newspaper in February 1978 and as part of the feature Jenny had made a request for UFO witnesses to come forward. Jenny received a letter from a young witness known as Trevor P. An interview with the young man was arranged and UFO investigators Andrew Collins, Barry King, Graham Phillips along with a psychologist and a trained hypnotist.

Trevor, his parents and his brother were in Mid-Wales on holiday, and on the day concerned, Tuesday, July 22, 1975, the family journeyed from the area of Dovey Dale near Machynlleth in Powys. Trevor's parents were to view a cottage in the area for possible future accommodation while in Wales. The time was 5.00 pm and the cottage was located on the A487 road near Wyfla Hill. Trevor being a bit of a 'loner' decided to go for a walk, away from the activity, and chose to walk slowly up the 250 feet hill which lay to their south. Trevor reached the brow of the hill and, casually looking forward over the ridge, was puzzled by what he saw on the ground in front of him. Realising his vulnerable position, he ducked behind one of the nearby boulders that litter the area and watched carefully.

In front of him, not fifty feet away, was a strange stationary object apparently resting on the ground. It consisted of a large circular base, like a 'paddling pool' approximately forty feet in diameter and seven to eight feet high, with large circular lights approximately five feet in diameter positioned around the base. Each of these were shining brightly, and each were of a colour not recognised by Trevor. Evidently no light was cast off on to the ground.

Between each light (there were about seven in sight) there were deep grooves or curves set into the base, which itself was 'silvery' in colour and rounded at its edges. On the base sat a hemispherical, transparent dome which, if viewed from the horizontal plane, rose vertically from the base, and then arched over into the hemisphere.

At the central apex of the dome was another large light which seemed to be fitted to the apex from the inside, and not interfering with the curvature of the hemisphere. Again, the size seemed to be about five feet across, a colour being emitted that was unknown to Trevor. The dome itself seemed to be lesser in diameter than the base.

It the centre of the base, inside the dome was a big 'metal unit' about fifteen feet long and seven feet tall at its highest point. This consisted, from left to right, of a vertical side, eventually sloping away towards the right at a forty-five-degree angle, then levelled out into a horizontal top which stepped down twice in an irregular pattern. As stared, it appeared to be made of 'metal' being silver in colour. No marks, switches or knobs etc could be observed on the unit at all.

Also inside the transparent dome were two forms which appeared to be what have been termed 'entities'. These were described as looking like "massive pieces of jelly", irregular in shape and some seven feet across and of a similar height. The forms were translucent whitish colour, and inside them were hundreds of white discs like English-style 'doughnuts' each possibly six inches in diameter. The masses were constantly changing shape to a considerable degree, although from the movement of the white discs it appeared that the centre of each mass remained inactive.

No real shape or shapes could be attributed to the changing forms, other than that attributed to the changing forms, other than that they were irregular. The surface of the jelly seemed smooth although Trevor is not certain on this point. Although the forms changed shape, their masses seemed to remain constant. No other details were visible.

119

One of the forms was positioned in front of the metal unit, whilst the other half was obscured behind it. Trevor waited some twenty-twenty five seconds, frightened but inquisitive trying to fathom out the situation. He was still couched behind the boulder. Then Trevor noticed a 'panel' or section was beginning to open on the right-hand side of the base, slowly pivoting down about a horizontal axis towards the ground.

This was approximately seven feet by seven feet in size. Trevor had no idea what he saw inside the base where the panel was opened. The movement took about seven to eight seconds to complete after which the entity, which was in full view, started 'floating' towards the opened section, gradually lowering itself down a possible duct or hatchway and out through the opening. Trevor, realising what was happening proceeded to do a 'four-minute mile' back over the ridge and down the hillside.

On reaching the bottom he said something to his father, something he cannot remember and then for no apparent reason ran back up to the position of the landed object. When it was gain in view, he saw that the entity had moved back to its original position and the 'hatch' or 'panel' had now closed. He also heard a strange constant noise which he likened to a car 'revving' up but quieter.

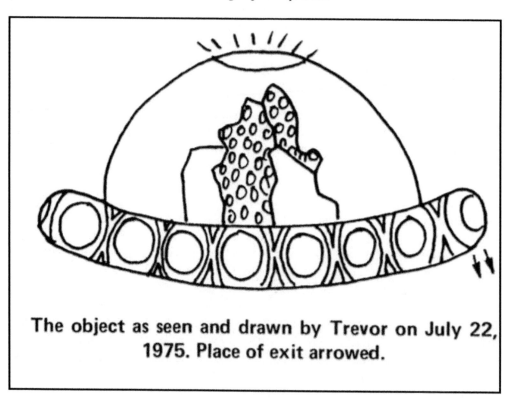

The object as seen and drawn by Trevor on July 22, 1975. Place of exit arrowed.

Illustration courtesy of the Flying Saucer Review

At this point the large circular disc of light on the object's side, together with the light on the apex, began to flash simultaneously in the colours of the surrounding countryside, i.e., green grass, brown soil blue sky, etc, which seemed to accelerate faster and faster and became larger and larger, until they were almost enveloping the whole craft, eventually blending more and more into the background until the craft was no longer visible, or apparently there. Just like a chameleon blending into the background.

Evidently the lights did not take on the shape or forms of the natural objects, but just their colours. Trevor had incredible problems trying to explain this process and had no idea how really to express what actually happened. Nor had he any idea regarding what happened to the objects inside the craft, and it seems that they too were enveloped in the strange light process.

Once the object was totally invisible, Trevor again ran at top speed over the ridge and down the hillside, back to his father who was waiting impatiently at the bottom. Here is what Trevor's father had to say.

Evidently, Trevor, on reaching his father (the first time) said "You won't believe me – come on," then ran back towards the ridge. His father then saw him lie down for a short time, then get up and run back down the hillside, tripping over and falling at his father's feet. This time Trevor was, in the words of his father "really petrified."

"A jelly-man got out of it" shouted Trevor. His father, Mr. P, realised that something odd had been seen by Trevor on the ridge, and asked him to accompany him back up the hill to see what all the fuss was about. This they did, although on reaching the place of the observation, nothing that could be possibly connected with the object was to be seen. His father noticed that a strange noise was being produced as the wind passed through the grass, which could hardly have explained the phenomena claimed to have been seen, and certainly nothing to support what was claimed to have been seen in the first part of the encounter.

The family holiday continued but in the coming weeks and months Trevor would suffer from both medical and psychological problems. Even in June 1978 when interviewed by the UFO investigators Trevor was still seeing a doctor. According to the investigators of this case they were convinced that Trevor did have an objective encounter with a craft and entities that were very real to him. (Source: FSR 1978 V 24 N 4).

This case must surely be one of the most bizarre on record. Although it only had one witness it has bags full of high strangeness. The young boy Trevor was observed by his father during the sighting although he could not see the landed object from his vantage point, only Trevor crouched down behind a rock. Trevor ran down to his father and then returned to view the UFO again. I have come cross UFO researchers who would dismiss such a case simply because the entities observed were not the typical small grey humanoids. Well, I'm not one of them and I would put this case right up there with the best when it comes to high strangeness.

John and Susan Harris and Paul Smith
North Redditch
Stockport
Cheshire
England
August 1976

I would like to thank Steve Mera of MAPIT for this following account. The following incident came to the attention of MAPIT during February 1977. The encounter was witnessed by three children (two of them twins aged ten years old).

Their parents are very respectable people and due to possible bad publicity, they do not wish their names to be used. Therefore, the children shall be referred to as Susan and John Harris. Before I go any further, I wish to point out that the third witness, whom shall be referred to as Paul Smith, was not interviewed; the reason being that when he was contacted by MAPIT, he denied all knowledge of the incident. Upon speaking to John Harris, it became clear that Paul's parents had told him to say nothing to anyone.

The incident took place in North Reddish, Stockport, Cheshire, England. The exact date is not known, but the events took place in the latter part of August 1976, on a Friday afternoon between the hours of 12.00 noon and 1.00pm. The area in which the observation occurred is a long plot of waste land overlooked by Reddish Vale Golf Club with railway lines running alongside. Further to end of this land is a local Primary School and reservoir. The children were playing on the waste land, around a hut which had been constructed for them by a neighbour. Susan was tired and thirsty, so she went into the hut to make herself and the boys some orange drinks. The boys remained outside playing by some bushes. Suddenly the boys saw a flash of silver pass before their eyes and heard a crackling noise coming from the direction of the bush. Then, from within the bushes, there appeared a figure wearing a silver, one-piece garment. He had a short grey beard and yellow, longish hair. The boys stood aghast because he was floating about six inches above the ground! Then all of a sudden, the figure vanished.

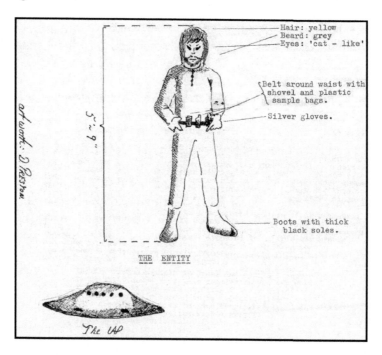

Drawing of the entity and the UFO (courtesy Steve Mera)

Meanwhile, Susan was completing the drinks as was unaware, at this point, of the incident outside: But then she heard a rustling noise outside the hut and then as she looked through the window, she saw for herself the same bearded figure, who was staring into her face. She did not know who it was so she stared back at him. The figure then removed a small shovel from a belt around his waist and began digging up samples of soil and placing them in a small see-through bag around his waist.

Susan for some reason then felt scared and screamed for the boys. As soon as she did this, the figure again vanished into thin air. She ran outside and after discussing the incident the children agreed it was the same figure. The children then decided to look around and see if he was still about the area. They all began to walk towards the school playground nearby, and then spotted him; he was near the school fence, bent over taking more samples. After a few minutes the figure appeared to go into the ground and again had disappeared. As they walked nearer the school fence they saw a silver, saucer-shaped object rises slowly from the playground and move off in a westerly direction until out of sight.

The figure was as tall as Susan and John's father, who is five feet nine inches; it had a very pale complexion and was wearing a one-piece silver garment, "like a track suit". The pants at the bottom did appear to be "elastic-like" and there were also four or five buttons running down along the chest. The hair was yellow with a grey beard; the eyes were like "cats" or with a shovel and plastic (?) sample bags hanging all the way round. The footwear appeared to be boots with thick black soles on them; the hands were covered with silver gloves. No sound or smell was emitted at any time from the figure. It is unfortunate that we found out about this case after so long a delay, since any possible traces had long since disappeared. One part of the encounter which does sound like fantasy is when the figure allegedly went into the ground.

First appearance was here -- near the bushes.

Photo courtesy the Flying Saucer Review

On Investigation at the exact spot where the figure had been bending, a possible explanation was uncovered. As the children were about 400 yards away from the figure, they could have mistaken his bending down in a hollow and ducking under the fence (which was broken at the exact spot) and walking into the playground, as going into the ground.

This is quite feasible remembering the rough land in between the figure and the young witnesses. In closing, may I say that I was very impressed by the Harris family, and I am keeping in touch with them in case of any further developments. (Source: FSR-MAPIT).

Two un-named witnesses
Fencehouses
County Durham
Cumbria
England
September 3, 1976

At 9.00 pm on September 3, 1976, two ladies (one aged 63 the other aged 18), were walking home from a friend's house in the small village of Fencehouses in County Durham. It was a dry, cool evening with a light breeze. As they walked past a piece of wasteland, they saw a very strange object. Both women stopped, and then walked towards it.

They said they felt "attracted towards it," and it was disclosed that "it" was an oval-shaped object about three feet high and five feet long, standing on chrome or steel runners. The main compartment was glass-like with an orange section on top. The whole thing was resting on a mound of earth.

When they reached the object, the elderly lady stated that the wind and traffic noise appeared to stop. She then touched the glass-like sides of the object and it felt warm. At this point two strange looking beings appeared inside the glass-like structure. They had long white hair parted down the middle, large eyes and claw-like hands. Both beings appeared to be frightened at the sight of the two ladies. Their size was like that of a large toy doll.

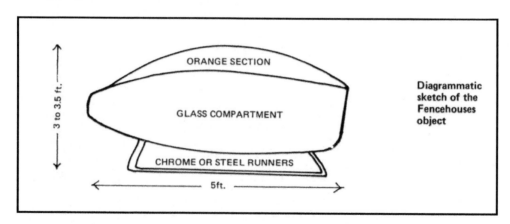

The Fencehouses UFO. Illustration courtesy of the Flying Saucer Review

Both ladies became frightened at the sight of seeing these two beings and the hurried away as a result. Once they had moved away from the object all the normal noise started to come back. The object then took off at a great speed and emitted a 'humming' noise. The entire episode last for only around ten minutes and it seemed like both witnesses were so badly shaken up by this encounter that they are unwilling to cooperate further with UFO investigators. Veteran UFO author Jenny Randles added that the older of the two witnesses did not want any publicity hence her name is not mentioned anywhere in this report. The younger witness was now untraceable. The location of the event has now been cleared for building work. Jenny pointed out one puzzling aspect of the case and that is the witnesses both stated that their watched stopped during the encounter but started again thereafter. Jenny thought it curious that someone would check their watches during such an encounter. The entities were reported as being only one foot or one foot six inches tall. It is understood that the only reason the encounter was reported was because the elder of the two witnesses wanted to 'get it off her chest' but had since 'clammed up' in fear of attracting any unwanted media attention. (Source: FSR 1976 V 22 N 6).

So, here again we have two witnesses one of whom even stated that she touched the landed UFO and that it felt warm. Both witnesses reported that all of the normal noises around them disappeared and perhaps the most unusual aspect of this encounter is the two humanoids and the fact that they were reported as being one foot six inches tall. Another aspect of this case that stood out to me is where the witnesses stated that they felt drawn towards the object. I have come across this several times in other cases. The witness does not want to get any closer to the UFO but somehow feels compelled to do exactly that.

Numerous school children
Broadhaven
Dyfed
Wales
February 4, 1977

This is a UFO case I recall from the mid 1970s as it was featured on TV and in the UFO literature. It rapidly spread to the national news in the UK and even received international coverage.

To this day it remains somewhat low key despite it being one of the few UFO cases that was investigated by the UK Ministry of Defence (MoD) as part of a number of sightings in the area during 1977 that were commonly dubbed "The Broad Haven Triangle".

Although there are brief mentions of it on the internet, the information is fairly sparse and rarely goes into more detail than a brief synopsis. With this in mind I will try and provide an overall picture of the events in question.

The story begins on the 4th of February 1977. According to the regional newspaper the Western Telegraph of Feb 7th, 1977, fourteen children at Broad Haven junior school near Haverfordwest, South Wales, had witnessed a landed UFO in a field close to the school but it was somewhat obscured by shrubbery. The report also confirms that 6 of the youngsters reported seeing a humanoid figure.

Observer Magazine 19 June 1977 (courtesy John Hanson)

A local BUFORA (British UFO Research Association) co-ordinator, Randall Jones Pugh, was telephoned at 4:50pm on the day by one of the children's parents. Apparently, the sighting had frightened the pupils and they were adamant they had something out of the ordinary. The pupil concerned, David Davies described a silver, cigar shaped object the size of a bus, hovering up above the trees as if trying to take off. It seemed to stop for a few seconds and disappeared back behind the tree line again. Davies agreed to accompany Pugh to show him the area where the sighting occurred. However, it was now around 6pm, it was raining heavily, and the light had all but faded. Given that the alleged landing site was obstructed by a fence bordering a fast-flowing stream, Pugh noted the location and decided to make further investigations the following day.

Randall James Pugh (courtesy John Hanson)

On the Saturday morning (5th Feb 1977) Pugh phoned Hugh Turnbull of the Western Telegraph. Both men accompanied 10-year-old David Davies to what was considered to be the landing site. However, the search proved fruitless and no tyre marks, tracks or other evidence of anything large being in the area was found. There did, however, appear to be damage to a nearby telegraph pole with the support beam left at an angle. Pugh considered that the heavy rain may have accounted for washing away some traces of evidence but found it implausible that he found nothing at all in the area.

The headmaster, Ralph Llewellyn, and his staff had at first been sceptical of the children's excited verbal reports and did not make the effort to go outside and investigate. They were eventually convinced the pupils had been shocked by something they had seen. So, Llewellyn asked the pupils to sketch and report what they had seen under examination like conditions so they could not compare notes. Here are some of the descriptions given by the pupils at the time when asked to recount their stories:

David John Davies (10): said that they were standing at the top end of the school playing field watching a bush where the object was sighted. Philip (Rees) was trying to get a close look when up from the bush popped a cigar-shaped object. It was silvery, bright and humming. It seemed to be tugging. Then we all ran. The time was around 3.35pm as they had just finished school.

Philip James Rees (10) stated that he saw silvery object at ground level around 1.30pm after school dinner and was still there when he went back into school at 2.00pm. "My friends and I asked the headmaster to have a look at the object, but he refused. A couple of my friends saw movement of a figure, but I did not. I was frightened. Two friends, Tudor and David, were very frightened."

Michael Mathieson Webb (11): "It was silver and a cigar shape with a big dome and a red light flashing on top." David R. George (9) saw both the object and the humanoid. Initially after 1.00 pm and then at 3.35 pm.

127

He stated that the object was huge and silver-coloured. It was shining and humming and looked like a saucer with a point. He saw the occupant who was silver suited, and whose features were not seen apart from "odd long" ears. He also said that one boy was so frightened that he cried.

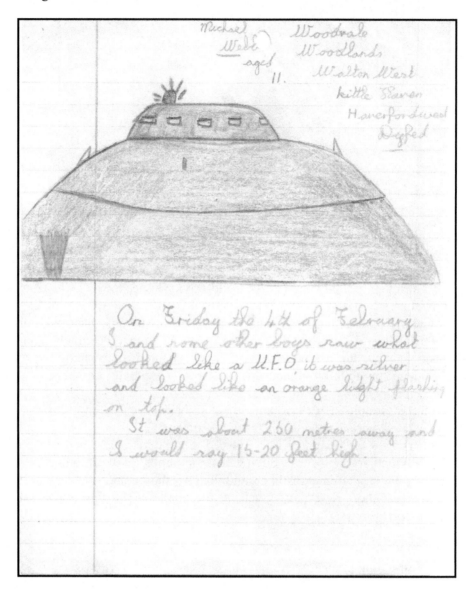

Michael Webb's drawing and description of the UFO (courtesy John Hanson)

Tudor Owen Lloyd Jones (10): Reported an object at ground level and behind a bush and stated that he saw a "man" and admitted to becoming very scared.

Jeremy Passmore (9): "I saw the UFO when it was dinner time. It was silvery green, and it had a yellowy orange to red colour light. It was a disc at the bottom and a sort of dome on the top with the light on top. It was about 300 yards away. It moved a minute and then disappeared. It did have a noise, but I didn't hear it. We felt very scared. David George wanted someone to go to the toilet with him. Tudor Jones was nearly crying because he was scared, he was going to be disintegrated or something, so we all rushed in. Some of our school did not believe us.

128

We tried to make them believe us, but they would not." In answers to specific questions, Jeremy stated that the sighting last not less than 5 minutes, the object was on the ground, and he saw a "person" in a silver-ish suit about 350 yards away.
(Source as above/Brenda Butler/Tony Pace/Norman Oliver/John Hanson)

A selection of drawings made by the school pupils (Courtesy John Hanson)

Of course, there were more children who witnessed this event and I have used only a selection here. The same goes with the illustrations that the children provided at the time.

There are many more available, but I think the few that have been used here will give you a good idea of what the children were describing. This encounter has of course become quite controversial at times with the suggestion that what the children actually observed was a sewage wagon and that the 'creature' was the result of a hoax or somebody wearing fancy dress.

These children have now grown up and many of them have children themselves. Interviewed down the years all of the children have stuck to their stories and are not convinced that what they saw was a misidentification of a local council sewage wagon.

Mrs Rosa Granville
St Bride's Bay
Little Haven
Pembrokeshire
Wales
April 19, 1977

Mrs Grenville and her husband owned the Haven Fort Hotel. The hotel stands on a small hill overlooking St Bride's Bay in Pembrokeshire, Wales. On April 19, 1977, Mrs. Grenville was witness to the sighting of a strange blue light and had reported the incident to Randall James Pugh who was a co-ordinator for the British UFO Research Association in Wales. Pugh drove down to interview the witness in late April (1977) and it was at this point that she mentioned that not only had she seen this strange blue object but two humanoid beings as well. Randall James Pugh interviewed the witness, and this is a transcript of that interview:

Q: What is your full name please?

A: Rosa Grenville, Haven Fort Hotel, Little Haven.

Q: And your occupation?

A: Hotelier.

Q: Can you describe for me the extraordinary events of Thursday, April 19, 1977.

A: About 2 o'clock I went to bed and picked up a book to read, and I realised I was getting a humming noise similar to the one I get from my central heating.

Q: This was not normal at this time of the morning?

A: Yes, it is normal if I have switched it on. But owing to the explosions of gas and what-have-you I have been very cautious. Last thing at night I always switch off the central heating and all electrical appliances for safety reasons. I thought at that point I had forgotten to switch off the central heating.

Q: So, the noise resembled the sound from your boiler, motor and so on?

A: Yes. So, I was debating for a good ten minutes whether to get up and go down and look.

Q: So, this sound was present all the time?

A: All the time, yes. Eventually I decided "Well, I'd better", and got up. I then decided to go a point above the boiler and listen if I'd left it on. So, I came out of my bedroom, past the public bathrooms and to the fire escape door which is just above the boiler-house. I realised that the noise was not exactly like my boiler. Although it sounded the same in the bedroom, on coming nearer the boiler I realised that it was different. I then thought of a ship, because we do get a lot of ships in the bay, and I went out to look. When I had gone to bed it was quite damp and dark, it wasn't a nice night. But now when I looked out, I saw it was quite lit up, a moonlight night.

Q: So, when you drew your curtains apart you saw a light in the field?

A: In the field, yes. I looked and saw this light was like a painter's blowlamp, you know, it was a sort of bluish colour, sort of off and on.

Q: Pulsating?

A: Yes. So, I thought "Oh dear, I thought someone was trying to break in here!" I've got a cottage out there and chickens. So, I looked again, I'd got my binoculars by this time, and I saw two figures. But first of all, I saw this object.

Q: It had a shape?

A: Yes, it was a round object.

Q: Large?

A: oh, yes.

Q: What would you say the size was?

A: Well, IO would say about two yards.

Q: I see. It was a round object the size of.... cartwheel size or something like that?

A: It was an oval-shaped thing, you know, oval-ish, round.

Q: Like a rugby football?

A: Not quite. Give me a pencil and I'll draw it for you.

Q: I see. So, it was resting on the ground?

A: Yes. This part was resting on the ground and this part was upwards, you know. Now in this corner of the field there's a gate and between this object and the gate were two long-legged figures.

Q: How tall would you say they would be?

A: Oh, six and a half or seven foot. Rather tallish men.

Q: And what were they dressed in, Mrs. Grenville?

A: It was a sort of white; plasticated....I don't know what it was. It was definitely not silvery.

Q: What did the clothes resemble?

A: Boilersuits.

Q: Did they have anything around the waist?

A: No, I can't remember that. It looked like a boilersuit. It was as if it from head to toe, the same thing.

Q: Presumably they had arms and legs?

A: That is what I was trying to tell you. They had rather longish legs.

Q: Were they thin or stout?

A: Medium, I should say. They had longish arms because they seemed to be measuring something and then climbing the bankside.....at least that is how it seemed to me and don't forget that this was half past two in the morning.

(GATE)

UFO and Humanoids, based on Mrs. Grenville's sketch

Illustration courtesy Flying Saucer Review

Q: Did you see the features?

A: Yes, they did turn round. They were turning round and observing......but they had no features at all, it was just a blank face. They also had pointed heads.

Q: No eyes or......?

A: Nothing! I couldn't even see a spot. They just had a blank face. They were definitely not ghosts.

Q: Did you go and examine the spot the next morning?

A: What happened when I saw it was that I was very frightened; I thought something was going to happen to the house. So, I switched all the lights on.

Q: You switched all the lights on then went back to the window?

A: Yes. And it was pitch dark. I tried hard with my binoculars to see if I could see something, if I could see them hiding. But there was nothing.

Randall James Pugh and Mrs. Grenville went to site of the encounter after the interview but there was nothing to be seen. Mrs. Grenville did stare that the day after the encounter she had observed a crescent-shaped depression in the grass. She also added that at one point during the sighting she saw one of the humanoids climbing up the side of the UFO. She then realised that this was not the case but in fact it was climbing up an adjacent grassy bank. She was also now convinced that the humming noise she had heard came from the UFO as it went as soon as the UFO disappeared.

Mrs Grenville summed up her reaction by saying: "I don't know what it is, but I was petrified. If I see it again, I am definitely moving from here."
(Source: FSR 1977 V 23 N 2).

Mrs Shirley Lewis
Walthamstow
London
England
May 1, 1977

This next case first came about after an article in the Waltham Forest Guardian newspaper dated 6th May 1977. The case eventually ended up with UFOIN investigator Andy Collins who managed to locate the witnesses and obtain the details of a double UFO landing case.

Mrs Shirley Lewis lived on the 9th floor of Whitebeam Towers with her husband and daughter. She seemed very honest, sincere and genuinely puzzled by what she had seen.

The sighting took place after Mrs. Lewis had just got out of bed to make a cup of tea as she was unable to sleep. It was around 00.45 and the date was May 1st, 1977. She walked out into the kitchen and switched on the small strip light above her cooker.

Looking towards the window, she was puzzled to see a white glow coming from outside.

Curious, she walked across to the window, pulled up the net curtains, and was astonished to see two objects one above the other, identical in shape, descending vertically towards the ground. Each was shaped like pear-drops or light bulbs, with the pointed ends towards the ground. The top one was white in colour, like a light bulb, and the bottom one was fluorescent dark green in colour. When she first saw them, they were at an angle of about twenty degrees up, and at a distance of about three hundred to four hundred yards. They descended smoothly and in complete silence for around one minute before the bottom one started to obscure or go into what is thought were houses about three hundred yards away. It continued to move behind or go into the building until it was totally obscured. The second object also disappeared in the same manner without any hesitation or slowing down. It was if both objects had disappeared down a hole.

After both objects had disappeared, the witness went into her lounge to get a pair of binoculars, and with these she scanned the area where the two objects were last seen. To her amazement she saw an area of green, in a rough square-shape, on what she thought was a roof top. It did not appear to be self luminous. She did not keep the binoculars focussed on the area so did not see the green area disappear. Mrs. Lewis, after making the tea, went back to bed. The following day she telephoned the Waltham Guardian newspaper who took details of what she had seen and subsequently published a small article in the next edition. Mrs. Lewis stated that she got up at 03.30 the following morning to see if the objects would return, but there was no sign of them.

MORE ODD OBJECTS IN THE SKY

GHOSTLY "electric light bulbs" in the night sky have been seen on two occasions in the past fortnight, but a Walthamstow woman's UFO sighting last Thursday was a little different.

An early morning thirst got Mrs Shirley Lewis out of bed at 1 am and, as she put on the kettle, she saw two bulb shapes glowing in the sky above the Billet Road industrial estate.

"They were huge, one a vivid green colour and the other one glowing white," said Mrs Lewis of Whitebeam Towers, Higham Hill Road.

"They descended slowly for a couple of seconds, one above the other, then vanished leaving a green patch on the ground which later disappeared."

Mrs Lewis says she will keep a nightly vigil with binoculars in case the "light bulb" spaceships come back.

Newspaper cutting courtesy of UFOIN

UFOIN investigator Andy Collins visited Mrs. Lewis and was shown the general area of where the two objects had descended. He could not locate any obvious mundane explanation for the sighting. Enquiries at the MoD, Heathrow Airport and so on, al draw a blank and no other witnesses came forward either.

Police Constable Bill Hefferman (and an un-named colleague)
Chigwell
Essex
England
May 3, 1977

Another UFO incident which involved the attendance of the police happened following a 999-call made to the Police by a Mr. David Samuels, at 3.55 am on the 3rd of May 1977 who told of having seen something strange hovering over the lake in Hainault Recreation Ground, at Chigwell Essex. As result of which Police Constable C 369J, Bill Hefferman, from Barkingside, along with another Officer, attended. After interviewing Mr. Samuels about what had been seen, the officers unlocked the gate that led into the grounds of the park, at 4.12 am and proceeded along the small road, when they noticed 'a large bright red light, near ground level, over the eastern part of the lake, about 300 yards away'. They then stopped the police car and made their way on foot when they were astonished to come across an object they later described as "red in colour. Its shape was like that of a bell tent - the size of a thumbnail, at arm's length. It continuously pulsated from dull to bright red, hovering silently off the ground.

Artist impression of the UFO witnesses by the two police officers in Hainault Recreation Ground (courtesy John Hanson). Artist Steve Franklin (courtesy John Hanson).

Suddenly, it seemed to dissolve on the spot." With some understandable reluctance, the officers split up and made a search of the area. Almost immediately, Bill Hefferman's colleague noticed a large white coloured inverted crescent shaped object directly above him, which 'dissolved' from sight, followed by a smell of burning. They made their way back to the car and radioed in a report of what had happened. After dropping off his colleague, PC Hefferman went back to Barkingside Police Station and later contacted the Essex UFO Hotline number, as a result of which he was later interviewed about the matter by Barry King, the following morning. On the 4th of May, Barry drove over to Hainhault to examine the scene and found recent damage to a large bush at the location given by the Officer. Barry: "It was flattened in the centre and damaged in several places; one part in particular was broken cleanly almost in half, at a height of about 5 feet. I took 35-40 photos of the scene. I then drove home and telephoned Andy Collins, asking him to bring his equipment over to the site to make a further examination of the area."

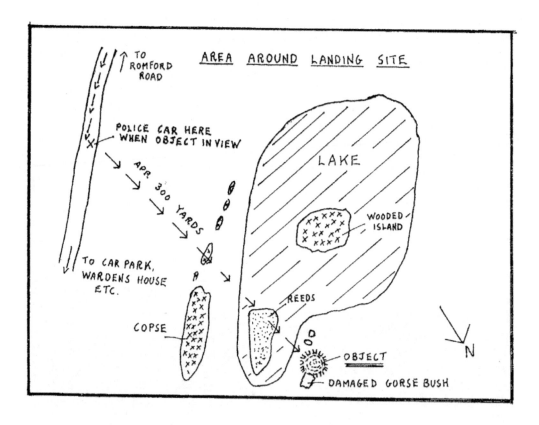

Coincidently at 7pm., 8th May 1977, Barry's brother, Steven, was driving home from Stapleford Airfield, near Abridge, along the B196 Road, which runs alongside Hainault Forest, when he noticed a blue and white Austin A60 Cambridge car emerging from the entrance leading into the park and move up behind him. The driver then began to flash his headlights behind him. Steven stopped near the foot of Hog Hill and two men got out of the car and walked up to him, explaining they had seen the UFO sticker on his car windscreen and wanted to tell him about a strange experience .They told him they had parked their car over the other side of the forest, near the Public House, about half a mile from the lake, near the area known as 'the Swamps', close to Taylor's plain and Cabin Hill, and were exercising their dog, when:

"Suddenly, we heard a rustling close to us and saw this large 'figure' loom into sight and disappear into the bushes and shrubs. It was dark blue in colour, brighter than the surroundings, resembling a large person in outline, with no discernible arms or legs. It was about eight feet in height, four feet wide, and was some 25 feet away when we saw it."

Steven contacted his brother, Barry, who made arrangements to meet the two men, who never showed up, which left their version of the events to be only taken at face value, although Barry significantly points out the men could not have known of the earlier incident involving the Police. (Source: Barry M. King / Steven King / Andrew Collins, UFOIN report published by FSR, Volume 1, 23 No. 2 1977/ The Recorder Newspaper (Ilford) 8.10.77/BUFORA Journal Vol. 6, No. 3, September/October 1977. John Hanson).

Karen McLennan and Fiona Morrison
Elgin
Morayshire
Scotland
May 18, 1977

A local UFO investigator by the name of Bryan Hartley had placed a request in the Sunday Post newspaper for any UFO witnesses to come forward and as a result it wasn't long before he received a letter from a Mrs. Caroline McLennan. The letter went on to describe a UFO landing account. As Bryan lived some distance from Mrs. McLennan his investigation was conducted via letters and phone calls. There was initially some confusion of the date of the incident, but it was narrowed down to May 18, 1977. The witnesses lived in Elgin, Morayshire in the north of Scotland.

At 6.30 pm on May 18 (1977) two young girls, Karen McLennan and Karen Morrison (both aged 10) were playing in some fields near their home. The area consists of a new housing estate with adjacent woods surrounded by fencing. The first thing that attracted their attention to anything unusual was a strange humming noise. This sound they described as something like a helicopter when it hovers, but more of a hum, and softer. When they heard the noise, they were round a corner from the woods, but the noise appeared to come from there, so they moved towards this spot to see what was causing it. It was at this point that they saw the object.

The object was made up of a long cylindrical shape with rounded ends and a small dome on top. The size was difficult to judge but they estimated it was thirty feet in length. The colour was basically that of polished metal, and there were no visible makings, and no doors or windows. However, on top was a red light which was steady and did not flash. In the middle of the bottom section was a red band about one quarter of the width of this portion of the object, and it seemed to be rotating.

The two girls were approximately four hundred yards from the object, and as a result the accuracy of any approximations of sizes cannot be guaranteed. However, both girls were very certain of what they saw, and can give vivid descriptions. The object was apparently hovering just above the ground at about the height of the fencing which surrounded the woods. This is about two feet in height. In fact, the object was seen to be just above the fencing.

By the side of the object both girls insist that they saw a "man". He was hidden partially by the bushes, but they were able to tell that he was tall and thin (it seems at least six feet in height) and seemed to be dressed all in silver. A detailed description from Karen Morrison was that he looked rather like a telegraph pole (this means that his arms looked disproportionally short). Upon seeing this figure, the girls became quite frightened. He then began to step out from the bushes and move towards them, and at this point they turned around and fled.

After a few seconds they gained their composure and looked back. The "man" had disappeared, but the object was still in the same position. Almost instantly it began to take off. The departure was unusual, as the object moved in three jerky steps. In other words, it moved to the left a few yards, and then rose upwards few more yards. It then moved to the left and rose again. After doing this for a third time the object took off vertically at a terrific speed and was soon out of sight. The total duration of the sighting was in the region of around one minute.

The girls returned home and informed their parents of what they had seen. It was taken seriously for the simple reason that Mrs. McLennan and Mrs. Morrison had heard the humming sound and had realised that it was something peculiar. Mrs. McLennan described the noise as something like a vacuum cleaner. Mrs. Morrison said it was just a humming noise. Other witnesses on the estate had also heard the humming noise but no one came forward to report seeing the UFO. Mrs. McLennan immediately phoned the police who took a statement and promised to look into the matter. They were unable to find any cause.

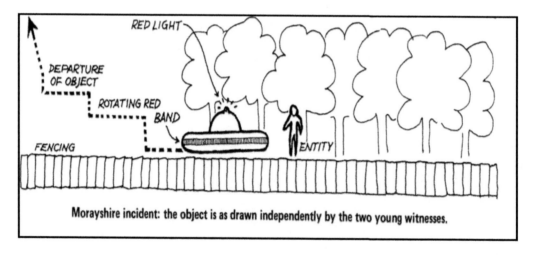

Morayshire incident: the object is as drawn independently by the two young witnesses.

Illustration courtesy of the Flying Saucer Review

The investigators involved at the time are convinced the girls were not making things up and that their sighting was authentic. One of the reasons for this is that the information provided by Police Constable Grant of the local police force tallies almost exactly with what the girls had to say. PC Grant was the one who took their statement, and it did not differ from the account given to the UFO investigators. (Source: FSR 1977 V 23 N 4).

GRAMPIAN POLICE

'A' .... Division/Subdivision .... ELGIN .... Station

19 September 1977 .....Date

Subject : ALLEGED UFO SIGHTING ON 18 MAY 1977

I have to report that on Thursday 19 May 1977, Mrs Caroline McLennan, 27 Robertson Drive, New Elgin, Elgin reported to the Police Office, Elgin that about 6.30 pm the previous evening her young daughter and a friend had both seen a strange object at the rear of the Cottar Hoose, Public House, New Elgin. She further stated that she had heard a strange noise at the same time, which she described as sounding like a vacuum cleaner.

I can add no further constructive information to that of the statement already given to the Northern UFO Network by Mrs McLennan. Mrs McLennan has also already sent several soil and bush samples to the network.

I request that this report be forwarded to the Northern UFO Network, per Miss J Randles, 23 Sunningdale Drive, Irlam, Greater Manchester M30 6NT for their information.

DnGrand .

Constable A 153

Submitted

DH M· 20/9/77.

Our Ref.

A153/Misc/77

Your Ref.

Forwarded to Miss J Randles, 23 Sunningdale Drive, Irlam, Greater Manchester M30 6NT

E.J. Elmslie

Chief Superintendent

Police report from Elgin

Although this case features two ten-year-old girls there is no reason to hold that against them. Their parents thought the matter serious enough to contact the police. The police not only logged the encounter but looked into it as well and were unable to come up with a conventional explanation. There was also a degree of circumstantial evidence to accompany this case as the witness's parents also heard the weird noise as did other residents on the estate. We have to say that this incident does, as a result, have a good degree of high strangeness and we should not dismiss it simply because of the young age of the witnesses.

Mrs Frater
East Bierly
Bradford
West Yorkshire
England
July 1977

"It was a flying saucer" is how the witness to this event Mrs. Frater described her close encounter. Mrs. Frater was walking through a field beside Copley Springs Wood taking a short cut to where she kept her horse. The field she was crossing was 8.75 acres across and is bounded at the bottom by a hedgerow and Cliff Hollins Lane. Midway across the field she would turn off onto a track to lead her to where she was going.

It was a beautiful evening after it being a lovely warm day. The temperature was around 75 degrees F, and there was virtually no wind. Mrs. Frater was finding it hard going on the hard ground with its undulating surface.

For no obvious reason she glanced to the north across the meadow and "froze to the spot in fear." She saw a very strange object which, as she says, "should not have been there....this made me afraid of it."

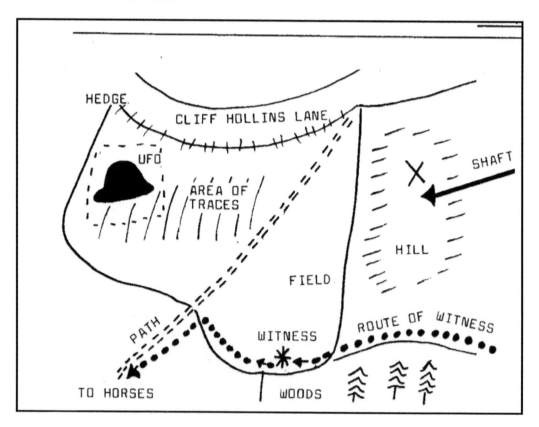

Map of the area where Mrs. Frater encountered the landed UFO (courtesy BUFORA).

The object was hovering only about one foot off the ground and it was totally silent despite the country location. It was circular in shape and approximately thirty feet in diameter and was a dark grey gun-metal colour. There was a dome on top and a row of portholes lined the point between the two places. From the underside came a short burst of red flame that was directed downwards. There was no sound with this at all. After about five seconds of stable motion the craft wobbled slightly and then began a swift clockwise rotary motion. Then, in an instant, it rose upwards, accelerating dramatically, and shot from view, heading straight into the sky.

Mrs. Frater was convinced that the object was at the point of take-off from the field when she chanced upon it. She stated that she found herself wishing "if only I had a camera." She went on to wonder if she would have had the composure to use it even if she had one. It was such a shock to see such a thing. She felt the object was hiding from view as the tall hedgerows hid it from the traffic on Cliff Collins Lane. She could not get over the way that in a few seconds your life can change from being a total sceptic to a firm believer. Confronting something so real and solid that no one could explain away which was so sudden and unexpected.

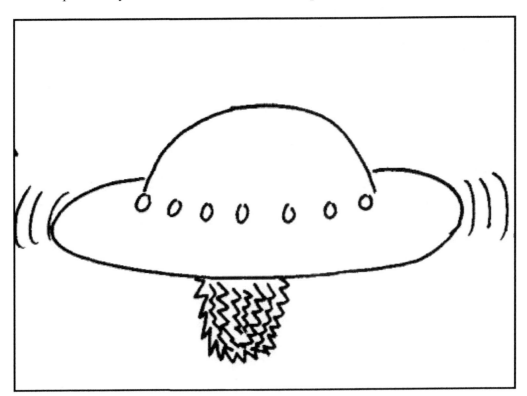

Mrs Frater's drawing of the UFO (courtesy BUFORA)

This case was investigated in 1983 by BUFORA investigator Nigel Mortimer. Nigel's conclusion was that he had no explanation for this event. In his opinion the witness was either lying or deluded or that she actually did indeed see such a strange object as described.
(Source: BUFORA Bulletin No.14 Aug 1984).

I must say that I agree with Nigel Mortimer here. The witness is either lying or telling the truth, there is nothing in between and I can see no reason why she would lie. One curious aspect out of many in this case is that the witness reports that the UFO emitted flames from its underside. This is something that rarely crops up in UFO reports but there are some such accounts in the UFO literature.

Bridget Chivers
Warminster
Wiltshire
England
August 28, 1977

Bridget Chivers was driving along the A36 road near Warminster, Wiltshire on August 28, 1977. She was approaching the turning to Upton Scudamore just after 11.30 pm, when she noticed a bluish oval-shaped light in the sky: she slowed the car down and wound down the window-the object was now a dark silhouette and much lower. She drove a little further along the road until level with the object, then stopped the car, by which time the object was resting in a field by the side of the road. Its shape was that of a large, inverted cone standing in a shallow dish, having a string of green and pink lights about halfway down the cone with one large 'searchlight' type at the top.

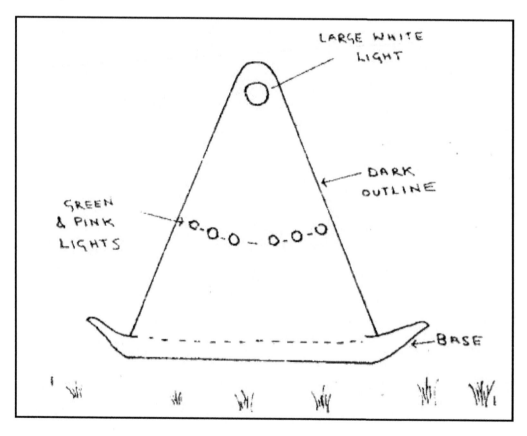

Bridget Chivers drawing on the landed UFO

Bridget Chivers stated that she grabbed her camera which would not work, then tried another and managed to take three photos before it disappeared leaving in its place a yellow musky type of smoke. The total duration of this sighting was said to be around five minutes. A UFO group at the time called 'UFO INFO' carried out analysis on the three photos in question but they "do not show what Bridget saw". Apparently the photos had previously been handled by numerous individuals Although BUFORA investigator Ken Phillips had some doubts about this case the UFO INFO group were of a different opinion and called Bridget Chivers as a reliable witness. (Source: BUFORA Journal Volume 6 No.5 Jan-Feb 1978).

Mrs. Pauline Broadhurst and three children
Clifton Campville
Staffordshire
England
December 7 & 12 1977

This encounter is in two parts, the first of which involved the sighting of an oval-shaped light on December 7th, 1977, and is witnesses by several people. This first UFO sighting was followed up by another event on December 12, 1997. Both sightings took place at Clifton Campville which lies just outside of Tamworth in Staffordshire, England and was investigated by Martin Keatman and Stephen Banks.

The first sighting took place on Wednesday, December 7, 1977, and was brought to the attention of the investigators by Mrs. Pauline Broadhurst, mother to one of the witnesses to the main event, informing them that she and three of her other children had seen a 'strange thing' some time ago. On the day in question, they had been returning from a Christmas shopping trip in Lullington.

Along with Allison, Wendy and Peter, three of her children all aged less than ten years, walked down the quiet road that connected the two villages. The time was 4.00 pm and it was starting to get dark as they walked along the unlit road. As they walked Mrs. Broadhurst suddenly noticed an orange light to the east. She pointed it out to the children, and they continued on their way as the light descended. It was a bright orange oval of light that looked solid with a haze around the periphery.

Maintaining a steady speed of approximately four miles per hour, it suddenly swerved through sixty degrees to assume a new course parallel to the road. This took it over a hedge some 90 cm high, and it proceeded to follow this mere 20 cm above it. The light gave the hedge a faint illumination.

As it changed direction the witnesses stopped to watch, and they now saw it travel along the hedge one hundred yards before disappearing instantaneously. Mrs. Broadhurst described this as "like a light being switched off." No sound was heard throughout the sighting, and this was the most curious part of the sighting so far as the witnesses were concerned.

It was a typical December day, with temperatures down to near zero and a slight breeze blowing. There had been a slight ground frost and a few stars were visible during the sighting.

On Monday December 12, something else was about to happen. It was 6.30 pm when four young girls, Sally Johnson, Linda Broadhurst (daughter of Mrs. Pauline Broadhurst), Gina Ward and Lynne Watkins, were tending to Sally's pony in Ward' field. This lies just to the south of Clifton Campville's main street.

Sally had been riding the pony for only a short while when Lynne pointed out a mysterious metallic looking object approaching them from the north. On catching sight of it Sally was so surprised that she fell backwards off the pony and on to the grass. Fortunately, she was unhurt, and her three friends managed to stop the pony (Blackie) from running away.

The four children involved in the main encounter: from left to right: Linda Broadhurst, Sally Johnson, Gina Ward, and Lynne Watkins.

Photo courtesy the Flying Saucer Review

144

By now the object was very close, its physical attributes being plainly visible in the fading light. It was shaped like a convex lens, perfectly symmetrical about a central horizontal axis. The strange craft was rotating slowly in an anti-clockwise direction as they looked at it. The diameter was approximately two and a half yards, and it appeared to be made of a dull white metal. Around the central axis were two coloured bands, one red and one blue. On the underside was a small, curved protrusion, this being the same dull white colour of the craft. Surrounding this were four metal protrusions, these the girls likened to "landing legs." On top of the object were two flashing lights on silver cylinders. There were the same blue and red colours of the bands around the centre of the object.

As the object approached they heard a quiet buzzing/humming noise. They all said this was like the humming of a swarm of bees. It passed directly overhead and was later estimated to be about six yards from the girls.

They watched spellbound as it circled over them and headed back from where it had come. As it moved away the humming noise decreased, and the object slowly descended into Lullington Woods some two miles away. After a few seconds it suddenly shot up from the wood and disappeared into the sky in a near vertical ascent.

The total duration of the sighting was difficult to estimate although a suggested thirty seconds to three minutes was estimated. As the object descended into the woods the girls became very frightened and ran off down the field. Lynne and Linda went to Lynne's house, and Sally and Gina hurried to Sally's. Sally was scared and her mother phoned the police. Later that day a constable from Tamworth Police arrived and took a statement.

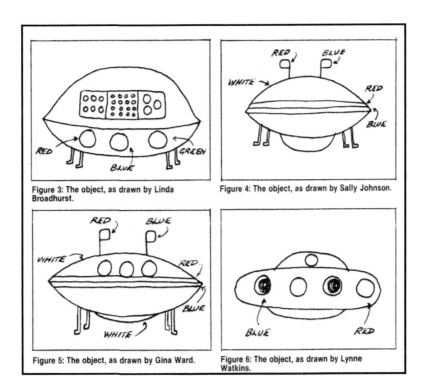

Figure 3: The object, as drawn by Linda Broadhurst.

Figure 4: The object, as drawn by Sally Johnson.

Figure 5: The object, as drawn by Gina Ward.

Figure 6: The object, as drawn by Lynne Watkins.

Illustration courtesy of the Flying Saucer Review

After interviewing all of the witnesses the investigators looked to see if there was a conventional explanation for this second close sighting and landing. They could find nothing that could have been misidentified as something unusual, there were no helicopters in the area etc and what the witnesses had seen was labelled as unidentified.

(Source: FSR 1980 V 26 N 4).

Four un-named men
Frodsham
Cheshire
England
January 27, 1978

The following account came to UFO investigators Jenny Randles and Paul Whetnall via a quite circuitous route and unfortunately they never managed to interview the witnesses in question. However, they were convinced that the source of the information was more than reliable. The witnesses had requested anonymity so their names are not featured anywhere in this account.

The evening of January 17, 1978, was said to be a cold one. At around 17.45 four young men (aged between seventeen and nineteen) decided to look for pheasant on the banks of the River Weaver. This would entail poaching on a farmer's land (the principle reason for requesting anonymity). The River Weaver is one of Cheshire's main waterways flowing into the Mersey Estuary about a mile from the town of Frodsham. Where the rivers runs into the estuary there is a wide-open expanse of land with cows grazing in the farmers fields. The pleasant surroundings are only occasionally interrupted by a nearby railway line.

The four men were in a place known locally as Devil's Garden which is situated by the weir where the water broadens towards the mouth of the river. The men were here, waiting patiently in the undergrowth, when suddenly one of the spotted a strange object coming along the surface of the river from the south-east. Their immediate reaction was that this was a satellite that had gone out of control. Shortly before this there had been a scare story of a Russian satellite complete with an atomic motor crashing in Canada, and this was instantly brought to mind. The object traversed the surface of the water horizontally and apparently in a controlled manner, no more than twenty feet above the ground.

The men watched silently as the object approached, passed by them and landed in some bushes very close by. The object was making a faint humming sound but intermixed with this was another noise – like the rushing wind.

The made the whole scene very spooky. The object was spherical and silver in colour, but at the base there was a kind of skirt or rim. The overall size was approximately fifteen feet, although it was hard to assess in the gloom. There were flashing lights on the side as well as what looked like windows that emitted a very peculiar glow. This was an ultraviolet type of light and was hard to look at for any length of time. The light made the interior look fuzzy, and it was therefore hard to see any details.

Needless to say, the men had now forgotten about looking for pheasant and were watching with equal amounts of both fear and apprehension. They still believed that it was a satellite, but remembering the atomic motor scare, they were terrified of becoming contaminated. As they were about to run, however, a figure appeared from around the side of the "satellite." Naturally it was almost impossible to see any detail because of the darkness, but the man looked reasonable normal and was wearing a silvery one-piece suit. The only peculiarity that they saw was a lamp like a miner's lamp, on top of the helmet section of their suit. This illuminated the surroundings with a violet glow at which the witnesses still could not look at directly.

The figure appeared to survey the surroundings, at about the same time as the men, some cows in a nearby field. These were standing absolutely still. Whether they were simply frightened, or were paralysed, the men did not know. The figure moved back to the spherical object which was no longer emitting flames from its underside (these had appeared as if from retro-rockets as the object landed). He was gone only seconds, returning with another man with a piece of equipment that looked like a large cage or frame made out of silvery metal. The witnesses assumed it must be aluminium, or something similarly light, as the two men had no trouble in lifting it.

FLYING SAUCER REVIEW

Volume 26, No. 3, 1980   £1

POACHED!

A NASTY SURPRISE FOR HUMAN POACHERS. . .   Our artist's impression

See page 5

The figures approached one of the cows with this cage. The cow remained totally still. Placing it around the cow they proceeded to move parts of the cage (struts and bars), as if performing an intricate measurement of the animal's size and shape.

It was at this point that the four watching men realised that enough was enough. They thought that after the cow it might be them next. With this in mind they all tuned and fled, without looking back until they reached the bridge which took them over the river. It was about a mile back to town from this location. They saw nothing further, but one of the men felt a 'tugging' as he ran away. He was quite embarrassed about this as he says the invisible pull was on his testicles which apparently remained sore for several days afterwards.

Jenny Randles and Paul Whetnall were convinced that there was something to this story despite not being able to speak with the four witnesses direct. In fact, they pointed out that there were a number of other close encounter cases around the UK in January of the same year. In April of 2020 while writing this book I contacted Jenny Randles about this case. Jenny remembered it well but could not add any further information. (Source: FSR 1980 V 26 N 3).

Lynsey Tebbs and Susan Pearson
Meanwood
Leeds
West Yorkshire
England
February 22, 1979

My own personal interest in UFOs really took hold in 1979. In April 1979 I returned home from working overseas and I joined the British UFO Research Association (BUFORA). In 1980 I went on you join a local organisation just a few miles from where I lived called the Yorkshire UFO Society (YUFOS). This local UFO group was put together and run by Leeds based brother Graham and mark Birdsall. These two gentlemen already had a few years of UFO investigation under their belt and in the years that followed I would learn a lot from both of them.

Graham Birdsall (left) and Mark Birdsall (right) photo by the author taken in the 1980's.

When I first joined YUFOS in 1980 Graham and Mark Birdsall gave a number of presentations some of which detailed some of the UFO sightings and encounters that they personally had investigated. One such close encounter was that of Lynsey Tebbs and Susan Pearson. The incident took place in Meanwood a suburb of the city of Leeds in west Yorkshire.

On 22nd February 1979, schoolgirls - Lynsey Tebbs and Susan Pearson, from Meanwood, Leeds, were out sledging in the Meanwood valley, at 6.45 pm., when they noticed a large cluster of lights hovering about 200 feet above their heads, which consisted of three green lights, with a red one in its centre. Without warning, whatever it was gave off a high piercing whine and began to descend, in a spiral movement, but straightened up when a hundred feet off the ground - the whining sound giving way to a low hum. Frightened, the girls ran but stopped some distance away, and looked back, describing what they saw as a grey object, approximately the length of a car and four feet in height.

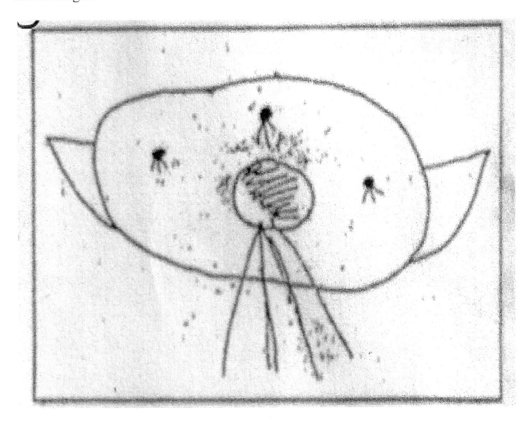

Lynsey Tebbs drawing of the UFO seen by her and Susan Pearson (courtesy John Hanson).

A few minutes later, the object began to rise into the air, accompanied by a soft humming noise, until it reached a height of about one hundred feet, when it hovered for a short time and veered away, descending downwards into the snow-covered valley, where it landed awkwardly onto a steep bank 80 feet away from the two girls. After a couple of minutes, it wobbled and rose upwards, in a straight line, where it was soon lost from view.

The matter was brought to the attention of Graham Birdsall - Chairman of the Yorkshire UFO Society, and his brother, Mark, who visited the families of the two girls, and after interviewing them, concluded the sighting to be genuine in nature.

A local newspaper covering the UFO landing by Lynsey Tebbs and Susan Pearson (courtesy John Hanson).

A search of the locality revealed a curious depression in the snow - now ice hardened and compacted in the form of a letter 'E', with a circular hollow in the centre, 6 inches in diameter – the shape found at both 'landing sites. Samples taken from these sites, and analysed at Leeds University, failed to identity anything unusual.

Following details of the incident being published in the 'Yorkshire Evening Post', two ambulance drivers, from Pontefract - Michael Duke and Lesley Evans – (who were on duty that evening), contacted the newspaper, confirming they had also seen an identical object pass overhead. An illustration provided by them *matched the one drawn by the girls.*

Following the incident, they received a visit from a man who told the father he was from the government office that dealt with such matters and told them, " *I can't say what it was at this point but it is best if you and the girls don't discuss it further* " (Source: Mark & Graham Birdsall).

Mike Sachs
Stacksteads (near Bacup)
Lancashire
England
February 24, 1979

At 2am 24th February 1979 Stacksteads farmer Alf Kyme and one of his farmhands were helping a cow to calf when they saw an object "*the size of two double-decker buses', pulsating different colours, but mostly orange, move across the* sky and descend towards the quarry at 2am.At about the same time, Mike Sachs the owner of a tailors business in the small village of Stacksteads, near Bacup was attending to his son Aaron) ill with asthma when the room was filled with pulsing light.

Mike Sachs photographed on site of his UFO encounter holding a drawing of the UFO he saw (courtesy John Hanson).

Wondering what was going on Mike and his Wife went to the window which faced nearby Lee Mill Quarry to look out and looked out, seeing an orange ball of light travelling across the sky heading in a northeast to southwest direction, at a speed estimated to be 100mph and approximately 800 feet high.

We then ran into the back bedroom, past the gable end of the house, some three quarters of a mile away, it was still coming down towards the quarry, silhouetted against the sides of the quarry, the clarity of observations was clear it was a cold night

It passed close to us heading towards the direction of the quarry and came to a perfect halt, after completing a 90degree U-turn, it was uncanny the way it which performed that manouevre the orange glow then extinguished leaving an arc of bluish light. Suddenly a superstructure appeared beneath it consisting of three dull red bands or rings /with blood red lights on it pulsing and rotating slowly in the air, illuminating the top of the snow-covered quarry below as it slowly descended into the quarry.

Mike then telephoned UFO researcher Jenny Randles to report the incident who was then living some 30miles away; unfortunately, she was unable to respond as she had no transport and then contacted the Police who told him two of their officers were already up at the quarry.

Mike continued his observations but after seeing no sign of the UFO remerging drove over to his brother Ray's house and after telling him what he had seen, the two men then made their way to the quarry where they parked the car and met up with the two Police Officers one of whom was Police Constable Wright, by now a good three quarters of an hour had elapsed so whatever was there could have gone.

Mike", *We slid down the quarry on our backsides fearing we could have broken our necks if we had attempted to walk down, with the two officers one at the front the other at the back, I said to Raymond what's those weird lights down there, tucked into the side of the quarry? It was slightly murky in the quarry; Ray agreed he could see them as well. After arriving at the bottom of the Quarry we started to walk along all of a sudden we heard this swishing noise coming through the air like a tish-tish-tish-tish sound but fast over our heads instinctively we all ducked what the hell that was I haven't a clue.*

We then fell into single file, and I found myself being left behind, with no thoughts of catching up with the others it seemed so surreal by now I was about 25feet away from the others. All of a sudden I am aware of this 'black mass at the side of me that's the only way I can describe it at the side of me some ten feet high showing dull orange lights, that's if they were lights set on this black thing whatever it was

I reached out to touch it and received telepathically the words three times saying Porta-Cabin, Porta-Cabin, Porta-Cabin which startled me. I never thought rationally how men could see out of these windows set into the side of the object about eight feet off the ground realizing they weren't windows what they were I don't know. I went to touch again and heard the words telepathically again' not for your eyes Porta – Cabin'.

A drawing of the UFO by Mike Sachs (courtesy John Hanson)

Then the event was completely forgotten as if swiped from my memory, and I am aware of having caught up with the rest of the group, it was weird everything seemed to have slowed down. There's not a day that goes by that I don't reflect on it to this present day (2010) we finally found another way out after looking around and made out way to Bacup Police Station with the two officers and made a report amidst the inevitable 'Mickey taking' from the other officers."

After some publicity in the Bury Free Press about the incident, Mike made his way to the Quarry approximately a week later and spoke to a workman at the Quarry who confirmed the only structure was a small shed at the top.

Mike also telephoned the MoD at London to report the matter and was transferred to three separate desks before he could explain what he had seen. Mike also made enquires with the local airport, but they were unable to help.

Another witness was Stephen Alexander a taxi driver who was taking a fare home at 2.45am through the village of Brynn, near Wigan approximately 25miles away from Bacup, when they saw an orange ball flying through the sky to the north, important enough to stop the car to take a closer look.

Between 2:30 and 2:50 am, the same morning over a dozen sightings of UFOs were reported from Lancashire and Merseyside. A Dr Ian griffin suggested a satellite re-entry may have been the culprit, while others suggested they were aircraft. The MOD released a statement that between February 21st and 24th, 1979, military exercises resulted in a low flying F-111 aircraft over the UK, which had inadvertently strayed into restricted airspace, during a 24-hour Exercise, based at RAF Upper Heywood worse another UFO researcher suggested to Mike it had been an optical illusion.!

Mike who starred in the Fire Fly Productions for Chanel 5's documentary British Close encounters, in 2008 had this to say about the program, "*I felt distinctly uncomfortable about the way in which I was interviewed at my house during the making of the film, mainly because after blacking out the windows in the lounge which created a dungeon effect, the camera was aimed at my chest and head, so I didn't feel relaxed, what I felt unhappy about was that when the film was screened on TV they had edited out most of the important parts of what I had said! Why they did this I do not know*"

Following this event Mike joined the Manchester UFO research Association as an investigator and became involved in a number of investigations. (Source Jenny Randles /*The Pennine UFO Mystery* Granada Publishing 1983/Brian Fishwicke MIGAP (Merseyside Investigation Group into Aerial Phenomena/ Norman Collinson/ David Tarry MUFORA (Manchester UFO Research Association/personal interview with Mike Sacks by John Hanson).

Philip Shepherdson
Easingwold
North Yorkshire
England
February 1979

I met Philip Shepherdson at A UFO Conference staged by Outer Limits Magazine in Hull, East Yorkshire in 2018. I was already aware of Philip's encounter and had in fact been in touch with him for some time via email. I asked Philip to put together a small article detailing his encounter and I am glad to say he obliged.

It was a crisp, 1979 February morning and my newly built scooter ran smoothly along the twisting country lanes near Easingwold (near York, North Yorkshire, England). As I turned left towards Huby, my personal world seemed to abruptly switch off into a hushed silence. I looked to my left and my heart flipped at what I saw. Hovering in a corner of a small field was a black triangular-shaped object. I stopped to get a better look not believing what I was seeing. The object was smooth with no control surfaces and no sharp edges and at the top was a cockpit with a figure inside it.

All I could see was a black shaped helmet and a black overall of some kind. By the side of the craft, I now realised there were two more slim looking figures who too wore black overalls and they were trying to push the vehicle into the next field perhaps to conceal it amongst the standing crops. They abruptly stopped to look in my direction; the cockpit figure too, turned to gaze at me. I felt transfixed with fear. I was shaking. The silence was stifling as we gazed at each other and I felt some form of contact taking place but I just don't know what that was. Time appeared to stop.

Suddenly my mind couldn't take anymore and I got on my bike and took off to work. I don't remember getting there, in fact everything after that seemed surreal. I appeared to forget the experience as if told that this was something I shouldn't have witnessed. What struck me at the time was this was nuts and bolts technology, no fuzzy lights with a smudgy image.

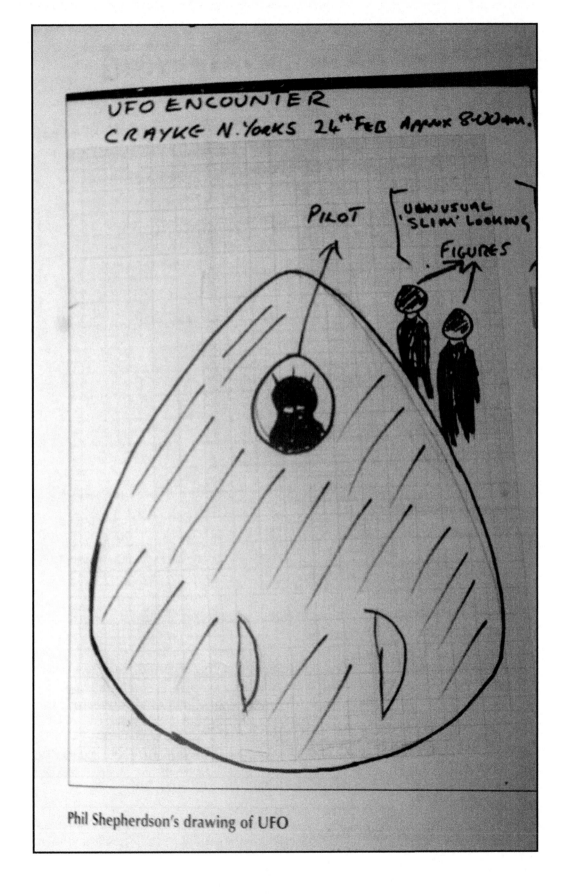

Phil Shepherdson's drawing of UFO

I freaked at the fact that an aircraft floating like a silent kite with not a blade of grass out of place and without jets, was way beyond our technology! My nightmares didn't start right then but I was in the impression that WW3 was very close at hand and, "for my own safety," I was to join a military establishment. Frankly I have hated anything official– but the Royal Observer Corp was looking for recruits. At York, which was a major Control Centre, they had sections consisting of Crew One, Two and Crew Three and the latter - Crew Three suited my requirements precisely: they worked hard and played hard. Only military personnel can appreciate what that means: you make firm lifelong friends and I gained many. And let's face it – this was the height of the Cold War and if an imminent WW3 developed, you would need them.

The author (left) in conversation with Philip Shepherdson at the UFO conference in Hull in 2018.

The York area suddenly became a UFO hotspot area and with puzzling crop circles suddenly appearing as well, it looked as if something was about to happen. I appeared on Arthur C. Clark's Mysterious World programme regarding York's crop circle as a scientist investigator. At the time of my sighting many more were witnessed. A UFO was spotted (Jenny Randles UFO Retrievals) in the Rossendale Valley near Todmorden around 2.00 am and was then tracked to Blackpool where a guard at Blackpool Pier, claimed it could have gone in and then came out of the sea when chased by military jets.

At 3.30 am, a man driving to Easingwold (near Huby) claimed a black triangular-shaped object flew alongside his car. "It had an orange light in the centre and there were lights all around it.

Then it shot off at great speed into the sky." Then at approximately 8.00 am, my own experience took place. I had to find out more. Going back to my field near Huby I walked across the small field to where my UFO had landed. What I found strange was that there was a bald triangular shaped patch where nothing had grown, and for many years afterwards that continued to be so.

Philip Shepherdson at the site of his close encounter

Then misfortune struck me when I had a motorcycle accident which left me concussed. However, it seemed to have triggered deep unconscious memories which now began to trickle into my dreams: nice to start but then with horrific nightmares. My first was being held in a dentist like chair with a masked face bearing down on me. Black eyes appeared to sooth my senses and then I witnessed a laser swan like instrument being used upon my upper face and body. The next nightmare consisted of being in a dark cavern like room; the only illumination came from an oval shaped window above my head.

I appeared to be on a soft to touch leatherette slab. Also, about this time my life appeared out of synch with the time of our world. A classic case was where a girlfriend of mine ditched me for being an hour late, yet I had arrived on time by my watch. The fact that I had gone to a previous meeting in perfect time added to this mystery, a displaced missing hour out of time mystery. I was lucky enough to obtain brief counselling with none other than Dr John Mack Professor of Psychiatry, Harvard Medical School, who became an expert on alien abduction and he appeared very impressed with my case and included it in one of his England lectures.

Trying to get rid of my demons and have closure, I spent some years writing my novel EarthZoo. This is purely science fiction but fact and fiction can be extremely blurred!

My nightmares became relentless until I knew I needed help, but from where? With the help of a spiritual healer who gave me regressive therapy, more disturbing memories surfaced, but were now controlled due to my guiding friend.

Further from my dentist chair experience, I now appeared walking – or more aptly hopping (due to a feeling of weak gravity) along winding corridors which held gothic like archways. Abruptly 1 reached a cave like small room which held a weird triangular table. It had uneven odd, shaped legs and should have fallen over but it was held in perfect balance by an unseen force. There was a box upon the table which had a lens on top.

Artist impression of Philip Shepherdson's encounter (artwork by Daniel Ramirez).

At my approach it flickered into life and through the lens I saw what I assumed was our sun – but it had a luminescence like ring around its inner core which behaved like a skipping rope. I gained the impression this was paramount for our solar welfare, yet totally unknown to our science at this time. Suddenly the view changed and I gazed at close quarters upon our home galaxy festooned with bright tiny multicoloured dots – all suns in their own right. My line of sight was along our galactic arm, but at (by rule of thirds) 35 thousand light-years there appeared behind our galactic centre (and therefore invisible to us) a smaller 'Z' shaped bar like galaxy. I awoke in a cold fearful sweat. Luckily my spiritual friend first gave me a brandy to ease my shredded nerves and then valued words of advice:

"We reside in many altered states of consciousness, and so treat your experiences as such. Whether these are mere dreams or past interwoven memories allow them to be as guides of enlightenment towards truth; there is nothing to be afraid of anymore." His words gave me extreme peace even to this day.

However more trapped memories surfaced whilst writing this article. My last sessions with my healer were very enigmatic indeed. So much so that fearing ridicule if I attempted to scientifically clarify what I am about to reveal, I have left this to the last. It also unnerves me due to its importance.

I am regressed back inside my UFO craft where a solid wall becomes transparent revealing a solid mass of multi coloured stars. I am not alone this time. By my side there is a humanoid figure about the same height as myself, but my focus is outside. Abruptly but without any sense of feeling the motion of speed, we are chasing a small red disc at tremendous velocity. It plunges deep into our Earth's atmosphere and suddenly we are flying at tree height through a forest type jungle. I gain the impression that this is subtropical – perhaps Australian bush land. Suddenly we stop and close by in front of us is a strange pineapple shaped tree. I gain the impression that this is extremely important to them and they have come here to collect samples. Apparently this is the first tree type/ plant type that evolved here on our planet. I cannot comment here because I am scientifically completely ignorant regarding what I have witnessed. I am now completely exhausted both physically and mentally and my healer allows me to rest. It is our last session together; I inform him that I have had enough! I can give no logical explanation to my story but hopefully catalogue this strange narrative for reference amongst the many other UFO experiencers. We all give witness to this enigma of the UFO who appear to be examining our world; let's hope with benign intentions.

In previous chapters I have intentionally shied away from what are known as alien encounters or alien abduction accounts. Philip's encounter of course happened the year after the movie 'Close Encounters of the Third Kind' was released here in the UK so I therefore thought it appropriate to use this case in this chapter. Philip is still contemplating what may have happened to him that day in February 1979. He has of course no doubt that something from another world is visiting the Earth and he has witnessed it first-hand. Having corresponded with Philip and of course met him in person I have no doubt in the authenticity of his encounter. It has bags of high strangeness and I will leave it to you what you make of his regression released 'memories'.

Lynda Jones
Didsbury
Greater Manchester
England
August 19, 1979

I have personally met Lynda Jones on several occasions. I interviewed her at her home near Manchester, have met her husband Trevor and she is even featured in my 1994 book 'Without Consent'. She is a lovely lady and one whose encounter has always stood out.

Rather than just use what I have published before about Lynda I would like to use an article provided to me by UK author and all-round paranormal researcher and author Steve Mera. Steve's account of what happened to Lynda and her two children in 1979 details their account in full.

Lynda Jones (left) with the author in 1994

It was August 19, 1979, when Lynda Jones a thirty-six-year-old housewife from Didsbury, Manchester was in her kitchen when she received a telephone call from an old friend. Lynda arranged a meeting and over a long leisurely lunch she and her friend chatted about the old days and lost acquaintances. It wasn't long before Trevor; (Lynda's Husband) had to leave for work. He was on a 2.00pm till 10.00pm shift at the local factory. Trevor left his wife and friend to chat away in the afternoon sun of their back garden looking over their children Christopher aged five and Lisa aged fifteen. Time quickly passed and Lynda's friend reminded her he had to be on his way before it gets dark, as he had visited on an old bike which had no lights on it. Lynda offered to show him a short cut home which would take them over the near-by fields. Lynda, her friend and children set off, it was around 7.30 pm when they had arrived at Simon's Bridge located near the River Mersey. After saying their goodbyes, Lynda and her children headed back, taking their time to look at wildflowers, which was one of Lynda's interests. With her Oxford Dictionary of Wildflowers in hand they regularly stopped to examine an intriguing flower. There was no rush, as Trevor would not be home for at least another couple of hours.

The location of the Jones family encounter (courtesy Steve Mera)

Suddenly Lisa shouted out 'Mum, the Moon is coming towards us'. Lynda turned to see a strange object racing across the sky, travelling towards them. 'It was like the shape of a rugby ball only a lot bigger' and was a bright orange in colour recalled Lynda. It had come into view from behind a crop of trees on the golf course situated on the other side of the river. 'The object had a spinning effect and it seemed to be travelling towards us at an angle'. 'Get Down! Lynda shouted out, 'get down in the grass'. As she crouched down in the tall grass with her two children next to her, she braced herself for an explosion, initially thinking it may have been a plane from the nearby Manchester airport in trouble or on fire. There was no sound whatsoever. Slowly looking up out of the grass Lynda saw the strange object pass overhead and then suddenly drop in a vertical motion behind an embankment which was part of the flooding defence of the River Mersey. It was then she realised the strangeness of the total silence, not even the sound of birds nor the traffic from the distant busy roads of Didsbury Centre.

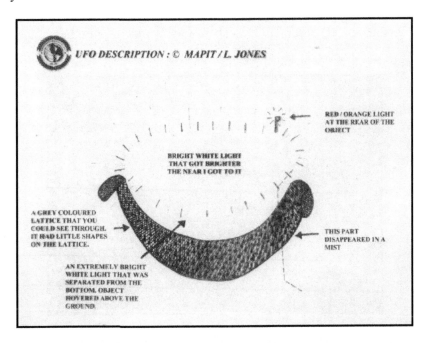

A description of the UFO seen by the Jones family (courtesy Steve Mera)

Lynda stood with her children in hand, taking a few steps towards the embankment, wondering if whatever it was had crashed. Lynda had a compelling urge to move closer to the top of the embankment. First walking then running up. She was suddenly stopped dead in her tracks by an amazing sight. There, about 25 yards in front of her lay an object which she could only describe as biblical looking. 'It was so weird'. Lynda did not know anything about UFOs nor had any interest in the subject. With her children stood beside her, Lynda stared at the object taking in all the detail. 'The object was about sixty feet across and hovering about two or three feet above the ground. 'The object was disappearing and then re-appearing'.

'The object had a light on the top of it'. 'It was a bright white light that was somehow separated from the object itself'. Lynda felt drawn to light, and as she got closer the light got brighter. As Lynda got nearer to the object an orange ball of light appeared from the far side of the object and started to move towards her in a slowly rotating fashion. 'As I walked towards the object I thought I would soon be looking in at them and watching what they were doing, 'said Lynda'. Suddenly Lisa shouted out: 'Mum, come back, come back'. The shock of hearing Lisa's voice jolted Lynda back to a terrifying reality. 'I had a feeling of Déjà Vu, really strong, then suddenly I realised what I was doing'. I thought 'Oh My God!' Lynda quickly turned and ran, grabbing her children by their hands and almost dragging them down the embankment. When they got to the bottom Lynda started running so fast that her son Christopher struggled to keep up. 'Oh No! 'It's there again Mum screamed Lisa'. The object was now travelling along side them. Lynda too scared to slow down picked her son up and carried on. 'Don't stop shouted Lynda, keep going'. 'Mum look, there are two of them now, Lisa screamed'. On the edge of exhaustion, Lynda suppressed the urge to turn around and look. 'Keep going!' screamed Lynda. 'Do not look back Lisa, just keep running she yelled'. As they ran across the grassland, Lynda noticed something really strange. The experience was having some sort of odd effect on their surroundings. Lynda noticed that the grass was terribly overgrown at least six feet in height and seemed to be folding down on itself as if it was being pressed down by some force coming from above and revealing an escape route. 'It was the strangest thing I've ever seen'.

Artist impression of the Jones family encounter (courtesy Steve Mera)

Lynda found herself still running when they had reached the edge of their housing estate. 'We never stopped running until we were safe inside our house', said Lynda. Lynda looked up to see Trevor standing there who said,' What's wrong, what's wrong with your eyes?' Lynda looked in the mirror and could see that the skin around her eyes was red and scaly.

'Lisa had ran straight upstairs to the bathroom presuming she may had wet herself in fear and Christopher though shuck up seemed okay' said Lynda. Trevor seemed concerned.

Lynda told Trevor what they had seen from start to finish and afterwards Trevor asked us all to draw a picture of what we had seen. He was later startled to find all the pictures looked identical. Then suddenly, Lynda realised Trevor was home, he should have not been home from work until 10.30pm. 'What time is it?' she asked Trevor. It was now around 10.50pm. Lynda had lost around an hour and a half of her life. She had left their comfortable semi-detached home in Didsbury around 7.30 pm and had seen the object around 9.00pm. She had run a good ten minutes, yet they had arrived home about 10.40pm?

Lynda would have to wait until the winter of 1980 before discovering more about her experience. In the meantime, Lynda and Trevor told very few about the incident. The local Manchester International Airport reported nothing out of the ordinary of that particular day and there seemed to be no other witnesses. Lynda eventually was talked into undergoing a series of hypnotic regression sessions. Each session was apparently recorded onto videotape and produced around ten hours of material. Lynda found the entire experience too disturbing and was so frightened she refused to view the majority of the video recordings. Lynda said, 'I was very upset watching myself under hypnosis'. 'At times I was becoming extremely upset by whatever I thought was happening to me'. 'It was just too much!' However, over the years Lynda had pieced together a vague account of what may have happened to her during the missing one and a half hours, based upon memories during her hypnotic regression sessions and numerous dreams and day visions. Christopher & Lisa also had recalled other events
.

'I remember at the point when we had turned to run away from the object, I saw several people running towards the object'. 'These 'people' looked like men, dressed in long dark coats and wearing trilby hats and holding what looked like satchels'. 'There was also a strange mist that surrounded them and when they got close to the object, they simply disappeared'. 'Also, the children and I remember seeing another cloud of mist around two or three feet high and in the mist was some more men, all around five feet tall, dressed in a one-piece jumpsuit, all carrying something'. Lynda recalled how odd it was that they all looked identical. She then recalled floating or a moving sensation. 'The next thing I remember is being inside a room watching six strange beings coming in'. 'They were human looking, wore dark suits with high necks'. 'They looked oriental; they had slanted eyes, dark hair and a yellow / olive complexion'. 'I seemed to know one of them'.

Lynda then went onto report the impression of being physically examined on a table. "I remember that they put something on my legs, and they went really cold." 'Every time I tried to see what was going on, a bright light would shine in my eyes'.

Even now all these years later, Lynda still gets frightened about her memories of the event. She refuses to speculate about what was being done to her whilst on the table in the strange room. Over the years since her experience Lynda like many other alleged abductees has suffered from a real-life medical condition.

She discovered that her menstrual cycle had been affected after about a month after her experience. Lynda tried to get on with her life and forget what happened to her; however, she would often find strange markings on her body which would disappear just as quickly as they had appeared. 'The marks would just suddenly appear, but after showing them to Trevor, they would have disappeared before I got to show my doctor'.

Artist impression of one of the men witnessed by Lynda under hypnosis (courtesy Steve Mera)

'The weirdest thing was a few months after my experience. I had what only can be described as a 'Show'. 'It was some type of waxy material; I immediately made an appointment to see my doctor'. 'After talking with him, he told me that I had had a miscarriage; 'But I wasn't even pregnant I replied! He seemed adamant about his conclusion'. Lynda's menstruation did not return, and she was referred by her doctor to a gynaecologist. Many examinations were carried out in hope of finding her problem.

It was not long until Lynda had to see a specialist at her local hospital. Lynda was told that the results from the examinations were successful and that they had found 'something'.

Her Fallopian Tubes had been examined and scar tissue was found on them. Lynda was told that the scarring was the result of an ectopic pregnancy. Even though this can be fatal and extremely painful, Lynda reported no discomfort whatsoever. 'I don't know what happened to me, but something did'. 'To tell you the truth, it's made me realise about other odd things in my life' Lynda stated.

Immediately after her experience a strange mark had been found on Lynda's jeans. The strange mark mysteriously even looked the same shape as the object she had seen. The mark on the jeans were later analysed at a University Institute and concluded to be printer ink, however why was it in that same shape? And Lynda did not even own a printer. Over the years Lynda has discussed the incident in depth with her children. Their memories of that day have never altered, the only one thing of further interest is Christopher's memory of seeing a large TV type screen with a picture of his mother and themselves on it. Lisa also remembers the object jumping back a couple of times as Lynda approached it. As if to say, 'Stay Away'.

During 1987, Lynda was working as a beauty consultant and was required to wear a plastic name badge whilst on duty. Her name mysteriously disappeared from the name badge within hours of wearing it. This happened numerous times to replacement badges without explanation. Lynda was now keen to report unusual things in hope of them never manifesting into anything disturbing. Investigators had arranged to have some analysis conducted on the name badge. The conclusion was rather odd, 'Radio Waves'. Scientists stated that the badge was adversely affected due to radio waves. It was not long afterwards Lynda left her job, due to the fact of feeling uneasy. 'Staff thought I was some sort of Witch or something! Lynda stated.

Lynda Jones at the scene of her encounter (photo taken in 1994 by the author)

I asked Lynda to describe the object she had seen back in 1979, simply for the fact that human perception does alter as the years pass and, I was privy to the original information reported. 'The object was nothing like what is generally reported as a UFO'. 'It was not a disc nor triangular in shape'. 'I have looked through many UFO books but never seen anything that looks remotely like what I saw'.

'The object was as if it was in two parts. The bottom of the object looked like the shape of a boat and seemed to be made of some type of lattice. It was grey in colour with small round things all over it. The top part of the object was just all 'light'. I have thought about this a lot and I believe there was something there but I could not see it because of how bright the light was. Directly above this entrance light was a pole or rod of some kind with a strobing red or orange coloured light on it. I thought this to be at the rear of the object. Between the bottom part of the object and the light at the top part I could clearly see the field behind it, as if it was see through. You could also partially see the lattice as well and it hovered about two or three feet off the ground without making a simple sound. In fact, there were no sounds at all. The object was pulsating backwards and forwards. After a minute or so, or what I thought was a minute, the bottom right side of the object seemed to disappear and was replaced with a strange mist.

At that point I grabbed the children and ran for it'. Lisa did give mention to when they were running away, the object flew off and followed a civil aircraft for a few seconds before rushing back towards them and splitting into two separate objects. I quickly realised that Lynda's account had never altered from its original reporting.

All Lynda's has ever wanted is just a normal life, but her life is filled with anomalies which are anything but normal.

Steve Mera ends this account perfectly. Lynda had only ever wanted a normal life but due to her close encounter and the things that happened afterwards that simply has not been possible. Again, here we have what is known as an abduction experience. There is a lot of debate regarding the use of regressive hypnosis but even if we were to ignore this part of Lynda's encounter, we still have some highly unusual to deal with. Most encounters of this nature have only one witness involved, but here we have three, Lynda and her two children. In the early years after the encounter Lynda, like any mother, was very protective of her children. Their encounter that day while picking wildflowers has a very high degree of high strangeness. I think Lynda sums this up in a much better way than I could ever do when she refers to their sighting as something 'Biblical'.

Robert Taylor
Livingston
West Lothian
Scotland
November 9, 1979

Foreman forester Robert Taylor was 61 when he almost became the victim of a Close Encounter of the Fourth Kind. Only a combination of his Scottish stubbornness and luck meant he could claim to be ' the one that got away'. So credible a witness was he and so graphic his description of events that the police and other authorities launched a full investigation. Although the case did not go down in the annals of police history as 'assault with a deadly UFO', the official investigation provided a catalogue of evidence from a number of truly independent observers - the boys in blue. In fact, 15 years on Robert has become so such a local legend that a memorial has been erected on the site of his encounter with a UFO....the only such official commemoration of a flying saucer mystery in existence.

But Robert needs no help in recalling that fateful winter's morning in 1979. To the married father of five grown up children it was just another working day with the forestry department of the Livingston New Town Development Corporation in Scotland. He had just enjoyed his usual breakfast break at the house he shared with his wife Mary at Deans, just outside Livingston, and climbed into his pick-up truck for the short drive to inspect some forest plantations at Dechmont Wood near the M8 motorway which links Glasgow to Edinburgh.

A punctual man, Robert left his home shortly after 10 am and headed off, knowing that he would have to make the last leg of his journey on foot as the rough forest track was impassable to vehicles. At 10.15 he left the truck parked by the side of the road and accompanied by his dog, set off through the rough woodland vegetation on the half mile trek that would take him to his destination. Robert had worked on the land all his life and had been with the Livingston forestry department for the last 16 years, so there was not much he did not know about this patch of bonny Scotland for which he was responsible. But as he rounded a bend in the rough forest track Robert was totally unprepared for what would confront him in the clearing ahead. A 30 feet high dome-shaped object, grey in colour lay before him. Dominating the clearing, the strange mass, silent yet ominous caused him to stop in his tracks. Mesmerised Robert noted how its surface seemed to become translucent and then changed back to a dull grey, the same colour and apparent texture as emery paper, he thought. For some reason he found himself wondering whether this bizarre machine, if machine it was, was trying to camouflage itself.

UFO investigator Dave Kelly (right) Robert Taylor (centre) the author (right). Photo copyright the author.

What he later described as a 'flange' girdled the strange structure, and antenna-like protrusions with what could have been rotors on top jutted out from the flange at regular intervals. Transfixed to the ground at the end of the 30-yard-wide clearing Robert's eyes scoured the surface of the massive object trying to make some sense of it. He noted several round porthole-type apertures in the top section of the dome. It was while he was absorbed by the portholes when the "sea mines" appeared. That was how Robert described the two objects which suddenly came at him, apparently from thin air. Spherical and with six or more legs or spikes protruding from them they rapidly rolled towards him. Measuring about a yard in diameter, and of the same colour and texture as the larger object, the sea mines made a sucking or popping sound as each spike or leg touched the ground, Robert recalled later. Within seconds they had stationed themselves at either side of the now stunned forestry workers, each having a spike or leg attached to the material of his trousers. Immediately Robert could feel himself being pulled forward, the spheres tugging him by his trousers, urging him in the direction of the large object. He could see the material of his trousers, just below the pockets, straining under the powerful pull of the spikes or the legs. Robert stubbornly resisted them. He wasn't going to run away but he would certainly try to stand his ground against this damned invader. The spheres steadily increased their pull to such an extent that at one stage Robert could feel his wellington boots dragging on the ground as he fought to keep his distance from the gloomy grey object. A foul acrid smell that he had noticed as soon as the spheres approached now seemed to invade his nostrils. The intensity of the appalling stink increased as he struggled with his would-be captors. Invisible choking fumes overwhelmed him as he summoned all his strength to resist the incessant pull of the spheres.

A strange pressure built up under his chin and he recalls a burning sensation in the same place. Struggling for breath and exhausted from his battle with "sea mines" Robert lost consciousness and fell forward into the damp grass
.

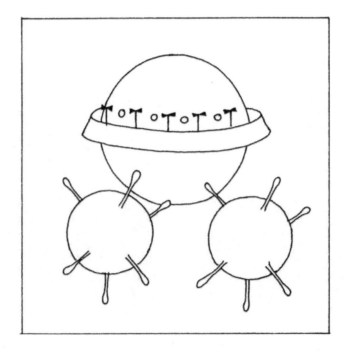

Artist impression of the objects witnessed by Robert Taylor (courtesy FSR)

"The next thing I hear a whooshing sound and my dog is racing around me barking loudly," remembers Robert. "But I'm not sure if that was before I lost consciousness or after I came round." When I did come round there was nothing there. The object had gone. I felt extremely weak and was unsteady on my feet. I dragged myself up and half crawled, half staggered to my vehicle." On reaching his pick-up truck Robert automatically went to his two-way radio to report the incident to HQ. But as soon as they responded he found he could not utter a word. He could not speak. But losing his voice was the least of his worries. After climbing, with some effort, into the drivers' seat of his truck, Robert struggled to co-ordinate his hand and leg movements to enable him to drive. After several attempts he managed to start the vehicle and steer it along the forest track for a few yards before it went veering into a muddy quagmire.

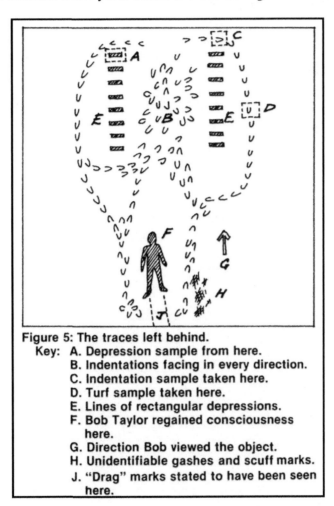

Figure 5: The traces left behind.
   Key: A. Depression sample from here.
         B. Indentations facing in every direction.
         C. Indentation sample taken here.
         D. Turf sample taken here.
         E. Lines of rectangular depressions.
         F. Bob Taylor regained consciousness here.
         G. Direction Bob viewed the object.
         H. Unidentifiable gashes and scuff marks.
         J. "Drag" marks stated to have been seen here.

Illustration courtesy of the Flying Saucer Review

Dazed and confused Robert made his way home on foot. Gradually his strength and his voice returned. Mary, his wife, saw her husband walking up the road towards his home through the kitchen window. She noticed his face was dirty and his clothes dishevelled. Rushing out to meet him she cried:" What's happened. Have you had an accident? "No, I've been attacked," he replied. "With men?" "No, a spaceship thing." "There's no such thing.... I'll phone the doctor."

Robert stopped his wife calling the GP and asked her to run him a bath. He wanted to get rid of that awful smell that he said clung to him and his clothes. Mary could not smell a thing, but she did notice his jersey was dirty. And his trousers were torn on either side near to the pockets as well as being grubby at the front. He had obviously fallen.

Mary could see her husband was unwell. He was very pale. He seemed drained and exhausted and complained of grazes on his left leg and under his chin. While he was in the bath, Mary telephoned her husband's boss, Malcolm Drummond, the forestry manager. When he arrived at the house Robert told his story, describing the domed object as like a large spinning top, accompanied by two smaller objects. Mr. Drummond listened without interruption. He knew old Robert was a man of few words, not one for exaggeration. If this is what he said had happened, then he was prepared to believe him. Mr. Drummond said he was going to look at the site for himself and left. When he returned, he brought Robert's truck and said that despite a cursory look around the location had nothing to report.

Robert insisted on returning to Dechmont Wood with his boss to see if the object had left any marks on the ground. There must be some sign of it having been there. Indeed, marks there were, and they were enough to convince Robert that he had not imagined his experience. Track-like marks and holes, three inches deep and at a slight angle into the ground. They suggested a heavy object had been sitting there.

'Track' marks found at the location of Robert Taylor's encounter

170

Close up photo of one of the 'track' marks found at the site of Robert Taylor's encounter.

Mr. Drummond had to agree they were strange. The police were immediately called in to investigate. In his report on the incident PC William Douglas of Lothian and Borders Police at Livingston described the marks in detail. "The central marks were similar to that of a caterpillar tractor and were uniform in size," he wrote." They indicated that an object of several tons had stood there but there was nothing to show that it had been driven or towed away. "I made a wide sweep of the area checking for fresh marks which might suggest a mobile crane, but I found nothing." The central marks were surrounded by holes approximately 3.5 inches in diameter and the same in depth. Each hole had a tow which cut under the sod, in some cases by as much as four inches. There appeared to be no rational explanation for these marks." PS Douglas's search for signs of a mobile crane implied that he thought the object, whatever it was, must have been lifted from the spot. An object, weighing several tons, according to his estimation, would certainly have left further marks when it moved off.

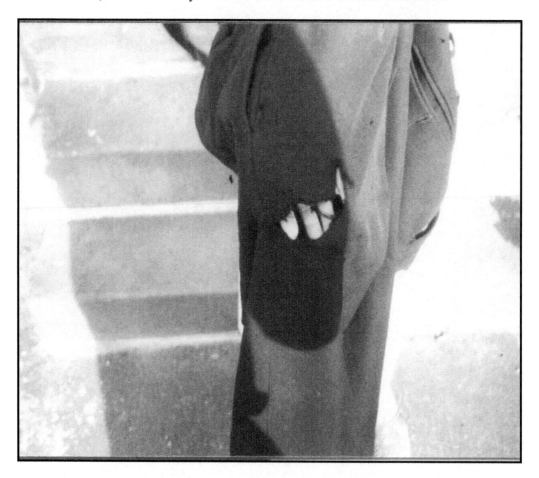

Close up photo of the damage to one side of Robert Taylor's trousers (copyright the author).

The official report by the Livingston Criminal Investigation Department concluded:" Despite extensive inquiries made. No information has been gained which could indicate what, in fact, made the marks on the ground at the location. "Mr. Taylor is a respected member of the community and is described as a conscientious and trustworthy person, not likely to invent a story."

The police investigation included a report from the Forensic Science Laboratory, where Robert's clothing had undergone testing. Nothing of significance was found. But the report confirmed that the tears in the hip area of the trousers he had been wearing, and in a corresponding area on the Long John underpants favoured by Robert were "consistent with the material having been pulled up while the trousers were being worn." The report from Robert's GP, Dr Gordon Adams, was equally inconclusive. He found no signs of a head injury or concussion.

APPENDIX 3.

WILLIAM DOUGLAS, Police Constable 'F' 29, Lothian and Borders Police, stationed at Livingston.

States:-

I am 36 years of age and have completed 6 years Police service.

About 2.00 p.m. on Friday, 9th November, 1979, I was on duty at Livingston Police Station when I was instructed to attend an incident at Woodlands Park, Deans, Livingston.

I was informed that a Robert Taylor, a forestry worker with the Livingston Development Corporation Estates Department, had alleged being attacked by alien beings from a space craft in the forrest(sic) behind Woodlands Park.

On arrival at Woodlands Park, myself and other officers were led into the forest and shown the location by Mr. Drummond of the Livingston Development Corporation Estates Department. Mr. Drummond did not witness the incident, but he had been shown the locus by Mr. Taylor.

The location was a clearing in the trees on the north side of Deer Hill and approximately 200 yards south of the M.8 motorway. (Map ref. 703 035 on Sheet 65, O.S. map for Falkirk and West Lothian). The clearing was approximately 50 yards x 30 yards with rides leading off north towards Dechmont Law, south towards the M.8 and west towards Woodlands Park. Mr. Drummond indicated some marks on the ground which were located on the northern side of the clearing where the craft was alleged to have stood.

The central marks were similar to that of a caterpillar tractor and were uniform in size. They indicated that an object of several tons had stood there but there was nothing to show that it had been driven or towed away. I made a wide sweep of the area checking for fresh marks which might suggest a mobile crane but I found nothing. The ground in this area is very soft due to the recent rain and any marks would remain for some time.

The central marks were surrounded by holes approximately $3\frac{1}{2}$" in diameter and the same in depth. Each hole had a 'toe' which cut under the sod, in some cases as much as 4". There appeared to be no rational explanation for these marks.

I took measurements of the locus from which I prepared a sketch. I was present when Detective Constable Wark of the Identification Branch took photographs of the locus.

The area was fenced off by the Livingston Development Corporation Estates Department.

In company with Detective Inspector Macdonald and Detective Sergeant Dickson about 6.00 p.m. same date, I called at the Livingston Development Corporation Estates Department and examined the motor vehicle which Mr. Taylor had been using that morning. There was nothing to indicate that he had been involved in an accident and there was nothing on board which might give off fumes likely to cause hallucination.

About 7.00 p.m. on Sunday, 11th November, 1979 in company with Acting Detective Constable MacDonald of Broxburn, I called at 4 Broomieknowe Drive, Deans, Livingston, and interviewed Mr. Robert Taylor and noted his statement regarding the incident. I also took possession of the clothing he was wearing at the time. I later passed these to Detective Constable Wark to be taken for forensic examination.

Mr. Taylor complained of a burning sensation under his chin and grazing on his left thigh which he showed to me. Other than these he appears to have suffered no ill effects from the experience.

43

A section of the official police report

He had seen him earlier in the year when it was suspected that headaches, he was suffering could be a return of meningitis some 14 years previously. However, hospital tests ruled this out. The flurry of press reports of Robert's experience were mostly the usual tongue in cheek Forestry Worker Meets Alien type, typical of a media which is unsure how to handle such stories. Another observer at the scene at the time explained away the incident as an encounter with ball lightening. But Robert is hardly likely to have mistaken this natural phenomenon for the object he described in such detail, and it certainly cannot account for the very physical effects of his encounter. But the British UFO Research Association's own files throw up some interesting sightings from the same area and at about the same time as Robert's meeting with his "spinning top thing."

The evening before, Peter Caldwell, a 35-year-old clerk at a factory at nearby Uphall, saw a dull, white, round object traveling from west to east across the sky. Behind it was a large red patch "as if the air was on fire." That same evening postman James Forsyth saw two white lights pass in the sky above him. First, they approached each other, then passed, then approached and passed yet again as James walked his dog through a park in the Craigmillar area of Edinburgh. At 9.30 am, possibly on the same day as Robert's encounter, an Edinburgh woman reported a bright light in the sky traveling west, towards Livingston. She described it as a dull, white grey in colour with "neither wings nor tail." Mrs. Barbara Gerrard of Leslie in Fife saw three orange/pink lights in the sky on the afternoon of November 9 and at 10 am on the same day 35-year-old Violet Connor of nearby Bathgate saw a bright light in the sky to the west, over Armadale, which is just across the M8 from Livingston. Robert Taylor's encounter baffled the Development Corporation of Livingston, the police, the medics, his wife and most of all himself.

The plaque on the cairn at the site of Robert Taylor's encounter. (Photo copyright Malcolm Robinson.

174

It still sparks fierce debate among ufologists. Were the occupants of the UFO trying to abduct Robert? He believes they were and fought back. Is he sure it was a UFO? Robert is convinced and neither the police nor the other authorities have been able to come up with an alternative explanation. And as far as other witnesses are concerned, couldn't at least one of those people making sighting reports to BUFORA over that period have seen the same object that Robert encountered? Happily, Robert, now in his 80s (At the time of this interview) and still pleased to recount his event, has not faced the sneering ridicule that many witnesses have experienced. In fact, he has achieved something of a celebrity status in his local community. So much so that local councillors voted to erect a Cairn or monument to the Close Encounter at Livingston. Erected in May 1992 the commemorative plaque and Cairn was the result of collaboration between the Livingston Development Corporation and the Scottish UFO research group Strange Phenomena Investigations. Robert Taylor passed away in 2007.

I have not commented on each case as we go through them as I think they can all pretty much speak for themselves. What I would say is that the 1970's saw more than its fair share of high strangeness encounters. In fact, I might take the risk and go on the record and state that these encounters got even stranger in the 1970's. Why that is I simply do not know. They seem to get even stranger as the decade progressed. Some no doubt will point out that in 1978 in the UK Steven Spielberg's block buster movie 'Close Encounters of the Third Kind' was released in cinemas. I remember going to watch it myself at the Odeon cinema in Leeds with my best friend at the time Jimmy Lockhead.

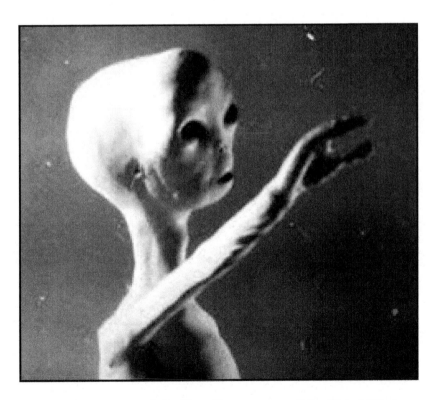

Alien from the movie Close Encounters of the Third Kind

I was a mere nineteen years of age at the time. UFO sightings in general were on the rise in the 1970's but there could be an argument to say that what the movie did was to encourage witnesses to come forward. I personally can see no connection either direct or indirect between the movie's release and the rise in encounter reports and their high strangeness factor changing. The aliens from the movie were cute little things and nothing like those reported around the UK by real life close encounter witnesses.

*****

CHAPTER FIVE

JOINING UFOLOGY-The 1980's

The 1980's in the UK were a time of division, political unrest, riots and war. Britain's first even woman Prime Minister Margaret Thatcher led the conservative party to power in 1979. In total she would spend eleven years as Prime Minster before finally being forced out by her own colleagues. Thatcher's premiership was one of deep division in the UK. After she introduced a new tax called the 'poll tax' there were protests and riots. The UK coal mining industry was brought to a standstill by a year-long strike which was marred by more protests and violence. The UK also went to war with Argentina after their invasion of the Falkland Islands in 1982. The war lasted just ten weeks before the Argentine military forces surrendered. On a happier note, Prince Charles married Lady Dianna Spencer, home computers and the first mobile phones were introduced. On a personal note, I had joined the British UFO Research Association in 1979 (BUFORA) but found it too London-central and I lived 200 miles north of the capital. In 1980 I joined the newly formed Yorkshire UFO Society and my life changed forever. It wasn't long before I jumped in with both feet to learn the ropes of UFO research and investigation and the rest is history. In among all of this of course UFO sightings continued as did close encounters with their own flavour of 1980's high strangeness.

Steve Glen and Mike Burns
Hendon
London
England
January 13, 1980

The pop song 'No Doubt about It' by Hot Chocolate was a big hit in 1980 reaching number two in the UK singles chart and going on to be a success in many other countries as well. The band, lead by singer Errol Brown, had a string of hits but none of them were like this one. This song told the story of a UFO sighting which was not quite what we were used to hearing in 1980's or at any other time for that matter.

It was also completely different to anything that Hot Chocolate had ever recorded. It was released on the RAK record label, and it spent 11 weeks in the charts. So, what's the story behind it? Was Errol Brown singing about a real event or was this a song simply from its writers Mike Burns and Steve Glen?

For those unfamiliar with this song, you can see it on YouTube at:
https://www.youtube.com/watch?v=WeiufBduVE8

I had always been curious about this song and remember it well from my days as a young man. I was therefore extremely pleased to obtain the contact details of one of the co-writers of the song, Steven Glen and managed to conduct a brief interview with him on the telephone in late January 2019.

North London resident Steven Glen started out in music business as a singer-songwriter before moving on as a songwriter/record producer working with artists such as Cliff Richard, Gloria Gaynor, Roger Daltrey, Bucks Fizz, Suzi Quatro and of course Hot Chocolate. He had been taken under the wing of legendary music producer Micky Most who had advised Steven that perhaps his future lay in writing and producing rather than that of a singer. Steven took that advice and signed to RAK as an in-house writer/producer and has had a long and successful career as a result, and one that still continues to this day.

The UK pop group HOT CHOCOLATE

While speaking with Steven it wasn't long before I realised that the song 'No Doubt About It' was not a figment of his imagination but was in fact based on a UFO close encounter, a close encounter that he had been witness to along with his writing partner Mike Burns and a pop group by the name of 'The Toys' and not Hot Chocolate. This is what Steven Glen had to tell me about his close encounter.

"It's a true story," says Steven, even though a lot of people find it hard to believe! "I was driving on the Hendon Way with my writing partner Mike Burns and he pointed up in sky and said, 'what's that up there?' I nearly drove off the road. We were actually on our way to the RAK recording studio in St John's Wood at the time. I was producing a band called 'The Toys' at the time and the band was following behind us in a van. Mike had looked behind us to check that the van carrying the band was following us and noticed that they were pointing towards the sky. Mike looked up and could not believe his eyes.

He now drew my attention to what the others had been looking at. As I turned off the A40 onto The Finchley Road at Hampstead I veered off onto West Heath Road and stopped just below the Leg of Mutton Pond. All I can say is that the UFO, well it was right above us. It was massive – about four or five houses wide and when we got out to have a look, it created an orange cloud." The date and time of this incident was about 5pm on Sunday January 13th, 1980.

Steven went on to explain that he and Mike got out of the car to take a look at this thing which was literally right above them and the members of The Toys got out of their van to view this unusual sight as well. While standing there almost transfixed viewing this large grey, brown object it suddenly created an orange cloud which hid the large UFO. The lyrics in the song 'No doubt about it' describes a cloud of white and green and not orange, this is because the songwriters could not find a rhyme for the word orange, so they changed orange to white and green! After a short while of calm and staring at the orange cloud suddenly several small objects shot out and started heading towards the assembled on-lookers and almost 'dive-bombed' them. These small objects were described as having only wings with no fuselage and they too were also a grey, brown colour. Steven didn't hesitate to duck out of sight in a nearby hedge and he's pretty certain that The Toys band jumped back into their vehicle.

The UFO remained above the two vehicles and thinking fast Steven noticed that there was a telephone box right next to where they had stopped. He jumped up and headed for this where he called the army first and a spokesman told him that there is no such thing as UFOs, so he then called the police. To his surprise the police did turn up and they too observed this UFO and the whole sighting lasted for about 40 minutes after which it shot off into the sky at a terrific speed and was completely silent. Two police officers even came to visit them the next day at the recording studio to take down some more details. Steven was very surprised that other motor vehicles on the road at the time didn't stop as they were on a busy road (A41 by Henley's Corner).

Steve Glen

After this encounter Steven went to Mike Burns' house where he discussed what had just happened with his co-writer before he wrote the song and they asked each other 'did we just see a UFO?' both agreed that there was NO DOUBT ABOUT IT! He said it was one of the fastest songs he'd ever written, and it went on to be one of Hot Chocolate's biggest sellers. Some years later Steven also wrote the song 'Is There Any Body Out There' for Roger Daltrey (lead singer with The Who) which was a sort of frustrated plea to whatever or whoever is out there in the galaxy. Steven said that this song also pretty much wrote itself. I asked Steven why he hadn't talked about this event much and he told me that he had talked about it at the time and was interviewed by the press and TV, but he was annoyed with people hinting that because they were in the music business they must have been on drugs. He said that in the end he just told Hot Chocolate's lead singer Errol Brown to say that he'd seen it himself just to help promote the song. It obviously worked as it sold in its tens of thousands around the world.

Steven Glen still works in the music business and is currently working on a number of new projects. I thanked him for his time and asked him if he was now a believer in UFOs and it won't surprise you to know that he said: "No Doubt About It."

Mrs. Westerman and children
Normanton
West Yorkshire
England
Summer 1980

When I look back now I am amazed to find that I have been involved in UFO research & investigation for forty years. Over those years I have been a member of six UFO groups, four of which were in the UK and two overseas. I've always had an interest in all things 'paranormal' but for some reason UFOs gained my full attention in the late 1970's. I've been asked many times which UFO case most impresses me.

Is it the UFO crash at Roswell, or the events at Rendlesham forest in 1980, my answer to this question in none of those. It is without the UFO case that has most impressed me is one that I investigated with Mark Birdsall when we were both part of the Yorkshire UFO Society. Mark now owns and edits the successful 'EYE SPY' magazine and he was part of the hugely successful UFO MAGAZINE with his late brother Graham Birdsall for many years. I doubt if you have ever heard of the following case that Mark and I investigated, but I remember interviewing the witnesses like it was only yesterday.

The following account was first published in the July/August issue of QUEST magazine, at the time the hand printed publication of the Yorkshire UFO Society (YUFOS).

On Friday the 13th of October 1986 I had been featured in the regional newspaper the Wakefield Express. The article in question told of my involvement with YUFOS and it encouraged its readers to report any UFO sightings to us. We had a number of observations reported to us but one stood out among the others. I was telephoned by a lady by the name of Mrs Westerman. She began by stating that "I wouldn't believe her."

180

She repeated this several times before she eventually told me that she and a number of her children had witnessed the landing of a UFO near her house in Normanton, West Yorkshire a few years earlier complete with humanoid occupants outside it in a nearby field. I quickly took her contact details and along with Mark Birdsall arranged an appointment to see her and conduct an interview.

It wasn't long before Mark Birdsall and I interviewed her at her home in Normanton. There were seven witnesses to the events in question six of whom were the children of Mrs Westerman. In 1986 Normanton had a large mining community all of which has gone now. It lies just a few miles outside of the city of Wakefield and the M62 and M1 motorways run close by.

Mrs Westerman stated that the date of the incident was the summer of 1980. She could not remember the date but speculated that it could have been May or June. Mrs Westerman went on to inform us that on the day in question she was at home doing the washing. It was a sunny afternoon and a perfect day to get the washing done. Her children were outside playing a ball game and enjoying the sun. They were not on school holiday so it must have been a weekend.

It was around mid-afternoon when her eight-year-old daughter suddenly ran into the house shouting and crying and telling her mother to "come quick, an aeroplane had just landed in the field." The Westerman's house was an elevated property and was near the end of a cul-de-sac and beyond that were some fields which contained electricity pylons. Mrs Westerman switched off her washing machine and ran outside. Just a matter of a few hundred yards away, in the fields adjacent to her house, she saw an object on the ground. It was a dull grey colour and had the appearance of a Mexican hat'. Around the object stood three very tall 'men' all of whom appeared to be dressed in silver suits. These men seemed to be pointing a dark instrument at the ground. The children and Mrs. Westerman made their way over the field towards this object and stopped at a fence. The men walked to rear of the object and it rose vertically, stopped in mid air, and then shot off at an angle at a high rate of speed. Needless to say, they were speechless.

This was a brief description given by Mrs. Westerman but we also took advantage of speaking to some of the children as well. Unlike Mrs Westerman they had actually seen the object come into land as well. The children were interviewed separately and their story was very consistent. This is what they had to say:

The children had been playing ball behind the house where Mrs. Westerman lived. Eight-year-old Sandra told us how the ball they were playing with had been thrown up into the air as part of the game. As she went to catch the ball she observed a strange object in the sky. Sandra shouted to the rest of the children to look and pointed skyward.

They all observed a silvery coloured object, disc-shaped with a rim around the perimeter. The object was at low level and was seen just above the electricity pylons. It suddenly stopped in mid-air just a few hundred feet up, hovered for a few seconds, before slowly landing in the field. Sandra immediately set off at this point to get her mother. While Sandra went to fetch her mother, the other children ran towards the landed object but stopped when they reached a fence the enclosed the field.

The object itself wasn't very big, perhaps as long as a large Volvo car. However, the 'men' around the object all seemed to be very tall and the object in their hand looked similar to a torch. These three very tall humanoids had been seen to emerge from the rear of the landed object. Their heads and face were covered by some kind of 'visor'. Their silver suits had no zippers, buttons or seems, they had glove or mittens covering their hands and were wearing a wedged shaped boot. None of these men appeared to communicate with each other and their actions were slow and precise.

Artist impression of the UFO landing at Normanton. (Artwork by David Sankey)

It was at this point that Mrs. Westerman and her daughter Sandra caught up with the other children. They continued to observe this strange spectacle for about a minute or so. Suddenly, one of the humanoid figures looked up and noticed Mrs Westerman and the children all standing behind the fence. Now these three very tall men quickly walked away behind the object and were never seen again.

A few seconds later the object silently rose from the ground, stopped in m is air, before moving off at an angle at high speed. All seven individuals were amazed by what they had just seen and Mrs Westerman, the only adult there, had to calm the children down. All seven witnesses hardly spoke about this incident down the years and had never told anyone outside of the family about it until relating it to me and Mark Birdsall.

All six children related similar accounts to us. There were minor discrepancies but we expected to find that from different people and several tears after it had happened.

All of the children were of the opinion that the dark object the men had in their hands and were moving about looked like a torch but it had no light and gave off no sound. The 'uniforms' the men were wearing were metallic silver and it would crease when the men moved. All of the witnesses stated quite clearly that both upon landing and departure this object never made a sound.

The location of this event is interesting. The field lies at the end of the houses which in turn are part of a large housing estate. There are many electricity pylons in the field making it very difficult for such things as helicopters to land.

At our interview a young man by the name of Andrew Lewis was invited to attend by Mrs. Westerman. He was a friend of the children at the time and although he did not observe anything unusual himself, he arrived shortly afterwards and confirmed how excited they all were. Another friend was Danny Shore. He was one of the seven original witnesses and was thirteen years old at the time. He estimated that they whole incident last no more than between five and ten minutes.

Both Mark and I visited the location and were impressed by the credibility of the witnesses. At no time did they call the object a 'spaceship' of a 'flying saucer' and there was no way Mrs. Westerman wanted any publicity, she would not even allow us to take her photograph. They were honest, hard-working down-to-earth people. The children's accounts were consistent and all seven witnesses were in no doubt that they had observed something out of the ordinary.

Both Mark and I could find no reason for them to concoct such a story. Mrs Westerman did say that she was amazed that no one else had seen the object. It was a sunny day and it flew at low level over the housing estate.

So, there you have it. This is the one UFO case that most impresses me above all others. Why? Well, it's not just because I was involved in it, and it is not necessarily what the witnesses related to us. Instead, it is the witnesses themselves. Normanton had a large miner's community. In fact, Mrs Waterman's husband worked at a local colliery. My late father worked down the mines all his life and I grew up with people very much like Mrs Westerman. Added to that, and despite our best efforts, neither Mark Birdsall nor I could find any rational explanation for this event. It either happened as they reported it to us or they were lying and we could find no evidence of the latter.

In 2019 I was fortunate enough to establish contact with Sandra, one of Mrs. Westerman's children who witnessed the UFO that day. I have not revealed her married name but I do have it on file.

This is what she had to tell me about the incident: "I only remember that something which I thought at the time was an aircraft landing and when we ran over it was a circular craft, I remember seeing 3 of what looked like tall men in silver suits who looked like they were looking for something on the ground, I vaguely remember some sort of metal detector in one of their hands. When we were seen approaching they hurried back in the craft and sped off."

Wayne Didsbury, Michael Winley, Kevin Clarke, Mr. & Mrs. Richardson and Mr. & Mrs. Case.
Ashbury
Oxfordshire
England
July 9, 1981

At 6.45 am. 9th July 1981, schoolboy - Wayne Disbury, was out on his 'paper round', when he noticed a bright white object on the ground, close to the B4000 road, which runs between Shrivenham and Ashbury, leading to the village of Kingstone Winslow. Thinking it was a plastic bag, he continued on his 'round'.

At 7.35 am. Michael Winley - a member of the Royal Observer Corps, was driving to work along the B4000, heading towards Ashbury, when he noticed two horses in the field acting in an agitated manner. Thinking they were being worried by a dog, he stopped his car and got out, ready to chase off the animal.

"I was surprised to see a bright object on the ground, near to the horses, and assumed it might have been a meteorological balloon, and went over to pick it up. As I did so, the object, resembling a dustbin lid in shape, 2-3 feet in diameter, chrome top and black base, funnel or tube protruding from its centre, showing what looked like a small truncated cone on its front, with a number of small indentations around its perimeter, rose vertically upwards, between 150-200 feet off the ground, and flew silently over the head of Mr. Winley, and descended before coming to a halt, approximately 70 feet off the ground."

A business colleague of Mr. Winley's - Kevin Clarke, was driving along the same stretch of road, when he noticed Mr. Winley's car, and pulled up at 7. 45 am, curious as to what was going on. After making his way over the field, he was astonished to see the object hovering in the air. A few minutes later, another workmate - Raymond Millin, also turned up. He and the other two men stood watching it before it moved off towards the direction of Idstone, parallel to the B4000 - until lost from view.

At 8.05 am. Mr. & Mrs. Richardson, accompanied by Mr. & Mrs. Case, were travelling along the B4000, towards Swindon, in the opposite direction to the other witnesses, when they saw a small object approaching their position, 2-300 yards away, travelling slowly - no more than 10 mph. - described as being, *'Two feet in diameter, by 8 inches deep - a light metallic colour, (mottled on top), with a dark base, showing indentations'.* Mr. Richardson noticed a small hollow tube sticking out of the base, although the others didn't see this. He then stopped the car, adjacent to the field, and got out - in time to see it pass directly overhead,15-20 feet up – apparently, as if to land. At this stage, he decided to continue his journey to work.

The incident was later brought to the attention of Marty Moffat, of the 'SCUFORI' UFO Group, who launched a thorough investigation into the matter, wondering whether a remote-control balloon could have been responsible, but finally concluded, in view of the lack of any further information, to classify it as an unidentified object. (Source: Ian Mrzyglod / Marty Moffat, *Probe'* / SCUFORI).

Alfred Burtoo
Aldershot
Hampshire
England
August 12, 1983

The following encounter was originally investigated by Omar Fowler of the Surrey Investigation Group on Aerial Phenomena (SIGAP). Omar had received a phone call from a local newspaper asking him to investigate a case in the neighbouring county of Hampshire. These were Omar's findings.

Mr. Alfred Burtoo was fishing on the Basingstoke Canal Bank, near North Town, Aldershot, Hampshire. The time was 1.15 am and the date was August 12, 1983. Mr. Burtoo, aged 77 at the time, had written to the local newspaper to ask if anyone had seen a strange light but did not mention the UFO. One of the local journalists phoned Mr. Burtoo who told him about the UFO. The reported then phoned Omar Fowler for an opinion who in turn called Mr. Burtoo to arrange an interview. A tape-recorded interview with Mr. Burtoo was made on 10.10. 1983. Here is s statement by the witness:

Mr. Burtoo at the scene of his close encounter (courtesy David Sankey)

"One the one o'clock news on the 11th of August, the weather was going to be fine, and the moon was only four or five days old, which is what I consider ideal conditions for fishing, so I had my wife go and get me a loaf of bread, which she did (bait). I got all my tackle ready, and I moved off from here at quarter past twelve at night (i.e., the morning of Friday, August 12, 1983). On the way up to the canal, I stopped on the road to put the dog on a lead, when I heard footsteps behind me and it turned out to be one of the MoD (Ministry of Defence) policeman on his duties, so we stopped and had a talk.......After a short time he went his way and I went mine up onto the canal bank.

185

As soon as I got there I put my fishing tackle on the ground and un-did my rod-case, stuck the rod in the ground, and tied the dog to it. Then I started to unpack my tackle-box, then, just as I started, I heard the 'gong' at the nearby Buller Barracks, strike one (1.00 am). I got everything ready for dawn because that is your best time for fishing.

I sat there on my tackle-box watching the water for any movement of fish and decided to have a cup of tea. I poured out my cup of tea, when I saw a light suddenly appear from the south, so I put my cup down on the box and stood and watched it. It came in towards the railway bridge and I thought.....it's not going to land on the railway bridge? I straight away guessed it wasn't an aircraft or a 'chopper', because it was only about three hundred feet from the ground. Then it settled down (landed) further along the towpath and the brilliant light that had been showing was extinguished. I stood there watching it and presently I saw two 'forms' coming towards me.

The dog growled and wouldn't stop until I told it to; two 'forms' came up to me, just over four feet in height I would say, dressed in pale green 'overalls' and visors. I stood there looking at them, and they stood there looking at me and then the chap on the right waved for me to come, and that was all. I was curious, so I followed them. Well, when we got down to within fifty to sixty yards from the railway bridge, there was this object sitting on the towpath, with ten to fifteen feet over the water and about ten to fifteen feet over the bank. There were steps. They were offline to the towpath, and we had to step on the grass to get up them. One of these 'forms' went across the corridor, which was hexagon in shape, and the other one stood near the door, and I stood to the right of him.

UFO investigator Omar Fowler (courtesy John Hanson)

Presently a voice said, in broken English, 'come over and stand under the amber light' (question by Omar Fowler: 'did you actually hear the voice?') Yes I actually heard it say, 'come and stand under the amber light'. Well, right in the centre of the floor was a column that went up, about four feet in circumference. At first I couldn't see an amber light, but when I stepped to one side I could see the light on the wall. I walked over and stood under the light, and this voice that asked me to come over and stand under the light, asked me......'what is your age?' I said I shall be 78 next birthday.

186

There was a pause, then he said, 'turn around' and I turned around facing the wall, and after about five minutes he said to me 'you can go, you are too old and too infirm for our purpose'.

Now this column that was in the middle of the floor, there was a z-shaped handle on it, such as you might see on a well, and there was a 'form' (being) standing on either side of it. These two were different 'forms' from those that had accompanied me along the canal towpath. I took it to be that these two 'forms' were standing by, ready to wind the gear that drove it, but this in only my suspicion.

I looked around when he said, 'you can go', and I came down. As I was coming down, holding the banister-rail on the steps, I felt two joints in it, which gave me the impression that the steps were telescopic, and folded up in some way. Anyway, I came down, and got about twenty to thirty yards from them, and then turned and watched it. It had a turret on the top of it, very much like an inverted saucer, but it looked like a cowl like you have on top of a chimney, but instead of it going around clockwise, it went anti-clockwise. I carried on back to where my dog and my tackle were, and the first thing was to pick up my cup of cold tea and drank it.....still watching I saw it lift off to about three hundred feet and it shot-off to the south-west over the military cemetery. I saw it pass over Tongham (half a mile south-east of Aldershot) and over 'Hog-Back' two and a half miles in the distance and out of sight."

MR BURTOO'S SKETCH OF CRAFT

Illustration courtesy of the Flying Saucer Review

Omar Fowler went on to ask Mr. Burtoo some questions about the encounter:

Q: You seem very calm and collected about the whole thing.
AB: I was more curious than anything; at my age, nearly 78, what have I got to worry about? I can only die once. I had read a lot about UFOs, and I didn't believe in them. Well, I definitely do now, and seeing is believing. I don't care a damn who believes it or who doesn't, but I definitely went into that machine. When I came back I told my wife and her friend. Up until then I took it that UFOs were a lot of bunk. I definitely wasn't scared, just curious and I wanted to see what was going on. If they had taken off with me, then it would just have been my lot. It would have been just the same as me going out on the street and being knocked down.

Q: Let us just go over the beginning, when the beings came up to you.
AB: I got a bit of a shock when they came up to me with those green overalls on, I couldn't see any buttons or zips or anything; it was just as though it was moulded onto them. The dog sat there quietly after I told it to shut up. They had like pea-green helmets on their heads, but the visor on the front seemed to be blacked out, like smoked glass. You couldn't see their faces. I didn't notice their hands; maybe they had gloves on. I've been a gardener for fifty-two years and I've learned to notice things as I go along.

Q: Did they have any belts on.
AB: No, no belts; no buttons, no torches in their hands.....nothing. The overalls seemed to be a one-piece affair to my way of thinking.

Q: These steps, were they just a ladder or what?
AB: Just a wide set of steps, with a handrail up both sides.

Q: Had the two figures gone inside the craft?
AB: One went in ahead of me; because that is the way they walked down the path, and one behind me. The one in front of me walked across what I would call the corridor, into what I took to be a room on the other side, and the other one stood just inside the door, and I stood on the right of him.

Q: What sort of illumination was there?
AB: There was a light; it was very dim, and everything appeared black.

Q: Was the light attached to the ceiling or what?
AB: No, that's the funny part. I didn't see anything like that, but there was a light there. Whether it was around the ridge of the ceiling? The inside of the craft was all black, but the outside was like polished aluminium. When I walked across the floor I didn't hear my own footsteps, so I got the impression that there was some sort of cloth down on the floor. The ceiling was only about five feet high, and it was as much as I could do to get into it. The 'beings' were about four feet six inches (tall). I am five feet four and a half inches (tall), so they were shorter than me. I had to 'bob down' going into the door, and the light was good enough to see where we were going, but once we got inside there was a dim light, but this must have been due to the blackness of it. Whoever built that thing certainly made a good job of it; there were no nuts, bolts, joints, or welds that I could see. I reckon I was in there for a goof half an hour; I had to wait for a while with this chap standing beside me.

Q: So, you had a good chance to look around?
AB: I wasn't scared or anything like that, I was just curious. I've spent many years outdoors and tackled many things in Canada; shot a bear, rattle snakes, wolves; I don't think I'm scared of anything. (Source: FSR 1983 V 29 N 2).

I think it's fair to say that this case would be labelled as an alien abduction. I have purposely not featured this type of case in this book; instead, I have concentrated on cases that involve the observation of UFOs on the ground. UFO landing cases and nothing more.

However, this particular case is not that well known even though it has appeared in several books and magazines. I therefore thought it a good case to use as an example of something that has a great deal of high strangeness.

Mr and Mrs. W. (and their two children)
Stonehenge
Wilshire
England
August 2, 1984

Mr and Mrs W and their two children Martin (aged 11) and Trevor (aged 13), were returning home from a holiday in the West Country to their home in Potton, Bedfordshire. It was around 11.00 pm and the date was August 2, 1984.

They were driving home on the A303 and were directly next to Stonehenge when their encounter began. Mrs. W was the first to see something unusual. The sky had taken on a golden hue colour and two orange/gold spheres (with a haze around them) appeared in the west looking towards the town of Warminster. Then two more, and another two, lining up into a definite formation.

At this point the family claim that the headlights on their car dimmed but did not go out. After a couple of minutes these strange lights disappeared. Martin was the next to see something. He observed (but no one else did) a light moving across the sky which changed colour from white, to green and then red. This was almost certainly an aircraft.

Mr W slowed the car right down now and all of the family were on the lookout for UFOs. They by-passed the town of Amesbury and at just a few minutes past eleven they had an encounter with a landed object. This was first seen by Mr. W (who spotted it briefly through the hedgerow as they drove by). Mr. W was concentrating on his driving and the two boys were looking at the sky.

However, at the first convenient spot Mr. W turned the car around and drove past the field. All four now observed the landed object. Again, Mr. W turned the car around and went back (heading east on the A303 again). Only a minute or so had passed since they last viewed the object, but now the field was empty and the object had gone.

The object was described as a grey dome resting on the ground with a row of windows through which shone an orange/yellow light. The headlights on the car were now working perfectly and Mrs. W said there seemed to be "an unnatural quiet, as though we were moving in a somewhat dreamlike way, rather like watch a film."

From this point on more strange lights and more orange spheres were seen. Mrs. W entered a state of "euphoria" and Mr. W stopped the car (now on the M3) but gave no reason for why he did this. The family continued seeing threes lights until 1.30 am.

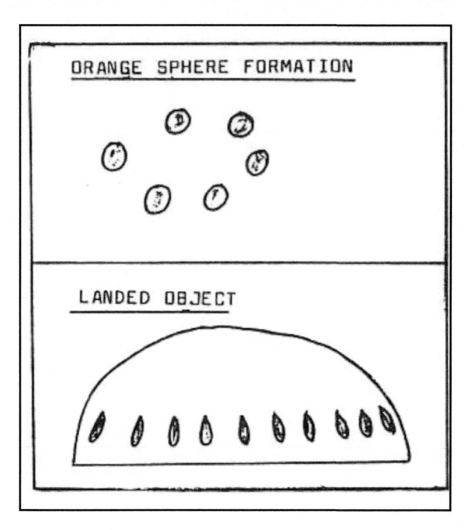

The formation of lights and the domed object seen by Mr & Mrs W and sons (picture courtesy BUFORA)

Mrs. W reported the incident to the police in Hitchin the following day. They claim that the police were initially quite sceptical but they did phone them back that they had not received any other reports and they would forward their report to the Ministry of Defence. Hitch police liaised with Wiltshire police and were informed that there were some military manoeuvres on that night in the vicinity of the sighting.

The witnesses were given the telephone number of a military air force base to call which they did but never received satisfactory reply. UK author and UFO researcher jenny Randles wrote to the MoD about this incident but never received a reply. In frustration the family turned to the media and their local newspaper did carry a story about their sightings.

Ken Phillips, the investigator for BUFORA which dealt with this case for the British UFO Research Association (BUFORA) was convinced that the lights the witnesses observed could well have been linked to the military manoeuvres, perhaps they were flares of some kind, but they domed object in the field was still unexplained. (Source: BUFORA Bulletin No.18 Jul 1985 August 1984).

Patrick
Worfield
Shropshire
England
May 1987

The following case was personally investigated by my friend and colleague John Hanson and his partner Dawn Holloway. John is a former CID Detective with the West Midlands Police and has published his own series of book under his 'Haunted Skies' banner. This is what he and Dawn had to say about the following case.

We spoke to Patrick a retired West Mercia Police Officer about what he witnessed while a village 'bobby' stationed at Bridgnorth Police Station Shropshire in May 1987. Patrick who asked that we not include his surname due to the sensitive nature of his job within the West Mercia Constabulary, told of having received a telephone call from Captain Robbie Evans, owner of the Wyken Estate who reported having seen a strange red glow in the sky over Chempshill Coppice near Worfield an area of mature woodland forming part of the Davenport estate

" I decided to visit the locality myself, wondering whether there was any connection with the nearby RAF Base, at Cosford, or the local Halfpenny Green Airport. As I was about to get into the Police car, I was aware of a loud humming noise resonating in the air - like an electrical buzzing - but thought no more of it at the time. I made my way to high ground overlooking the area concerned, close to Rindleford - a tiny hamlet, near Worfield - which gave me a clear view over the countryside. I was shocked to see a grey saucer shaped object, making a quiet humming noise similar to what I had heard when leaving the Police Station.

I estimated it to be 100-200 feet across, with a dome on top, hovering over a field. Projecting from underneath the 'saucer" could be seen three beams of orange light -diffused, rather than bright. I stood watching for a few minutes, feeling the hairs standing up on the back of my neck - then the humming noise increased in pitch to a droning noise. The next thing that happened was that it shot off at terrific speed and out-of-sight by now dusk was beginning to fall. I decided to leave any further investigation until the next morning. When I returned to the scene, the following day, I came across a local shepherd, who told me something odd had happened in the field because 'Moss', his dog, was too frightened to go anywhere near the area

We walked across the field, towards a clump of trees, where we discovered a huge area of dried grass formed in a big circle. My impression being through examination of the ground, was that it looked as if the circle had been created not through the application of any heat but as if all the moisture had been sucked out of the around only on the inside of the circle, in complete contrast to untouched plant growth on the outside"

Patrick told us he submitted a full report of the incident to his Supervising Officer, a copy of which was also sent to the Ministry of Defence and that he was later contacted by Mr. Mike Pryce - a Reporter for The Worcester Evening News' who interviewed him, details later being published in that newspaper.

We spoke to Mr. Pryce, who told us he remembered the incident very well because it was so unusual, although he regretted having not visited the locality himself. Patrick gave us details of another witness - a lady then employed in the Police Canteen, at Bridgnorth who was a passenger on a bus passing the scene at the time.

Unfortunately, we were unable to interview the lady concerned, due to health problems, but her son confirmed to us his mother had certainly seen something very strange, while a passenger on the bus, along with several other passengers.

We wrote to the Ministry of Defence seeking further information about any UFO incidents that had occurred in May 1987, in the Shropshire area. They told us they had no knowledge of any UFO reports during that particular period. (Source: Personal interviews by John Hanson and Dawn Holloway- Haunted Skies).

Miss S.
Bolsover
Derbyshire
England
August 8, 1987

The next case was investigated by my old friend and colleague David Clarke (now a PhD). The sighting took place amongst a spate of sightings across South Yorkshire, West Yorkshire and Derbyshire in 1987. I remember talking to David not long before this sighting took place and saying that we'd had just about every kind of sighting reported to us in recent weeks and months but not a landing report. Little did I know what would soon come our way.

Miss S. was a tax inspector and living in Bolsover, Derbyshire. At 10.55 pm on August 8, she was driving along a lane below Bolsover Castle ruins called Limekiln Fields. Upon reaching the junction with Hill Top Road which leads up to the castle ruins, she looked to the right and was about to turn left out of the junction and "saw something with white lights on it." She described this object as about the size of a "double-decker bus" at ground level, in the shape of a flat square, with ten to twelve white lights around its perimeter. These lights were bright, like car headlights, and may have gone across the middle of the object as well as the sides. "I couldn't see any shape unless the other half of whatever it was around the bend, because it is on a bend. But how can a vehicle curve round a bend like that, it seemed to me to be right on the bend." Miss S. only glanced at this object, and satisfied that it was not moving, turned left onto Hill Top Road and scared, drove home thinking, "What was that? I thought turn around and go back and have a look to satisfy your curiosity but I daren't, I was too frightened to." When she returned home she told her husband and son and they hurriedly returned to the spot within minutes but were unable to find any trace that anything had been there. Miss S. went on to add that: "on that particular night I never saw any people walking about on foot because quite often I do because there are people walking their dogs, and I do not recollect seeing another vehicle either on the way home.....certainly not on that part of the road and I do not recollect another vehicle passing me or anything like that, it seemed very quiet. It was a clear, fine evening, I don't know, I can't explain it and I still haven't been able to."

Bolsover Castle and ruins in Derbyshire

David Clarke was then part of the Independent UFO Network and along with a colleague inspected the area just a few days later. They also talked to local residents living in the area, none of whom reported seeing anything unusual on that August night. The investigators looked for a rational explanation for this sighting but were unable to find one. They left the case open to further investigation simply because the witness had only seen the object for such a short period of time.

I have included this case simply because I was partially involved in and around the investigation of some of the other UFO reports that we were receiving at the time. I was a colleague of David's and I am still friends with him today. David is well known for his sceptical approach to the subject, so if there had been an explanation David would have found it. The fact that he didn't find one speaks volumes for me.

I have also included it because it did, as I've already pointed out, take place among a spate of sightings being reported at that time. The witness also mentioned that fact of not seeing any other people or vehicles about. This type of thing has often been reported in similar close encounter events.

Mr. RM & Mrs. GM
Cannock
Staffordshire
England
August 4, 1988

The two witnesses, Mr. RM and Mrs. GM were driving home together after attending a meeting in nearby Cannock on the 4th of August 1988. Between midnight and twelve thirty, they were about to turn right onto the bridge that would take them from the A513 to Little Hayward when Mrs. GM noticed a large luminous cloud on her side of the road (passenger's side).

This luminous cloud was pulsating with red light and was shaped like a saucer. It was estimated to be around thirty feet in diameter and the edges of it touched the ground. Mr. RM then looked up and saw a large circular object within this diffused mist some thirty feet in the air. Mr. GM watched it as it moved north-west across the road and over the nearby River Trent, disappearing, then reappearing and then finally departing and out of sight. The estimated duration of the sighting was around one minute although the investigators of the case, Clive Potter and Kevin Flannery, thought it closer to thirty seconds.

The following day both witnesses were again driving along the A513 when they noticed a damaged section of hedgerow at the spot where they had observed the luminous cloud. The damaged hedgerow had not been noticed by either witness as they had driven past this spot previously. They were both convinced that it was the UFO that had caused this damage to the hedgerow. The location of this sighting is where the A513 has some minor crossroads between Rugely and the witness's home in Little Hayward.

When UFO investigators Clive Potter and Kevin Flannery visited the site of the incident they found the hedgerow not to be burnt (as had appeared in a local newspaper) but to show a crushed, dying section of hedge some three or four yards in size, with several other sections looking like they had been uprooted. Broken branches littered this section of hedgerow and many of the leaves on it had begun to wither. Parts of the hedge had also been pushed into an adjoining field (pastureland). Some of the branches had the bark scraped from them looking like 'scuff marks'. There were no skid marks from a car or truck but there was an old number plate found. No damage was found in the adjoining field, but a tree on the opposite side of the field was later found to have had several branches broken off, with some branches twisted around and pointing in the opposite side of the road. This tree would have been in the approximate direction of the initial movement of the object. Samples taken from the location (soil, leaves etc) were examined by Dr. Michel Clare of Sheffield University who found nothing out of the ordinary in them.

The investigators of this case were adamant that the luminous object did indeed cause the damage to the hedgerow; however, they went through various ideas of what the UFO may have been. A variety of different types of weather phenomena was looked at including a vortex or perhaps the little understood phenomenon of 'earthlights' was also considered. Whatever the outcome is was classed as a UFO and not the misidentification of a mundane, natural object. (Source: UFO Times No.6 Mar 1990).

Peter Simons, family & friends
Glenmalur Valley
County Wicklow
Ireland
Summer 1988

It was the summer of 1988 when Peter Simons (pseudonym) his family and friends went to the picturesque Glenmalur Valley, County Wicklow in the Republic of Ireland. They were spending a long weekend in this heavily forested area and on the day in question they all set off together for a walk.

It was late in the evening, although still light, and it was their intention to take in some fresh air, stretch their legs, and go straight to bed reasonably early. Mr. Simons and his friend had been working that day before they set off and this meant that any exploring would have to wait until the next day.

The children in the group chatted excitedly as they walked in front of their parents who, in turn, were catching up with the goings-on in each other's lives. Suddenly, just ahead and to one side of the road, they all noticed a small figure, wearing what looked to be overalls, busily tinkering with the mechanism at the top of a telephone pole. Though the figure's face was obscured by the on-coming dusk-and its lifted elbows-it was examining the device carefully.

It was an odd thing to see, especially at that hour on the Friday of a long weekend, but everyone in the group naturally presumed that it was a maintenance worker from the telecommunications company, carrying out essential work on a locally reported fault. The figure was unusually slight in stature, but perhaps a young apprentice had been tasked with doing the work, or maybe the worker was female.

Seconds later, just yards from the telephone pole, everyone stopped. They all realised that they were miles away from any depot the 'maintenance worker' could have come from, and he or she had no van. There was no gateway in which the vehicle could have been parked, nor any houses with driveways onto which a vehicle could have turned. There were no gaps in the hedges on either side of the road, so the worker's maintenance van couldn't have been parked in a field, out of sight. They turned to look at the figure again but it had vanished.

The group returned to their local accommodation, musing over what had happened. They all decided to shrug it off, then they planned their activities for the following day and went to bed. All, that is, except Peter Simons. He didn't like unresolved problems or unanswered questions, so he decided that a resolution might only be found by going back to where they had seen the figure on the telephone pole. The lack of a vehicle with the figure bothered him. There had to be a vehicle parker somewhere nearby and he wished to go and prove it.

With everyone else preparing to go to bed, Mr. Simons told his wife that he was going outside to smoke a cigarette. Once outside, he quickly walked back down the road towards where they had seen the figure a few hours earlier. Passing a gate, he looked across at the dots of light on the far side of the valley. Each was a light in someone's house, or in some locally sited caravans or mobile homes. Then he noticed another, closer light. Then several of them, various colours, clustered in one small area.

He zipped up his jacket, climbed the gates and headed off in the direction of the lights. Within moments, he realised that they were much closer than he had thought. They were not, as he had concluded, emanating from a farm building, that he hadn't seen earlier. The shape that came into focus as his eyes adjusted to the dark was not that of a van or a car, though the size was about right. He stopped in his tracks. In front of him, just yards away, was an object that was shaped just like a saucer. It had four legs supporting it on the ground.

For a man who had not believed in UFOs all his life, this was the exact moment when he changed his mind. He could not believe what he was looking sat, and it terrified him. The object had several lights around its middle, which were the lights he had focussed on ever since he had looked over the gate into the field. As he stared, his hearted pounded and sweat drenched his shirt, despite the chill in the late summer's air. Mr. Simons told UFO investigators Dermot Butler and Carl Nally, that on looking back at the incident; it wasn't the craft that scared him the most. It was his sudden thought that he was all alone in the middle of a large field, at night, hundreds of yards away from a road which had no traffic on it.

If whoever (or whatever) was in the object had decided to attack him, there was no one around to help him. A question he then asked himself really terrified him, where were the craft's occupants? What if they had been watching him all along and they were now behind him?

UFO investigators and authors Carl Nally and Dermot Butler (courtesy of Nally & Butler).

Lights began to flash all over the noiseless object. Mr. Simon's legs had turned to jelly, but instinct now took over. He just knew that he had to get away from there, and he turned and fled as far and as fast as he could. He didn't know what the object was, and at this stage that question was the last thing on his mind. Peter Simons had never been terrified at any point in his life before now. He got little or no sleep that night, and when he did work up enough courage to tell his wife what had happened, she laughed at him at first. She believed him later, but still insisted that he was not to tell anyone about it as he (and she) would be ridiculed and embarrassed about it. (Source: Conspiracy of Silence - UFOs in Ireland by Dermot Butler and Carl Nally).

You have to ask yourself in this instance of the person at the top of the telephone pole has anything to do with the subsequent sighting of the UFO on the ground. The answer of course is no one can say for sure. The witnesses have rightly pointed out this curious observation but whether or not it is linked to Mr. Simon's sighting a short while later we can only guess. What it does do of course is add a degree of high strangeness to the whole event.

When we look at the cases in this chapter it is clear to see as far as I am concerned that they all have a good degree of high strangeness. That chapter began with a UFO landing report being turned into a pop song and was recorded by the pop group Hot Chocolate.

This song 'No Doubt About It' went on to have a worldwide success. We have another case that could well have and explanation to it, and one that caused damage to a roadside hedgerow. With the case of Mr. Burtoo in Aldershot we have high strangeness almost off the scale. Probably the only thing that lets it down is that it was a single witness observation. And last but not least we have a landing case from the Republic of Ireland. Now I know this book is concentrating on such cases in the UK only, and the Republic of Ireland is not part of the UK, but as it is joined to Northern Ireland, which is part of the UK, so I decided to add it regardless. What is curious is that there is a distinct lack of cases in Ireland in general, be it north or south. Why this might be is not for me to answer here, but it is a curious fact, nevertheless.

*****

CHAPTER SIX

THE X-FILES DECADE - The 1990's

The 1990's saw UFOs and the paranormal in millions of people's front rooms via their television set as the US made TV series 'The X-Files' was launched in 1993. Hot on its heels just two years later the infamous 'Alien Autopsy Film' became 'the' hot topic. Hugely controversial and yours truly was right in the middle of it. Away from ufology the British all-girl pop group 'The Spice Girls, were an international sensation, topping the charts around the globe. On the sporting front England's football team, world champions in 1966 were knocked out at the semi-final stage by Germany in the world cup in Italy. On a happier note, British triple-jumper Jonathan Edwards broke the world record with a jump of 18.29 meters. There was a small step forward for women's equality in 1997 when they were allowed to become Anglican priests for the first time. And on the political front Tony Blair became the UK's Prime Minister in 1997 returning the Labour Party to power for the first time in decades. UFOs were a hot topic in the 1990's and the cases of high strangeness were still being reported.

Pat Macleod
Portobello
Edinburgh
Scotland
October 1992

One morning in October 1992 Pat Macleod was driving along Duddingston Park, heading for an appointment at her local health centre. The time was 9.30am. As she drove along, Pat became aware of an extremely bright flashing light in the sky. Half a mile further along the road, keeping the light in view, she realised it was getting bigger and the brightness was intensifying. In fact, it was coming much closer to her and as it approached she noted that the central sphere of light had a ring or flange around it. This reminded her of pictures she had seen of the planet Saturn. At about twenty to thirty feet from the ground, the object slowed down and appeared to hover. It was larger, very large. It was as big as an aircraft's wingspan. Around the circumference, at regular intervals, were squares of light, like glowing windows.

Pat had not been checking her watch while this bizarre event unfolded, but thinks it was now around ten o'clock. Her appointment at the health centre was for this time and she arrived there shortly after. As she turned 0ff the main road to carry on down a side-street to her destination, the object veered east in the opposite direction and slowly descended, seeming to land in an area of open ground called Niddrie Burn-a valley-shaped expanse of grass with a stream running through the centre. Although it is open land, the ground is, in fact, surrounded by houses and multi-story flats which have a clear view of the valley. Incredibly, in spite of considerable publicity over the incident, not a single person came forward to say that they had seen the UFO at the same time as Pat.

Pat Macleod told UFO investigator Ron Halliday that there were other cars on the road at the time of the sighting; they were travelling in the opposite direction, away from the landed UFO.

Pat Macleod in the Edinburgh evening news 28th November 1992 (courtesy Ron Halliday).

According to Ron Halliday he conducted an in-depth investigation into this case and he could not find a rational explanation for it. What is interesting is that another sighting did come in. Mr. Jon Jeromsom, who ran a plumbing business in Duddingston Park, was looking out of his showroom window when he saw a bright object descend to about fifty feet. It hovered for several seconds, and then vanished. The time? 10.00am-exactly the same time as the object Pat Macleod had encountered disappeared from view. (Source: UFO Scotland – Ron Halliday).

Arthur Moar
Sandwick
Shetland Isles
Scotland
January 6, 1992

Arthur Moar, an inhabitant of Sandwick, one of the remote parts of the Shetland Isles. A retired farmer, Mr Moar was used to getting up early, and on the morning of Monday January 6, 1992, was no different.

At five minutes past seven-he could be sure of the time as he has just checked his clock-all thoughts of continuing with his daily routine was disturbed by the appearance of a bright, flashing light which lit up the whole room. Mr Moar hurried to the window and observed a strange object on the ground about thirty or forty yards from his house. Mr Moar stated: "the object was about five or six feet high with flame all around it, and in the centre I saw the globe of the world.....all the markings on the globe." Mr Moar noted that the globe was grey-coloured and that the area around the globe was dark red. The object was enclosed by a flange about four inches across. From the rear of the object protruded a round, white tube, out of which flashed the intense light which had first caught Mr Moar's attention. The globe was made of a suede-like material and even appeared to have rumpled up in the manner of a hastily dumped coat. As he watched, the UFO raised up into the air, leaving behind the white tube which remained standing on the ground. This tube, which to all intents and purposes looked solid, gradually faded away until it eventually disappeared from view. Although Mr Moar observed the object for only a short time, it is an event he is unlikely to forget.

UFO Investigator Ron Halliday had this to say about Mr Moar's encounter. On a scale of strange events listing from 1 to 10, I would classify this as number 10. Why? Because there seems no obvious object in the first place which could provide a justification for claiming a misidentification and secondly, the UFO did not look remotely like a 'flying saucer'. But if it wasn't from outer space, what on earth was it? If further reports are received of a similar object we will, perhaps, be in a better position to find a solution. (Source: UFO Scotland – Ron Halliday).

Paul Baguley, Sonya Bailey and Robert
Silbury Hill
Wiltshire
England
July 30, 1994

My friends and colleagues John Hanson and Dawn Holloway bring us yet another close encounter report.

The witnesses were at the time on Silbury Hill which is one of many historical monuments in the UK and it is located not far from Avebury in Wiltshire. This encounter involved three witnesses, Paul, Baguley, Sonya Bailey and 'Robert'. They had decided to visit this area on the evening of July 30, 1994.

Paul Baguley is quoted as saying: "We sat looking out over the open countryside. It was a warm night and we noticed what we took to be a bank of fog rolling towards us from the direction of Calne, obscuring some of our view near the base of the hill. At this stage some of the others, who were assembled on the hill decided to move away (it was now around 2.00 am) when I noticed the smell of burning tyres.

I looked around and saw a number of flickering orange lights appear near to West Kennet Long Barrow on the other side of the A4. At first I thought these lights were bicycle lights, then realised that this was not the case, as the light given off was illuminating the ground below the 'lights'.

Silbury Hill, Wiltshire (photo by the author)

Then an incredible thing happened. Two objects appeared on the road. They were tetrahedral in shape with what appeared to be a humanoid lit up shape – with the light given off from these 'shapes' cutting a swathe through the fog."

West Kennet Long Barrow (copyright Maria Wheatley)

Sonya Bailey went on to add: "We could clearly see the head and shoulders of the occupants, who seemed to be looking for something on the ground. I flashed my torch at 'them', which made them turn round to face us as if acknowledging our presence, at which point I knew from their lack of facial features-such as hair-that they were not human. The next thing that happened was that the entities seemed to be kneeling down inside the tetrahedron. I shone my torch again at which point the 'craft' started to move over the ground into a nearby field, before rising up some ten feet into the air. Robert, our other companion, was so frightened by what was happening that he fell over backwards, at which point everything seemed to slow down. I felt as if I was walking through water. I turned round and saw what I can only describe as what looked like a black tarpaulin material covered in wet mist or dew, covering the form of some other people who had fallen asleep.

What this material was I cannot say except it wasn't tarpaulin sheeting. Robert told me to stay put. We looked out over on to the A4 and could see two or three 'light beings' still in their 'craft', although by now these had been joined by three or four other similar beings.

At this stage we could see car headlights approaching from the Marlborough direction which could not have been seen from the lower position. They just knew-it is as if they were synchronized with our thoughts, moving out of the way of the car, when more strange things happened.

We saw them decrease in size to what looked like a slit of orange light like a door closing, until all that was left was a globe of orange light hovering over the road, which then faded away from sight as if it had never happened."

The investigators, John Hanson and Dawn Holloway know this location very well and went on to state that they had no reason to disbelieve the witnesses. The whole location is mysterious with its ancient monuments scattered across the countryside. I have visited this area several times myself in the past. The account provided by the witnesses has a high degree of high strangeness with the main factor being that there were three witnesses.

Robert Shawe
Urmston
Manchester
England
December 25, 1994

In the early years of my involvement in UFO research and investigation for some reason we always seemed to have something reported to us at the Yorkshire UFO Society on Christmas day. Why this should be is open for discussion. The reason I mention this of course is because the following event happened on Christmas day. This encounter was investigated by Steve Mera of MAPIT with assistance from NARO, Tony Eccles & Peter Hough.

It was on Christmas Day, 1994, that Robert Shawe claimed to have seen a UFO outside his Urmston home. He had decided to head out to Manchester City Centre to sample the nightlife so he ordered a taxi for 10.00pm. At approximately 9.40pm, Shawe glanced out of his window and noticed an aircraft at what he considered to be at high altitude. He continued to watch in horror as the aircraft started to plummet towards the ground. Robert breathlessly waited for the impact, which never happened.

Puzzled, Shawe looked out of the window towards a clearing no more than thirty feet away. Hovering silently, about one hundred feet above the trees, was the aircraft that Shawe thought had crashed.

It was now that he realised the craft was nothing like anything he had seen before. The large column-shaped craft had five red lights in a sideways formation which, although they were shining brightly, surprisingly did not illuminate the surrounding area. The craft slowly descended into the clearing and Shawe noticed that there did not appear to be any sound emanating from the object.

Eager for a closer look, Shawe headed outside towards the clearing. He had not travelled far, when he claims that he was overtaken by an innate kind of fear - the hairs on the back of his neck stood on end and his mind was awash with negative thoughts.

Understandably shaken, Shawe turned tail and fled back to his home, to wait for the taxi he had ordered earlier. Shawe claims that he cannot remember anything after returning to his flat until he woke up in his bed the following morning. Despite repeated attempts, Shawe could not clearly recall anything about the previous night, except the mysterious craft. A daylight investigation of the clearing yielded some interesting findings. We came across some flattened reeds, which were broken at the base, covered in a black substance and all facing in the same direction.

Following his unusual incident, Shawe was plagued with a succession of bizarre dreams, involving himself being manipulated by humanoid-like creatures. Shawe was completely convinced that these dreams were memories of actual events, rather than a product of his imagination.

UFO and entities as described by Robert Shawe (courtesy Steve Mera – MAPIT)

It wasn't until nine months after his encounter that Shawe eventually contacted MAPIT with his story. It appeared, initially at least, that the investigation would rely solely upon witness testimony, since it seemed unlikely that there would be any physical evidence left at the site of the incident. But surprisingly, we managed to obtain soil and plant samples from inside and outside the affected area.

The photographs that were taken indicated a circular shape within the clearing measuring just over 18 feet in all directions. The circle appeared to be due to a lack of normal plant growth - the flattened reeds, incidentally, have never grown back. Three trees to the east of the site seemed to show extensive heat damage from the base to about forty feet up the trunk.

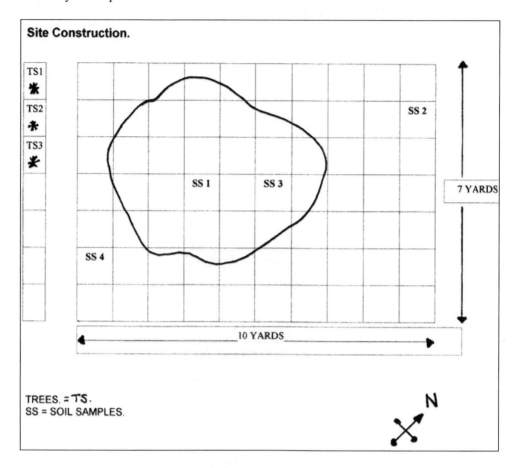

UFO landing site (courtesy Steve Mera – MAPT)

With some assistance from investigator Tony Eccles, we were able to have a professional analysis carried out on the samples by the Environmental Science Department of Manchester University. Shawe was interviewed and was clearly still attempting to account for the missing time from that night. Shawe was found to be an intelligent and rational person, who simply could not make any sense out of his experience. Following several interviews, Shawe gave mention to having hypnosis. He was informed of the procedure and of course the problems that could occur.

He was adamant; therefore, hypnosis was conducted in an attempt to regain his lost memories. Shawe's hypnosis was undertaken by a professional psychoanalyst, with over twenty years of experience in his field.

At this point I would like to mention that MAPIT now operate a No Hypnosis Policy as we believe hypnosis is rather useless at eliciting the truth, however, some interesting details can be obtained.

During the regression, Shawe retraced his steps and it became clear that he had in actual fact ventured farther into the clearing than he had previously thought. It was at this point that Shawe began to feel uncomfortable and decided to head back to his flat. When he arrived back, he checked the time on his watch, which read 10.30pm.

However, the journey should have only taken a few minutes when, in fact, over 40 minutes had elapsed. Shawe also remembered that his shoes were covered in mud, yet his conscious mind was convinced that he had only walked on the concrete path. As a result of the hypnosis, Shawe was now able to draw what he had seen; he paid particular attention to the craft, portraying the entities around it as secondary items. Shawe believed that the column shaped craft was organic in nature and he also claims to have spoken with one of the figures, although the nature of that conversation has yet to be revealed by Shawe.

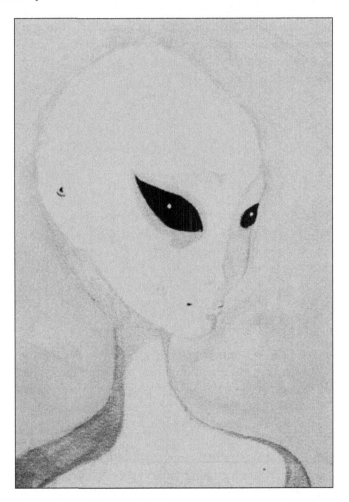

Alien as described by Robert Shawe after his hypnosis session (courtesy Steve Mera – MAPIT).

MAPIT tracked down the taxi firm who Shawe claimed to have contacted on the night of the incident. Unfortunately, they were unable to help unless the information was required for an official police investigation. However, they did confirm - off the record - that there was a 'No Show' on that night. Indicating that Shawe was either not at his home when the taxi came or his was not aware it was there.

Air Traffic Control confirmed no scheduled flights over the Urmston area during the times given on the night. The results of the analysis confirmed that the bark from the trees had been burnt by intense heat. The soil also showed distinctly different mineral oil content between the controlled and affected samples. Outside the area, the mineral oil in milligrams, per kilogram, was 95% higher than inside the area.

There did not appear to be any reasonable explanation. The pH balance of the soil was also different, but it was suggested that this is quite normal for soil from the river Valley. For now, the case remains unsolved.

I have purposely tried to keep out any cases where regressive hypnosis has been used. I made an exception here as the witness, Robert Shawe, gave a description of what he had observed before undergoing regressive hypnosis. As you can see from this account Steve Mera and his colleagues at MAPIT no longer recommend the use of regressive hypnosis. During my time at the British UFO Research Association, we also had a ban on the use of regressive hypnosis and one that is still in place today. With this in mind I leave it up to you to decide on the validity of the details provided by Mr. Shawe while under hypnosis.

Ken
Croydon
Surrey
England
April 1995

Ken was heading home from shift work in his truck. He lives on the top of a very steep hill. Halfway up the hill he had signed off on his cab computer at exactly 04.00 and at the same time became aware of a deafening turbine like drone accompanied by an ear piercing high pitched whine or whirr. We have to bear in mind here that he was driving a turbo diesel truck that was pulling up a very steep hill at the time, which would make the truck engine very noisy, but the other noise drowned the sound of his labouring engine.

This curious deafening noise seemed to go overhead, across the road and he wound down the window whilst travelling and the noise appeared to be heading south where he could hear it in the direction of the nearby woods. On reaching the brow of the hill and turning right into the road in which he lived, he switched off the engine and coasted on to his drive-in order to avoid waking his family.

He then realised he could still hear this strange noise very close by and that it was still extremely loud. He felt it was emanating from his next-door neighbour's garden, and tried to use a frame of reference for how the noise sounded. He said, "It sounded like a Concorde in full reverse thrust, but with an extra electrical alarm type noise".

Feeling that there must be an explanation for this noise, maybe a helicopter that had come down in the woods behind the houses, he walked down the alleyway at the side of his home and climbed onto to some building blocks beside his garage to look over his neighbour's fence.

He told an investigator from the British UFO Research Association (BUFORA) that upon looking behind his neighbour's hedge to the left of his oak tree, he nearly fell off the blocks in sheer panic because here he could see a brilliant ball of light glowing and hovering just above the ground behind the hedge In his own words he goes on to say: "At this point I was petrified and was balanced over the fence staring at this glow with the noise piercing my ears. I thought to myself 'why aren't my dogs barking and why aren't the neighbours out?' I wanted to run indoors and tell my wife, but I couldn't seem to pull away from the scene.

After what seemed like a couple of minutes, the noise stopped and up popped this aluminium looking saucer shaped object to about 15 feet above the ground to the left of the oak tree; it was silent and hovering in the air. It was emitting a light around its centre and I couldn't decide if the object was spinning or the light was flashing on and off in a circular motion".

"I just stood there in total disbelief and thought to myself *"I'm dreaming, this is ridiculous*. After what seemed like a couple more minutes, the object moved off diagonally away from me in a south-easterly direction gaining height, and to my surprise, it went over the rooftops of the neighbours' houses. I ran up the alleyway out of my drive and into the middle of my road and froze when I saw it again, motionless, hovering more or less in the centre of the road at the junction of another road.

It was no more than 20 feet higher than the houses and I gauged the width of the object by the rooftops, making it between eighteen and twenty feet wide and roughly ten feet deep. From ground level, it was about fifty feet high and around one hundred and twenty feet away. I stood there in total shock and then walked near to it, even though I was petrified, because it fascinated me. I got to about one hundred feet from it and I could see under the object, the bright lights and that the underside was slightly concave. After a couple of minutes, the silent motionless object sped off at an unbelievable speed towards Croydon without making a sound. I couldn't believe it!'

Ken goes on to say that he ran into his house and shouted to his wife and went into his front bedroom and looked out of the window where he could see the brilliant ball of light in the crystal-clear night sky over Croydon in the distance. He checked the time and it was now 04.26. He had observed this light for about fifteen to twenty minutes, but it had only seemed like a couple of minutes during these events. His wife checked the following morning to see if she could see anything that would appear unusual behind the back garden and oak tree but saw nothing that she felt would be relevant to her husband's sighting.

This sighting was not reported to BUFORA until mid-1996 and Ken cannot understand why he took so long to report it but had only told his brother about it and didn't want to suffer ridicule from reporting this to anyone else. On his written report he feels that he was trying to deny what he had seen. A few months prior to him contacting BUFORA it was on his mind a lot and he feels that after the incident he was hoping to hear or read that another person had observed this too. It appeared no one had observed this. This case was followed up by a BUFORA investigator, who visited the witness in1996 and to date this case remains unexplained. (Source BUFORA - https://www.bufora.org.uk/).

Although not quite a UFO landing case I have included this encounter as it was literally just a few feet above the ground at one point. The witness, Ken, was able to see the UFO from underneath. Eventually Ken's wife also saw the object in the distance above the ton of Croydon. This incident was investigated by the British UFO Research Association.

For those who are not aware I was part of BUFORA for many years and even acted as their Director of Investigations for several years. As a result, I have a lot of respect for BUFORA and if they label this case as 'unexplained' then that is good enough for me.

Sacha Christie & friends
Gleyn Ciriog
Wales
February 1997

The following witness is a lady by the name of Sacha Christie. Sacha is providing here a first-person account on her close encounter and its aftereffects. I have had the pleasure of meeting Sacha several times and having the privilege of listening to her presentation at a UFO conference detailing the following events. The following account from Sacha is truly fascinating in many ways. Let's see if you agree.
.
"On the 4th of February 1997, I had an encounter with a group of friends in Wales. We saw two UFOs, one of them landed. Every February I get the anniversary jitters. I hate this week. I can feel it coming before I even know the date. It is like some internal alarm goes off. I remember one weekend a number of years ago, having a total breakdown over it at a crisis centre in Leeds and didn't even realise it was the anniversary of the event I was in bits over it. My friend who was with me during the initial event was also having a breakdown, she was in Spain and flipped out on the same weekend and contacted me, I didn't realise until later, we both had a breakdown on the same day without even knowing the date 'it' all happened. Steve was the only person who knew the date, I couldn't remember until he told me later. I am sat in the crisis centre this particular night having emptied myself all over this poor woman! I went for a cup of tea afterwards in their kitchen, I looked at my phone because I had been crying, there were people around, and I just tried to vanish into my phone. There was a message from Danya which she had just sent, saying everything to me that I had just downloaded on this poor woman who worked in the crisis centre. Thankfully she was Sikh and had beliefs that meant she could accept what I was saying. I was lucky, but I didn't care I was so overwhelmed I just had to empty myself of it. Lock me up, I don't care anymore, I can't live with this.

It was 1997 the first weekend in February. My boyfriend at the time was a guy called Steve. We used to go to Wales for rides out on the bike; we had stayed in cottages and camped. This particular weekend we went to Wales in Steve's uncle John's car with Danya, Steve's sister. Danya had her son with her and I had mine with me they were aged four and five. We drove for miles in terrible wet weather, I had no idea where we were going, Wales was all I knew. We were driving through fog a lot for the final part of the journey.

It was truly grey and miserable and we couldn't wait to get out of the car. Finally, we reached our destination, a cottage in a village called Gleyn Ciriog; I think the house is called Cairn Fern. Nice house, it had big out-houses full of old farm kit, lots of tins of nails and boxes of rusting things.

We had a quick nosey around the property outside, inside it was lovely a couple of living rooms, a games room, nice big kitchen, the best bit was the open fires. I remember we didn't know where the axe was so we were jumping on branches to snap them; it turned into a game because one of them was very springy. I don't really remember much about the Friday, it was just a travel day, settle in, have a nosey. On Saturday I remember we walked to the shops, I was completely irritated by something, I don't even know what, and we all were a bit odd that day. I remember walking ahead of everyone, I was probably hungry, I am a ratty bag when I'm hungry. That's about as much as I can recall of the daytime.

Sacha Christie speaking at a UFO conference in Leeds

It was about 7.00-7.30 pm on Saturday night. I was upstairs in the bedroom, I had my bag on the bed in front of me, I was taking things out of it to go have a nice relaxing bath in the overly pink bathroom when I heard Steve calling my name urgently. Because the children were loud and shouting I thought something was wrong so I ran downstairs to find the children just playing, Steve was poking his head into the kitchen doorway from outside saying "come here quick", he probably said something else but that is what I remember.

So, I went outside with him and we walked over to the wall by the outhouses and he pointed at the sky and said, "look there are some lights in the distance" and pointed off to I'll say the 1 o'clock position so we know the angles so you can picture it better.

I am looking out and all I can see is a thick low blanket of cloud. It wasn't raining but it was heavy cloud cover and was really, really low. For a long time after that night, I couldn't understand why the clouds were so low, I thought I'd exaggerated that in my mind, I had forgotten in the aftermath that we were on top of a mountain.

So, I am looking but I couldn't see anything for a while. He continued to point, I followed his finger trying to catch on to his line of sight, and then I see it. A little squiggle of light. It came on and went off. I immediately said, "It's lightning".

He said, "It's not, watch it" So I stood and looked and watched. Sure, enough the 'lightning' came back on again and went off, then back on again and off. After I saw the lights a few times it became obvious whatever it was had a very uniformed pattern to the way it lit up and it was moving away from us towards Merseyside, we were in North Wales five miles from Berwyn. After some minutes, maybe five minutes, it stopped. It stayed where it was but the flickering remained the same, after another minute or so we saw that it looked bigger than before. It was just a tiny flicker before, now it looked larger and brighter. It was then in a completely different place it had moved in a diagonal motion towards us, then it moved in a diagonal motion away from us, then again towards us, it repeated this as it slowly zig-zagged towards us.

When it was directly at 12 o' clock it was huge. We had to look from 11 o'clock to 1 o' clock to see the lights end. To me it looked like an enormous jelly fish rippling bright white but gentle pink, yellow and hints of green through the clouds. I don't think the craft itself was a mile wide but the lights it emitted were spreading to at least that. I have had people ask me how can you see lights in clouds, how can you see lightning in clouds? If it is bright enough you will see it. This was very, very bright, it made the clouds look like mashed potato with light beaming through it. We could see the different densities in the clouds as the lights rippled. The way the lights flickered out sideways through the clouds gave it an undulating effect, like a jelly fish's tentacles in water.

By this time all of us were outside. It was exhilarating; we were all literally awe struck. It came closer at an angle and eventually was above the field which was to the left of our original position where we had been looking out over the forest. It stopped over the field, opposite the house now, still in the clouds, still rippling this bright light. It then drifted so slowly you would hardly notice it moving until it was directly over us. We all stood gawping up at it in complete disbelief, none of us spoke much. I noticed that the sheep were all lying down and silent, something Steve noted too but we didn't comment at the time, we spoke of that later.

I know Steve went inside and left a message on the answer machine of the house we shared with others telling them what was happening. He didn't call the police or the airport. No such thing occurred to any of us. In fact, our behaviour throughout was as bizarre as the event itself.

We are all standing there looking up, I remember John stating "It's the aurora borealis" I laughed and said, "In Wales"!? I remember turning to my right to look at Danya who was stood on a wall that was about two feet high, a border of sorts, her eyes were so wide and her face lit with this very blue yet white light.

I can remember Steve being to my right slightly behind me, also standing on something, a large rock of some sort I think? He was just stood staring; my son was by my side when I saw an orange strobe light on the wall of the house to my right, and it flashed rapidly, bright orange. I turned to look and there was a large sphere on the ground. Tall enough for a man to get in. It was emitting steam or mist which was swirling all around it as it pulsed a very dull grey light every couple of seconds. I said, "Oh look another one", it was given very little attention. We continued to look up and forgot all about the sphere.

As we stood around staring up in disbelief, not knowing what to do, not even thinking what we should do, just standing there empty headed looking up, my son tugged hard on my clothes, when I looked at him he was terrified. His hair was shaking, his eyes were wide.

He said "Mummy, Mummy, a hand just came through the hedge and touched my foot! It wasn't my imagination, I saw it with my eyes, and I thought it was the hedge but it was a hand"!

At that point you would rationalise the situation by looking over the very small hedge wouldn't you? You'd think so wouldn't you? I didn't. Neither did Steve. I don't know why; the thought never entered our heads. Steve was right behind me at this point. I turned and said, "The kids are getting scared" and Steve said, "Come on let's get them inside". I still can't to this day figure out why I didn't look. If my son said there was a monster under his bed I would prove to him there wasn't. But nothing we were doing could be considered normal. We were not switched on at all.

As we turned to the others and we found John with Danya's son, and the axe for chopping wood, he was hacking into the door frame of the woodshed distracting Danya's son, his nephew, from what was going on. I think he was doing it for himself as much as the child, I think the children were the only ones who were switched on and had any idea of the potential danger we were in. We gathered ourselves together and went back into the cottage. As soon as we walked through the door it was like nothing had happened, like we'd watched some fireworks and got bored. John and Danya walked straight into the living room to watch TV, the children went back to where they were when I came downstairs and started playing again like they hadn't skipped a beat. Steve picked up a dishcloth and started drying the dishes! I just looked at them astounded. What the hell were they being so weird for? Not even registering that the whole thing was weird.

Thinking my next actions were entirely normal and suitable for the occasion, or not thinking at all more precisely, I looked at them as if they were crazy, I said "F*ck this! I'm off back outside"! And promptly marched back outside on my own, shaking my head in disbelief at their behaviour!! This still makes my head go cold all these years later.

I marched up the garden path without any thought. No thought to my son saying he had seen a hand, no thought to any kind of danger. I was so totally enthralled in what was happening, I wasn't in the least bit afraid, far from it, I was excited. I walked past the end of the house; looked at the sphere on the ground which had stopped pulsing and was just a very dull grey, I can remember shaking my head from side to side in disbelief but still was totally unafraid, totally switched off. I walked up to the object that had drifted over to us. Its central circle of light was about sixty feet across. It was so brilliantly white but when it hit the surface of anything the light was blue. Going outwards from the central circle of light were lines of light, like fluorescent strips, with the central circle of light it looked like the underneath of a mushroom, white circle in the middle, fins going to the edges, the lights rotated one way and at the very edges of those fluorescent strips was a tiny light that went the opposite way. It was so very bright but I didn't have to shield my eyes against it.

There was no sound, it was utterly silent, as was the sphere which had perched itself under the overhang of some trees at the back of the house somehow. I stood there looking up at this light thinking now what? This is crazy, I can't believe this, you know, that kind of thought pattern. Still completely oblivious to any danger I might be in. No one in the house came after me saying are you mad?! Don't go out there alone! As I'm standing there in this switched off state of incredulity. In four seconds flat everything changed forever. What I heard haunts me to this day. I have tried to rationalise it but there is no way to do so. Behind me was patch of dirt, the ground was hard packed mud, there was no growth of any kind on it, it was winter, wet, it was just hard packed earth, a chicken wire fence at the property boundary and the forgotten about (again) sphere. What I heard was two bare feet running towards me, fast, then I felt something bump into my lower back as if it was running past me, it dragged my jumper with it.

I don't know what it was or where it went because to my left was a four-foot stone wall, in front of me was the hedge my son said he saw the hand, there was nowhere for whatever it was to go, I'd have heard it hit the wall it was that fast. I don't know what it was that touched me, a sheep would never come near me, it would run away, but the sheep were all subdued. I think there is a clue in that because we were all subdued, well until that moment anyway.

It was like I had been hit by a truck. If you have ever had that full pulse of adrenaline in your body you will know that it literally feels like you have been hit by something hard and heavy. I was running before I even realised I was running but I couldn't see anything. I had gone blind. I couldn't see a thing and just kept running. I wasn't fully aware of anything this was pure flight, abject terror; I was literally running for my life. I don't know if that was what was called hysterical blindness in the war, people have suggested I was abducted, the tug was me going up into the craft, and then I hit the ground running with some kind of mental block in play from the aliens. Well, I don't say that because I don't know if that is true. I didn't see anything, I was blind. I remember what I heard and it sounded like my son running across his room at night, that kind of quick run grab a toy and leap into bed quick and pretend to be asleep after being told about ten times to stay in bed. That's exactly how it played out, rapid small fast slapping sounds like little legs running bare feet slapping on mud.

I literally ran for my life; I can't explain to you how that feels. Suddenly I felt danger, suddenly everything about the situation felt dangerous. We were in grave danger. I was panicked. I ran into the house and saw the children and stopped dead. I just stood there freaking out without moving. I quietly told Steve something just came up to me and touched me, his response was to look at the clock on the cooker and said, "Well you haven't been out there long so you haven't had any missing time" like that was the most normal thing to say. That was the end of me after that. Everything was super surreal. Everything was too loud, too bright, I was panicked beyond belief. I made him lock doors, close curtains, I wouldn't go to the toilet alone, and I was so utterly freaked out. I remember we had somehow got the kids to bed; I was sat in the middle of the bed and couldn't put my feet on the floor, like a child frightened of monsters under the bed grabbing my ankles. I remember Steve looking out of the window, he shut the curtains, didn't say anything. I didn't ask. Eventually somehow, I don't know how or even why but we went to sleep. The next day was awful, everyone was at each other's throats, John was foul, and Danya was screaming at me, we decided to spend the day apart. It was so bad in the end Steve booked a taxi and some coach tickets and we sneaked off at five the next morning, got the taxi to Wrexham and got the coach back to Leeds (back home), we never said a word to them. It was that bad.

I found out thirteen years later when we found each other again on Facebook that John's car wouldn't start, they had to stay another night. John was being strange, Danya was terrified. It was a horror show from start to finish. The vehicle recovery agency he was with came out the day after that and the car started, it was fine.

We didn't report this to anyone, we didn't really tell many people. It had a permanent effect on us all. In the immediate aftermath I couldn't go anywhere if the lights weren't on. I would open doors to rooms so fast if anyone was behind it they would be seriously injured and I would hit the light switch at the same time. We had a bend in the stairs and one day I remember reaching the bend and the landing being dark so I went back downstairs again to put the light on. My relationship with Steve didn't last long after that. We were all too wrecked. I was especially traumatised.

No one could understand the change in me. It was drastic. Even my mum in frustration one day shouted at me "You've never been the same since you went to Wales".

She was right. I have never been the same since. None of us have. When we found each other after thirteen years I was relieved, I had been singing this song alone on the net for about five years. I hoped for two things originally. I hoped that first of all Steve was going to have found some easy explanation and tell me it didn't play out as I remembered. I had over exaggerated everything in my mind and there would be a feeling of comfort, something I hadn't had since that moment. All ideas of safety gone. No lid on my life. Nothing from the top of my head to the furthest reaches of space. There is no bubble. It doesn't matter if you lock your doors or have the mightiest military in the universe. But he said it played out exactly as I remembered.

When you see something like that and you are not a UFO researcher or anyone from the military who might know of secret craft, your perceptions are "That's a spacecraft with aliens in it" Your perceptions are completely automatic and nothing conscious. To us that was an alien spaceship; the small one came from it and had occupants.

Those are the perceptions. It traumatised me to the point of eventually being suicidal. It was a slow disintegration of my psyche. I didn't know what life was anymore. Everything I knew was a lie. I thought the government must know about this; they are letting this happen. All of that stuff. I knew nothing. I wasn't a UFO researcher; I was a 27-year-old woman with a child who worked in kitchens cooking food. It doesn't matter if I now suspect we have that kind of technology, it doesn't matter if I now concede that could have been terrestrial. I knew none of that then. The second thing I'd hoped for was he would speak out too. Now I think that's the worst thing anyone can do to themselves. After all nobody really cares unless you allow them to sell you for their own profit, I see it happen to people all the time, this isn't exclusive to me. It's not MY whinge; it is just the way it is.

John didn't survive himself; he died maybe six years ago now. I came close, we have all struggled. The one thing that struck me though is that I was the only person who went outside and had that fight or flight moment. Even though John was obviously freaked out, they all seemed to take it in their stride. So, it was a total shock to me to find out that everyone had been utterly traumatised and that John was dead. I have seen and spoken to both Danya and Steve, initially I did hope they would want to share their side of events. Steve does, he told me he wanted a polygraph and hypnosis and all of that because he wants to know what happened to us. He wants to know if there is more from when we went to sleep. He wants to prove to the world this really happened. This is what he has said but in reality, I don't think he does because he would have by now.

I am not sure that we can have any answers, any closure. Hypnosis is dangerous, how would you cope with other memories if you can't cope with the memories you have? I certainly do not wish to traumatise myself again. I have just about learned how to live in my own skin. As for Danya, I think it would be one of the worst things she could do to herself. To her life. She isn't like me, she isn't a tough old boot, she's really quite refined and gentle, she certainly could not handle her normal life being turned upside down by this, and with the possibility of people around her thinking she has gone completely mad.

I have stayed in touch with them, but I don't badger them about this, I figure if they have something to say in public, they will say it. But they do support me and they can see the way I have been treated. Why would they want to be treated this way?

If anyone was truly interested in these things and there was respect in the community, there would have been a four-witness account available of a situation with two UFOs where one of them actually landed. As it stands, it isn't worth the risk to their personal health and well being. They can see that people try to bully me over me not being professional, when why should I be?

Just because I speak in public? Are they to be professionals too to come forward? Professional UFO researchers? Professional speakers? Witnesses aren't good enough these days unless they are all polished and ready to speak at a conference and do the radio circuit. There are no professional counsellors for these people; they are thrown to the lions. The UFO community tells me by its behaviour; it wants personas not real people. If I was a polished persona then I'd be part of a clique I really don't care for.

Well, I am who I am and I am what I am and as far as I am concerned the only thing that matters is the event and the data that can be gleaned from the event.

That doesn't seem to matter anymore but I also am castigated for even mentioning it. Being observational is playing the victim apparently. Pointing out my experience of the UFO community which is the exact same as everyone else's, BAD, means I am playing some sort of victim mentality. Well, if I was ever a victim of anything it was that night in February 1997 on a mountain in Wales, we were all victims. Victims of either humans playing with secret technology who did all of that to us on purpose, or it really was something from somewhere else with extreme foreigners at the controls. Now it seems to me more likely it was terrestrial than extraterrestrial, but on that day, in that moment, our whole worlds came crashing down on us. We had to rebuild ourselves with what was left of us. We have no lid anymore, no sense of surety in anything. No sense of safety or security, absolutely no safety net at all anywhere, the sky fell in on us. It makes you question everything, including your own sanity every single day. That's what something like that does to you, and then you try and tell people about it..... Well, you all know how that works out for everyone.

So, there you have it. This is my account of the events of that weekend. Whether you will ever see anything from Steve or Danya, I don't know. I really don't recommend that people speak in public anymore, not knowing the way we are all treated. There is so much damage caused by the community to peoples whose only crime is to have seen something they never asked to see, never wanted to see and in some instances wish they had never seen. Sometimes I wish I'd never seen it, sometimes I am glad I have. The one thing I do wish is that the technology for recreating memories into images becomes available before I die then you can all see it too. Until then, if ever, I am grateful to the friends I have made and the friends who stayed with me and believed me and didn't think I had just 'gone mad' for the fun of it. The one thing that does help is having other people around who you can talk to; it brings a kind of normalcy to it, that is a definite comfort!

So, keep your eyes peeled but don't be surprised if nobody is interested in what you have seen, they're mostly too busy yakking about what they think about everything. Generally, everyone else knows better than the witness and the only person who is ever wrong is the person who had the sighting!

C'est la vie!"

I think it's fair to say this is a fascinating and emotional account from a witness to a close encounter. There is no holding back by Sacha and I thank her for her honesty and openness. As a UFO researcher I know all too well that it is easy to forget the affect such an event has on the witness, however, I know from personal experience that at times I have had to act as a kind of 'counsellor' when discussing such events with the witness. None of us are trained in this field in general but I know it is something that I personally have done. As for the encounter as described by Sacha I have no doubt in its authenticity and it has a bag full of high strangeness. Down the years Sacha has now become involved in UFO research and has her own blog and podcast. (http://sacha-christie-nfomaniachousewife.blogspot.com/).

The cases in this chapter pretty much sum up a lot of the things I've been trying to put across. Ron Halliday sums it up pretty well when he says, "what on earth was it." This chapter has seen a very passionate, personal and emotional first-person account from Sacha Christie. As Sacha herself points out that after the initial sighting all of the witnesses returned to the house and carried on as 'normal'. This is a trait that I have often seen myself in such cases and it is one that the debunkers try to use to discredit them. The debunkers would say that if they had just had such an encounter why would they return to normal? It is a good question but it is simply a fact that some witnesses, rather inexplicably, do exactly that. Sacha, although a witness herself, was aware of the unnatural normalcy to which they returned in an instant.

This chapter features a case where regressive hypnosis is used. The witness in question is Robert Shawe who described the object he encountered as being 'organic'. There is still a huge debate on whether or not the use of regressive hypnosis is a useful tool in the investigation of such cases or is totally useless and mixes fact with fantasy. Personally, I remain in the fence but we should not forget that Mr. Shawe saw the landed UFO and reported it before he underwent regressive hypnosis.

When it comes to the sighting by Pat Macleod in broad daylight and in the middle of a busy housing complex, no one else saw this very large UFO land apart from Pat, so far as we know. I have come across this situation time after time. For example, Mrs. Westerman's account in the previous chapter. The UFO was seen in broad daylight at the end of a housing estate with a major motorway on either side of the town. The case has been in the local newspaper on several occasions but no one else has ever come forward. I have to ask the question; how can that be? Personally, I simply don't have an answer.

And if you want to have a case with a serious degree of high strangeness then look no further than that featuring Arthur Moar in the Shetland Isles. He described the UFO as looking like a globe and made out of suede. What can I say? UFO investigator Ron Halliday gave it a maximum of 10 in the high strangeness category and who am I to disagree.

*****

CHAPTER SEVEN

THE MILLENIUM-BEYOND 2000

Of course, the year 2000 was the millennium. To some prophets of doom, it was going to be the end of the world as for others the 'millennium bug' would render every computer in the world useless. Of course, none of this transpired and the world continued on as normal. There were a number of celebrations here in the UK and Prime Minister Tony Blair's Labour government built the Millennium Dome by the River Thames in London. A building that is still standing and still in use today. In 2000 the UK finally had its own Freedom of Information Act, one that would be put to good use by UFO researchers. In 2002 Queen Elizabeth II celebrated her Golden Jubilee and in 2003 England's Rugby Union team won the world cup in Australia. In 2005 terrorist bomb parts of London and fifty-five people were killed and over seven hundred were injured. The years 2008 saw Britain, like much of the Western World, plunge into a financial crisis and just two years later in 2010 the Conservative Party returned to power with David Cameron becoming Prime Minister. In 2012 Queen Elizabeth II celebrated her Diamond Jubilee and in 2015 she became Britain's longest ever serving monarch. The year 2016 was once again dominated by politics and Britain voted in a national referendum to leave the European Union. This was finally achieved in 2019 under new conservative Prime Minster Boris Johnson. As I write this in early 2020, Britain, like most of the world, is gripped in the Covid 19 (Coronavirus) pandemic killing tens of thousands across the UK and many more hundreds of thousands around the globe. With the UK's population in lock-down, myself included, all looking for ways to fill their days, I decided the time was now right to finish this book on UFO landings in the UK.

Mr. Robert
Ribble Valley
Lancashire
England
February 2000

I would like to thank my colleague Steve Mera for another case from his neck of the woods.

Mr. Robert had contacted MAPIT after obtaining our telephone number from UFO Magazine. Mr. Robert is 35 years old and has recently moved into a farmhouse in the Ribble Valley area. Mr. Robert does claim to have had a previous UFO experience when he was a child and that he has no interest in the subject and is level-headed. Mr. Robert has by all accounts assured us that his initial telephone call is not a wide up of any sort.

He claims that, approximately three weeks ago, (February 2000) he awoke about 10.30pm to a strange noise. At first he thought it to be a Quad Bike engine sound. He got up out of bed and walked to the window. (It was at this point Mr. Robert became agitated). He stated, 'I wish I had never looked out of the window'.

In the distance he noticed the noise was coming from a combined harvester, probably from one of the local farms, as there is sheep in a field nearby. He then suddenly looked to his right and was amazed to see, what only can be described as a metallic spinning top shaped UFO, just hovering completely silently about fifty feet away. Mr. Robert watched as the object slowly moved from left to right in a falling leaf motion about ten-foot side to side.

Location of the encounter as witnessed by Mr. Robert (courtesy Steve Mera)

He described the object to be shaped like a spinning top with a centre rim, and just above the rim was what looked like, portholes. One porthole had a blue light, as if there was illumination from inside the craft. There were belt type straps on top of the object and recalls how the moonlight reflected off the top of it, as if metallic in structure. Mr. Robert then described watching a small blue light move out of the object and move around. This light was flashing a blue colour, similar to the colour of the new type of headlight on vehicles. He turned his head and looked out over the field.

At first he saw the sheep that seemed obviously scared and huddled together, before they ran off out of sight. It was at this point Mr. Robert turned and ran over to his bed to awake his wife. In a matter of a few seconds he was back at the window trying to explain to his wife what he had seen. When he looked out he was once again amazed. This time there was nothing! The strange craft and the ball of light had completely vanished.

Mr. Robert claims that he has had no stress at home or work and things in his life are going very well. He cannot comprehend his experience nor really wants to. He is at a delicate point in his work at the moment regarding the sale of a company. Mr. Robert went on to say that there had been a few other incidents since the initial one approximately three weeks ago. On one occasion, he and his wife were woken up by yet another odd sound. He described it as a humming or buzzing sound that had a little bleep or something at the end of it. The sound was intermittent, about once every three seconds. On investigation, he noticed the sound emanated from the side of his house.

Mr. Robert also recalls his pet dog, (a 20-week-old German Shepherd) that was kept in the porch area due to not being fully house trained, whining constantly. He went down and opened the front door not switching any lights on whatsoever. He stood at the front door in shock as he watched a light on the ground disappear. He described the light as if there was something at the side of his house that had a door and inside was brightly lit. The light was as if being shone onto the ground through an open door which slowly closed. Mr. Robert dared not look around the corner and quickly locked the front door and ran upstairs. By morning, Mr. Robert had noticed his extremely clean water in his swimming pool had turned an unusual mucky green colour.

(MAPIT was currently unaware if this particular incident was related to his experience).

Mr. Robert claimed that his wife refused to fully believe him yet she did hear the strange sounds herself. Mr. Robert seems to have been psychologically disturbed by these experiences. He has found it difficult to concentrate and becomes extremely scared at night, so much so, he has resorted to going to bed early, whilst still light, in hope of sleeping right through the darkened hours. Mr. Robert claims to have reported his initial experience to Accrington Police Station, to which, two police officers attended his home and took a statement and issued him an incident number in case he needed to get back in touch with them.

Artist impression of the object witnessed by Mr. Robert (courtesy Steve Mera)

Mr. Robert indicated he had worked as a police officer at sometime in his life and thought it best be completely honest with them. He found the police were completely useless and unhelpful. Not long after his police report he received a telephone call from well known researcher and author Jenny Randles who was obviously attempting to obtain further information. Mr. Robert was unsure of who Jenny was and did not disclose much detail. He later learnt for himself that Jenny was a well-known author of the subject.

It was at this point Mr. Robert felt he needed to talk with someone but did not wish to discuss anything with Jenny Randles. Mr. Robert has at times become very upset and even found himself crying. He does not know what to make of his experiences and was extremely scared. At this point investigators informed Mr. Robert that he should attempt to record any of these events. He agreed and said he would set up recording devices such as a video camera etc.

He said that he would be back in touch with us soon and would agree to allow a couple of investigators to visit him at home in a few weeks.
Actions Carried Out:

■ House Plan.
■ Background Research.
■ Police Report Verification.
■ The attempt to obtain beneficial information from necessary officialdoms.
■ A basic psychoanalysis of the witness.
■ Environmental recording and appropriate field analysis.
■ Necessary documentation, photographs etc.
■ Geiger Counter sweep of locations.

Our second visit took place on Tuesday 11th of July 2000, at 10.30am.
Another preliminary interview was completed and we informed Mr. Robert that we had verified his police report and were awaiting other information. The two incidents took place in two different fields which belong to two different farms. Access is required to these locations via permission from the farm owners.

Necessary field equipment has been obtained and report forms and questionnaires completed. A water sample from Mr. Roberts's swimming pool was taken and sent off for analysis. The analysts believed there was a rational explanation for the discolouring due to PH levels and chlorine concentration).

Confirmation from Accrington police station of the incident was obtained. Mr. Roberts had telephoned the police station three times during the early hours of June 14th, 2000. Two officers did attend the location but apparently found nothing. Mr. Roberts also reported the incident to the Ministry of Defence via their telephone answering machine. No other officials or persons (apart from ourselves are aware of these incidents).

Mr. and Mrs. Robert have also reported a strange pulsating sound that moves around their living room. This has also been heard rushing over the roof of the house. Preliminary observations of the area show no anomalies. There were no marks on the roof nor any tiles missing. MAPIT investigators travelled on quad bikes to the first location in a field owned by the witness. Needless to say, some of us were not very good at riding them. We arrived at the location and conducted the following tests:

■ Radiation Sweep with a Geiger counter.
■ Resistivity Readings carried out.
■ Electromagnetic Baseline Tests carried out.
■ Magnetometer Sweep.
■ Soil samples taken for further analysis.
■ Metal Detector Sweep.

Plans, photographs and video footage were taken of the location and Geo-Position was noted. The same tests were carried out at the second location, which was in a field owned by Mr. Robert's neighbour. MAPIT obtained permission to carry out the baseline tests. Again, tests were carried out. Neither location showed any visual evidence and the results obtained from the test equipment were as normal.

As MAPIT was conducting its investigation into the sixth week, Mr. Robert contacted us and said he was leaving the farm and moving elsewhere and that he would leave his home to be sold by an estate agent. Mr. Robert was obviously troubled and worried of another visitation. He fled the farm and asked MAPIT to send on any of our findings. To this date, MAPIT investigators have found no evidence to support Mr. Robert's claims, but if he would go to the bother of ringing the Ministry of Defence and the local police station three times in the early hours, he must have seen something... surely!

Compiled by Steve Mera.

Special Thanks to Stuart Robinson.

Mr. Robert was obviously very upset by his encounter (encounters) which although is not common it is not unknown. In the previous chapter we saw how Sacha Christie was affected by her close encounter in Wales. And as Steve Mera says why would Mr. Robert telephone the Ministry of Defence and the police if he had not seen something?

Carl and Simon
Erdington
Birmingham
England
1999-2003

The following investigative report was provided by Dave Hodrien of the Birmingham UFO Group. Dave was the investigator of the case in question and released this report in 2010.

Introduction

Craft referred to as 'Flying Triangles' have been seen many times over the last couple of decades. There have been waves of sightings reported in numerous countries around the world. In many of these sightings, including some which I have previously looked into, the craft are only seen at a distance. However, this report covers a stunning case where a Flying Triangle was seen at extremely close proximity by two witnesses. The incident contains many aspects, some of which suggest that more than just a sighting may have taken place. As well as the main sighting, the report also covers a number of other incidents, including a possible second sighting of the same craft.

Background

The witnesses, Carl and Simon (Names changed for privacy reasons) were living on Holly Lane in Erdington, Birmingham, at the time of the incident. Running alongside part of Holly Lane is an area of wasteland referred to as "the tip".

Many years ago, the area used to be brickworks but was then levelled and covered in grass. There were a number of dirt paths across the area, and people would often use the area for walking their dogs. Today the tip is heavily overgrown so it is much rarer to see people crossing it. Carl had a pet dog named Champ which he would walk numerous times a day on the tip. At the time of the incident, both Carl and Simon smoked.

Simon's parents were not aware of this fact, so to keep things this way they used to take Champ for a walk as an excuse for having a cigarette. They would sometimes do this very late at night. It was under these circumstances that they were out of their houses on the night of the incident.

Sighting Details

Carl cannot remember the exact year which the sighting took place (for a very valid reason which will be explained later). He says he must have been between the age of 21 and 25, which would mean the incident took place between 1999-2003. He believes it took place between 11pm-1am. It was a warm, still and clear night. Due to the weather conditions, we may assume the incident took place in spring/summer, though this is not known for definite. Carl and Simon were outside with the dog. Carl doesn't remember whether they had walked Champ over the tip or not, but he assumes they must have. His first recollection of the incident is of him and Simon standing on the corner of the junction between Holly Lane and Holly Dale Road.

Carl and Simon suddenly noticed some lights in the sky above the trees at the far side of the tip to the East. There were three lights in a triangular shape. Carl remembers them being red in colour. At first both witnesses assumed it was an aeroplane.

But as they watched, the lights began to move from side to side a short distance. The movement looked erratic rather than smooth, as though the lights were shimmering left and right. The object was moving in a slow speed in their general direction.

As the object got closer, they could make out a black triangular shaped body around the lights, and it became clear that it was a single solid object – a craft unlike any known conventional aircraft. They also now noticed a central larger light on the underside of the craft evenly spaced between the red lights. Carl believes this was either a white or yellow colour. The witnesses stood in amazement as the craft approached their location. They realised it was completely silent and had no visible means of propulsion. As it got close to the road, the craft began to descend in altitude. At this point, Carl says the lights may have changed to an orange/golden colour. The witnesses began to get un-nerved by the proximity of the craft, and crossed Holly Dale Road to the opposite corner. Champ stood motionless by their side.

The craft reached the edge of the tip and continued to slowly descend until it was hovering over the road, about ten feet off the ground. It then slowly turned until one of its points (Carl assumes the front) was facing them. At this point they realised that it was aware of their presence. They were about 40 feet from the craft, and due to street lighting could have a clear view of it. Carl says the craft was about 25 feet wide by 10-15 feet in depth. There were no visible markings or openings on it at all; it was simply a jet-black triangular shape, with a flat base and angles converging to a point at its top. The corner lights were still visible even when it was down low over the road, although the central light could no longer be seen. This perhaps means that the corner lights were jutting out from the main body of the craft or wrapped around the corners. Or perhaps they were so bright that their glow could still be made out. Carl says that they were within a stone's throw of the craft, and if it had been a car they would have been able to give the make, model and registration number – it was that close to their position.

222

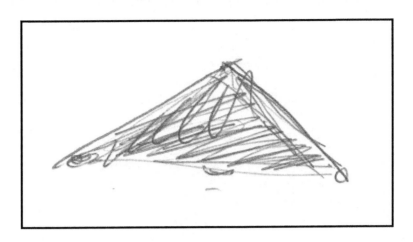

Drawing by Carl of how the craft looked up close:

As the craft halted over the road, it began to make strange sounds. Only Carl remembers it making these sounds, Simon does not remember it making any sound at all for the duration of the sighting. Carl describes the sounds as a deep pulsing humming noise similar to the sound of a didgeridoo. This noise continuously altered in pitch and tempo. Thinking back to the incident, Carl realised that he recognised the sounds and had heard them at other times (see later).

Photograph of the house over which the craft hovered (courtesy Dave Hodrien)

The witnesses stood still and stared at the craft for what seemed like a couple of minutes. Carl feels that the experience was very personal, and that it was aware of them as they were watching it. Both he and Simon were awestruck by the craft, and at no point thought about knocking on any of the house doors to get anyone else. Neither of them had a camera, and back when the incident took place mobile phone cameras were relatively new. Carl cannot remember whether his phone had a camera on it or not, but even if it did he did not think about using it at all.

Suddenly Champ bolted and ran back across Holly Dale Road past the craft towards Carl's house. Carl was very reluctant to follow as this would mean getting uncomfortably close to the craft. Soon after this happened, the craft began moving again without warning. It began to rise in altitude at a diagonal angle until it was directly over the roof of Carl's house. It was literally a few feet over the chimney top. Here it once again stopped moving and remained stationary for at least a minute.

After this it started moving again to the west and was lost from view behind the house. Behind the houses is a garden allotment area, and it was in this direction that the craft was heading. The witnesses ran down Holly Dale Road to where they could get a clear view of the area. But when they checked they found that the craft had completely vanished. Carl is not sure if it had flown away extremely fast or if it had just flown somewhere else out of sight, but it was gone.

Forgotten Experiences

After this, Carl cannot remember anything that happened. He assumes that they must have both walked back home and gone to bed. The following morning, both witnesses had completely forgotten the entire incident had taken place. They met up later in the day but had no recollection of it and did not discuss it with each other at all. They continued to regularly walk the dog over the tip but never once thought about what they had seen or experienced any unusual emotions.

On a number of occasions after the incident when Carl approached the tip with Champ, suddenly Champ would drop to the ground, start whimpering, and refuse to go any closer. Carl never understood this behaviour but looking back it seems probable that Champ either remembered or sensed what had taken place and was frightened to go where the craft had initially been located.

It was only when Carl and his family moved out of the house on Holly Lane a number of years later that the incident came back to him. He is not sure of how this recollection happened, but he came to the realisation that him and Simon had seen the craft and had then forgotten all about it. He got in touch with Simon and reminded him of the incident, and then he too remembered what had happened.

Other Encounters?

When Carl remembered the strange sounds the craft had been making while it was over the road, he realised that they were familiar to him and that he had heard them at other times too.

He recalled a number of times where he had been in his bedroom on his own and heard the noises. On some of these occasions he feels his girlfriend should have also been in the room but he doesn't remember ever seeing her there.

Sometimes he had been lying down in bed at night, other times he was sitting on his bed during the day. The sounds would resonate through him and make his body vibrate. He also remembers that these sounds would lull his senses and put him into a confused state of mind. Carl says he is a very nosy person and would almost certainly have checked to see where the noises were coming from, but he never did this and just remained still, listening to the sounds. He finds this very strange indeed.

As he had forgotten the incident with the craft for a number of years, Carl is unsure whether these other incidents occurred prior to or after the sighting. He feels that he must have been visited by the same craft at other times but has no other memories of these events. He is not aware of whether there was any missing time involved, however as some of these experiences occurred at night-time, if there was missing time it is unlikely he would have known.

A Second Sighting

On an evening in September 2009 around 7pm, Carl was in the back garden of his house on Warwick Road, Tysley. There was nobody else at home at the time, and he was hanging out some clothes to dry. He happened to glance up into the sky, looking to the North towards Birmingham centre. He noticed what appeared to be three red lights in a triangular pattern, hovering stationary in the sky. They were quite distant, but he immediately became un-nerved by the lights and assumed that they may be the same triangular craft.

He only watched them for a few seconds, before deciding to head outside the front of the house onto the pavement where there would be other people around. This made him feel a lot less venerable. When he again checked for the lights he could no longer see them and assumed they were now hidden out of sight behind the housing. Satisfied that the lights had not got any closer, he remained outside for a minute before heading back indoors. Carl cannot be certain this was another sighting of the same craft but feels that it may have been.

Other UFO Sightings

Carl has had two other UFO sightings in his life. Several years ago, he used to work at Land Rover in Solihull. He would often go for a break outside with his work colleagues. One clear night they were looking up at a star-filled sky. Suddenly they all noticed three or four white lights appear. They looked liked stars and appeared to be at very high altitude. They were not in an organised formation but were cluttered around one another and completely motionless. Several seconds went by, and then suddenly another white light appeared close to the other lights, and then moved at a very fast speed between them. They then all vanished simultaneously. On another occasion after the Flying Triangle incident (Carl cannot remember when exactly), Carl witnessed three white lights in a line. The middle one suddenly began moving. It appeared to drop down below the other two, then went into reverse and moved back up.

Carl feels that these sightings were completely unrelated to his experience with the triangular craft and does not feel that there were in any way personal to him, he was just at the right place at the right time.

Sighting Analysis

Carl certainly appears to be speaking about a real experience, and I fully believe that he is telling the truth about what him and Simon saw. I have visited the sighting location with him on a number of occasions and asked him to repeat the story of what happened numerous times.

He is fascinated by what he has experienced, and because of the sighting has become very interested in the subject of UFOs. There are realistically only three explanations for what took place. Either it was a very clever hoax, a secret military craft of some kind, or it was extraterrestrial in origin.

The object seemed much too large to be a hoax, and it seems very unlikely that someone would be able to make a model of such a size with a completely invisible and silent means of propulsion. Carl says that it looked solid rather than flimsy and hollow, so I do not believe for one moment that it was some kind of remote-controlled model or inflatable.

There is the possibility it was a secret military craft of some kind, but again this seems unlikely for a number of reasons. If it was, why would they fly it right over one of the most populated cities in the UK, let alone descend closely to multiple witnesses. There would seem no reason for doing this, nor for the strange sounds that only Carl heard being emitted from the craft.

The craft displayed highly advanced flight capabilities. It was able to hover and move silently, descend and take off slowly, and also appeared to vanish without trace. These are characteristic of many sightings of UFOs, not just Flying Triangles but of other types such as discs and saucer-shaped craft. Despite this, Carl believes that it was more likely to be military than alien.

You may feel the same, but I believe that this was a genuine Flying Triangle sighting, and that many if not all of these craft are extraterrestrial in origin. It is possible that the military have built their own based on alien technology, but in this case I feel it was not one of these for the reasons described above.

Flying Triangles vary in size – there have been some sightings of craft larger than a football field! In the 1990s there was a wave of sightings of craft of this type in Belgium, during which the craft were even seen to move around under the water and emerge from the sea.

There are also a number of sightings where Grey-type entities have been seen next to landed Flying Triangles, which may well mean that they are linked with this particular species of ET.

Artist impression of the 'flying triangle' when viewed close-up (courtesy Dave Hodrien).

Possibility of Contact

There are a number of signs that suggest that Carl may be a contactee, one who is currently mostly unaware of this contact. The triangular craft that he and Simon witnessed certainly seemed to be interested in them in some way. Not only did it descend to the road, but it also turned towards them. I do not believe these movement patterns were just coincidence. It looks as though it approached their position for a reason. It then began to make highly unusual sounds, sounds only Carl remembers hearing. Could these have been some form of communication directed personally at him?

If so it is possible the craft was there to interact with Carl, and the fact that another witness was present could have been regardless. Thinking back to the incident, Carl remembers hearing the sounds on a number of other occasions while in his bedroom. He also remembers the sounds putting him into a drowsy/confused state of mind. The sounds made his whole body vibrate.

All of these aspects I find very interesting indeed. The fact that he had heard the noises at other times suggests that he has been visited by the craft (either the same or of similar type) either before or after the sighting incident. Many contactees, including others I have personally investigated, have reported hearing strange sounds such as pulsing humming noises, beeps and clicks. Vibrations that pass through the body are also commonly reported, sometimes though not always accompanied by paralysis. These events appear to be signs that a contact experience is taking place or about to happen.

The noises that Carl has heard both during the sighting and at other times, may well have preceded other events which he is currently completely unaware of.

The fact that the sighting of the craft was forgotten about by both the witnesses for a number of years is also extremely interesting. In most cases when a UFO is witnessed, even at close proximity, the individuals involved fully remember the incident and can describe it in detail. However repressed memories are extremely common in cases involving contact. Missing time can be an indication of this, in other cases flashbacks or nightmares can reveal some details of what has taken place. Both witnesses had no recollection of the event, even when they revisited the location of the incident many times afterwards. Years later when Carl did remember, and then reminded Simon too, memories of what had taken place came flooding back. But something more may have taken place, something which still remains blocked out.

The sighting of the red lights in September 2009 could be another indication that Carl has been visited by the craft since the incident. There is no indication that the craft approached or interacted with him in this instance, but this does not mean that it definitely did not take place.

Another intriguing possibility suggested by Carl is that his girlfriend or another family member may be a contactee rather than himself. It is interesting that the craft hovered directly over his house before moving away from the area, even though Carl was down on the street corner. Also, he mentions that during the other incidents where he heard the sounds, his girlfriend should have sometimes been present, but he does not remember ever seeing her. Could these sounds have been used to lull him while she was being taken and experiencing contact instead?

As you have probably noticed, I have not yet had a chance to meet up with Simon to hear his version of the events of the night. I hope to meet him soon to get his side of the story, which I am sure will be quite similar to Carl's, other than the fact that he did not hear any sounds coming from the craft.

Attempted Regression

On Sunday 21st March, Carl was regressed around my house by hypnotherapist Rob Tudge, who assists me with investigations involving contact. However due to anxiety or state of mind, Carl could sadly not be hypnotised. He went over the incident again but was remembering consciously and simply closing his eyes rather than being properly under. He hopes to try again after a short while, as he sincerely wishes to know if anything else took place during this incident.

Conclusion

This is an absolutely stunning close encounter with a craft likely to be extraterrestrial in origin, and one of the best we have yet had reported to the group. The type of craft seen, with the corner lights and larger central light, has been seen many times before all around the world, though not usually at such close proximity. There are many mysterious aspects to the sighting which we have yet to find an answer for. Why did it approach the witnesses? Why did it make strange sounds that only Carl could hear? Why did it hover over the roof of his house? Why did both witnesses forget the incident afterwards? In time we may find out answers to these questions.

Perhaps Carl and Simon will learn more about what they experienced, either through future regressions or by other means. But whether they do or not, this remains a fascinating sighting and one which defies most alternative explanations. This report will be updated with any additional information as and when it becomes available. (Source: Dave Hodrien, Birmingham UFO Group - www.bufog.com).

Un-named husband and wife
Reading
Berkshire
England
September 11, 2004

The following incident was reported to the British Earth and Aerial Mysteries Society (BEAMS), and it is taken directly from their website at: http://www.beamsinvestigations.org/about.html

Name: ******* ********

Email: ********@btinternet.com

Date: 11/09/2004
Time: 6-7 am Town/Village/Dist: Burghfield, Nr Reading, Berks, UK.

Weather conditions: described below in the witness' own words:

"It was a bright morning... don't think I saw the sun up yet, but it was a bright morning... in fact the best sky I've ever seen... all light blue, not a cloud in the sky anywhere... none, not even a plane's energy trail... nothing; but there were two other objects in the sky... the moon and a shining, flickering, bright star."

Based on witness statement:
September 11, 2004, it was early in the morning between 6.30 to 8.30am, when I left my daughter's house in Burghfield heading for our Tilehurst home; as we approached Church Lane, my wife suddenly screamed "WATCH OUT!"

I quickly hit the brakes and just managed to stop before going into a ditch on my right; "what's wrong with you?" I asked... She said, "have a look out of the window - what does that look like?" she said "a spaceship" in a concerned voice - so I drove the van up the road a bit to get a better look, stopped, and then I got out.

WOW!!!!!!!... From being scared to death one minute, to amazement at what we were now witnessing the next! I felt privileged to see this... I felt as if I was gifted to experience such an event! The "spaceship" was Saturn-like in shape, and initially, the thought crossed my mind that this thing had just emerged out of the ground, although the idea seemed so far-fetched that I quickly dismissed such a notion: I also thought to myself that it was rather like a hologram, as the object didn't seem entirely solid.

Now hovering over a field, no more than 50 yards away, about 200 feet in the air, I estimated its size to be easily as large Wembley Stadium, maybe bigger: I wondered how something so huge could even get off the ground!

We watched this for about eight amazing minutes! The picture I've made up shows the size and the place where we had this experience; it was very close to AWRE Burghfield (now AWE - The Atomic Weapons Establishment) one of the most important nuclear facilities in this country's defence.

Reconstruction of event and location (courtesy BEAMS)

What we were seeing was so close to us I could have hit it with a catapult! The middle had what looked like square, rainbow-coloured windows... and small thunderous clouds were racing through it, which made this thing look like it was rotating. Like being in some sort of time warp, there was no noise, no cars or people about... and no planes in the sky either!

The 'ship' then moved off in an arc shape, going up as it moved; and its path took it straight over the atomic research base 500 yards away; then it went parallel to the M4 motorway towards London; that is the point where we lost sight of the UFO, when it disappeared out of our sight (too far off to see). I drove up the road 500 yards and parked the van but didn't observe anything else of note."

Possible sources where further evidence may exist:

(1) M4 motorway cams must have recorded it, the traffic Police, and the BBC, have access to these road cams.
(2) Weather photos of that morning... Sky news again the BBC and also weather stations possibly hold this evidence.
(3) Google Earth may also have evidence.
(4) The Burghfield MoD base itself has twenty or more cameras that could/should have recorded the flight of this UFO.

Update: It is our understanding that various UFO researchers, the Police, Google Earth and the Ministry of Defence have been approached by the witness of this case, and yet all of the aforementioned concerns have failed to satisfy requests made for further information concerning the event on September 11th, 2004.

Comment from BEAMS: Please, if you can shed any light on this or other possible UFO sightings in the Burghfield/Reading area, (and beyond) then please contact us here at BEAMS by email beamsinvestigations@sky.com

Again like a few other cases in this book the object was not exactly on the ground but was pretty close to qualifying. You would have to ask the question of why there were no other witnesses to this event, or none that we are aware of course. This case does of course have its own degree of high strangeness with no noise, cars or people being about and the UFO looking like a 'hologram' and not looking entirely solid'?

Mike Booth
Lockeridge
Wiltshire
England
June 21, 2005

On Tuesday, June 21, 2005, British bicyclist Mike Booth was out for his regular constitutional at about 6: 30 pm, pedalling along the road through Lockeridge, Wiltshire, toward the tiny rural village of Alton Barnes - for many years a center of crop circle activity. As he passed by the fields known as Boreham Down (which rise up from the road on both the left and right, near the village of Lockeridge) he was startled to observe three to four whitish, metallic-looking objects about two hundred yards away up in the field off to his left, slowly gliding along through the tops of the young wheat.

Photo by Mike Booth

Mr. Booth estimated that the objects were approximately six feet long and four feet wide, with dome-shaped tops sticking up above the seed-heads about two to three feet. His impression was that they were not touching the ground but were only flattening the upper portion of the plants, leaving random trails in the young crop behind them as they moved.

The photograph (above) here was taken on June 22, 2005, by Mike Booth and shows one of the tracks left by the objects in the young wheat; in this photo it appears that only the tops of the plants have been bent over, although later on in the season this track, and the others apparently made by the objects, were flat to the ground. Cars at bottom of photo show approximate location of Mr. Booth on the evening of June 21st.

As Mr. Booth stopped to watch the strange spectacle he realized that the objects had stopped moving and had a peculiar sense that they had done so because they were now "aware" of him sitting on his bike at the bottom of the hill. And in spite of the fact that he had a mobile phone with a camera with him and did consider taking photographs he -- for reasons he can't explain -- decided not to. As is often noted by people who have witnessed similar bizarre events, Booth later realized his behaviour at the time was uncharacteristically "passive," since he simply accepted the idea that he should "leave it alone" and continue on his way. Which is exactly what he did.

Artist impression of the objects witnesses by Mike Booth

On the following day a geometric crop circle was discovered in this same field, but in another section not fully visible from the road where Mr. Booth had stopped his bicycle, and it is not clear if this formation was in the field during his encounter.

This more typical "geometric" crop circle, however, was highly unusual in one particular: *the entire outer edge was formed by plants that had been cut – in fact shredded--* rather than simply flattened as is usually the case. These shredded plants were found piled up in various places throughout the outer edge area, as if placed there deliberately by someone. Subsequent conversation with the farmer is reported to rule out his involvement. (Source: http://www.beamsinvestigations.org/ufo-reports.html).

I must admit that I am not a fan of so-called 'crop circles' and have had little involvement with them. An old colleague of mine called Walter Black from the Yorkshire UFO Society (YUFOS) did venture down to Wiltshire in the 1980's when photographs of these 'circles' first appeared in the national news media. If you have been involved in ufology for as long as I have in the UK then you cannot escape them.

There is no way that I am going to get into the debate about crop circles here; we can leave that for another time. I did however want to feature this case as it does have a degree of high strangeness. Why did Mr. Booth not take any photographs? This is something that I have come across time and time again in such cases and I don't have an answer.

Un-named witness & Lenny White
New Milton
Hampshire
England
August 2005

Witness statement: 'Here is a drawing I made depicting what my neighbour Lenny White and I saw in August 2005. I first saw it as it was coming over the horizon, (we were on quite high ground at a working quarry at New Milton, Hampshire), and I thought at first it was lightning as it had a very bright strobe, but as it came closer I could see it was something shooting huge diameter laser beams that were contained inside some kind of field.

It came over the horizon and in less than twelve seconds had 'landed' inches from the ground about thirty to forty-five feet in front of us at the edge of the quarry, which is bordered by trees. The object stayed put for three to five seconds, still flashing the strobe and red beams, then it blinked out or shot off at impossible speed, or maybe just turned off its lights?

I could see the 'flat end' of the tree trunk diameter laser beams as they were cut off by the field. We were scared and I agreed to Lenny's pleas to go home, and we left with it still above the trees. It was a very scary walk home that night, past those very dark woods.'

Further witness comments: "I did not see what was at the center of the 'energy field', all I saw was the big red laser beams and the bright blue/white strobe, and the beams hitting the edge of the field, but Lenny said " I saw it through a gap in the trees, it was like two dinner plates stuck together, with a bit on top. It had just got dark at the time we saw it. The UFO landed a stone's throw away, and we were actually looking down at it slightly. I wish I had gone down to investigate now - it would have only taken a fifteen second walk, but I was darned at the time if I wanted to get any closer to it! And Lenny - no way was he going down there!"

There is a farmhouse fifty feet away and if the farmer was looking out his window, he would have got a good look at the object.'
(Source: http://www.beamsinvestigations.org/ufo-reports.html).

This is a short but sweet sighting as initially the object was only on the ground for a handful of seconds. As the witness stares the UFO landed very close to them a 'stone's throw away'. It sounds as if both witnesses were scared by this event and I cannot blame them. I have often wondered what I would do if I were ever in such a situation.

Roy Shaw
Exmouth
Devon
England
February 2010

Exmouth man Roy Shaw has exclusively spoken about the moment he came face-to-face with what UFO experts are calling a Close Encounter of the Third Kind, writes Becca Gliddon. UFO sceptic Mr Shaw, of Withycombe Village Road, is the latest resident to report seeing strange, coloured lights - and says he spotted what he can only describe as a spaceship landing in Phear Park.

The retired engineer and his dog ran for home when a white 'shimmering' shape began walking towards them.

Roy Shaw does not believe in aliens, ghosts, flying saucers or anything he cannot physically touch or explain. But recently Mr Shaw, a retired engineer, saw something unusual in Phear Park that frightened him so much, it caused him to run home so fast he twisted his ankle in the process, writes Becca Gliddon. Mr Shaw believes he saw a UFO land in Phear Park and witnessed a 'white shape' come towards him.

The Withycombe Raleigh resident calls the experience 'weird' and is at a loss to explain what he saw. An Exmouth UFO boffin believes Mr Shaw had a brush with alien life and calls the 'rare' event a Close Encounter of the Third Kind.

Roy Shaw and dog Sydney

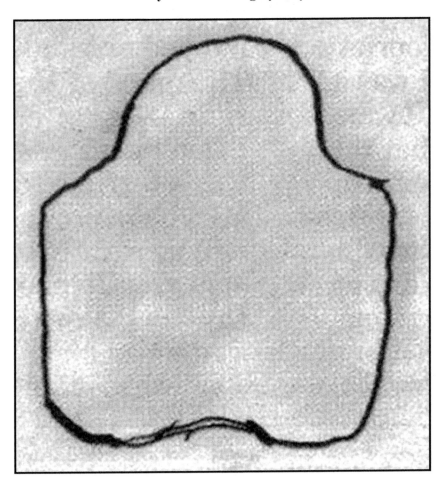

White figure drawn by Roy Shaw

Mr Shaw is worried people will think he is a crank after reading his account of the strange occurrence. But he is keen to point out that, far from believing in little green men, he remains a sceptic and still cannot give an explanation of what he saw that night. Mr Shaw said: "The object was round in shape and about 30-feet in diameter and 100-foot long, with blue and red flashing lights on its perimeter, and it appeared to land at the top end of the park by the bowling green.

"My dog started to growl when, what I can only describe as a white shape, came towards us."It was about four-feet high and seemed to be translucent, and moved very slowly towards us. "I was transfixed because it made a droning noise which sounded like 'my, my,' over and over again, which I could not understand."I didn't know where the sound was coming from but it was coming straight towards me. "I immediately ran back down through the park." Mr Shaw said the UFO appeared to hover over the hedge of the bowling green, and then flew horizontally from left to right, before immediately shooting off at high speed, back to the left at a 45-degree angle

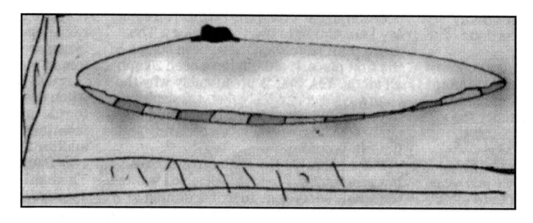

Drawing if the UFO by Roy Shaw

He said the UFO appeared from nowhere. He did not see it fly overhead, or land. Mr Shaw said his normally-placid border collie dog, Sydney, ran away from the object after baring his teeth at the approaching figure. "I twisted my ankle when I ran like hell," said Mr Shaw. "My dog Syd kept whimpering and kept looking out of the bedroom window towards the park until at least two in the morning."I had problems sleeping because I just kept going over in my mind what I had seen. "I still can't believe what I saw and I am still in a state of shock."Syd doesn't like going back up there now. Something put him off. "Everybody thinks you are crank when you report something like this.

"I am an engineer. I like to touch and feel things. If I can touch it, it exists, but there's no way I can explain this." Exmouth UFO expert Nigel Wright said: "This is a close encounter of the third kind."The definition of a third kind is having encountered an occupant of a UFO in close proximity to the craft itself. "This is a really important sighting."
(Source:https://www.exmouthjournal.co.uk/news/ufo-seen-in-phear-park-exmouth-1-43211).

It is not always the best thing to do and to take what has appeared in a newspaper article as being totally accurate. This case comes direct from the Exmouth Journal in Devon. It is written in typical poor journalistic language. A local UFO investigator suddenly becomes an 'expert' and a 'boffin'.

Is it any wonder that local newspapers are on the decline? I have used other newspaper accounts in previous chapters so I decided, with a degree of caution, to use this one here. If the newspaper report is accurate and Mr. Shaw did indeed run away in fright, injuring himself in the process, then he would not be the first close encounter witness to do so as we have seen from other accounts elsewhere in this book.

We can see yet again the high strangeness factor running through the cases featured in this chapter. Mr. Robert in the Ribble Valley reports his account to the Ministry of Defence and the police (three times) and eventually becomes so scared of living at the scene of his encounter he sells up and moves away. An un-named couple in Reading, Berkshire, thought that the UFO they observed looked like a 'hologram' and was as large as Wembley Stadium. It was so large they could not understand how such a thing could get off the ground. Other witnesses in New Milton, Hampshire were literally a 'stone's throw away' from the object they observed and wished they had taken a closer look. Roy Shaw in Exmouth, Devon was so scared of the UFO and 'white figure' that he saw that he injured his ankle while running away from it scared stiff. And let us not forget Carl and Simon in Birmingham. Having encountered a 'flying triangle' close-up they were so traumatised that the encounter was somehow pushed to the back of their mind only to surface at a later date. So puzzled and traumatized by the event they could not even remember the approximate year that the encounter took place. Each and every case has its own degree of high strangeness and has left both witnesses and investigators completely at a loss for an explanation.

*****

CONTEMPORARY COMMENTS

Now we have a plethora of UFO landing cases from across the UK and even into the Republic of Ireland. These cases also span the decades with a few pre-dating the birth of the modern UFO era in 1947. The question now then must surely be what is the nature and origin of these UFO landing accounts? To try and answer this question I have asked a selection of my respected colleagues from around the UK and the Republic of Ireland to offer their own opinions on these phenomena. As one might guess it is highly unlikely that we are going to get unanimous agreement here. I will of course add my own comments but first let us see what my colleagues have to say. The following come in no order of preference; I simply inserted them into the chapter as they arrived. I know and respect all of the following but that doesn't mean I will have to agree with them

Mike Covell:
UFO/paranormal researcher/investigator, historian and author.
To me, a landing is defined as a physical craft touching a physical object, in this instance the UFO landing on earth, I would also add that such an event leave some sort of trace evidence, such as burn marks, depressions in the earth, flattened grass, etc. For many years I have researched such cases, but occasionally I get the odd one where observers have witnessed this "high strangeness" with no physical trace afterwards, and a feeling of being there, but watching from another perspective, if that makes sense. Perhaps the most infamous of these cases was the Longhill UFO landing in 1967, during which several children claimed to have seen a craft land and leave burn marks. A large percentage of the people I spoke to saw no craft but saw the burn marks, of these most of them believed that it was caused by a fire created by the children. Another group, albeit small, claimed to have seen the craft and the burn marks, but the police officer on scene discounted these accounts. A third group, who didn't see the craft, or the burn marks, but had heard of one, the other or both, stated that afterwards the area felt weird.

Andy Roberts:
Founder member of the Independent UFO Network, West Yorkshire UFO Research Group, former BUFORA council member, editor of UFO Brigantia & The Armchair Ufologist, author, journalist and UFO researcher/investigator.
Philip's contention is that 'The closer a witness gets to a 'UFO' then the less likely it is to have a rational explanation'. On the face of it this could be seen as a logical argument and an analogy might be, you see a coloured blob in the distance and as you near it the colour and shape becomes clear and you realise it's a car, for instance. But in ufology we are not dealing with what we know or have experience of, we are dealing with - the clue is in the name- things which are 'unidentified'. We also know that when people speak of 'UFOs' and landings what they really mean, whether they realise it or not, is 'structured craft of unknown origin' or some such similar term. We also know from over seventy years of UFO study that, so far, all UFO reports that are identified are identified as earthly phenomena and/or are the result of 'radical misperception', i.e., something is seen, is not immediately identified and thus becomes a 'UFO' but is later resolved - by having more or more detailed information- into what it actually was.

The literature is full of such cases; people seeing stars, planets or the moon and misinterpreting them as 'UFOs' etc. Ah, I hear you saying, but what about the really close up sightings where someone or some people clearly report having seen a 'structured craft of unknown origin'. Well, what about them? We know if we study the history of anomalies and folklore that people have seen, close up, fairies, gnomes, elves, gods, goddesses, lake monsters, Bigfoot and so on. The list is endless. Yet not *one* of the foregoing, or anything like them has ever been *proved* to be corporeal and existing in our consensus reality. And so, it is with close up sightings of 'UFOs'. Many previously believed to be good or watertight sightings have been explained when more evidence has come to light. Classic example is the UFO 'landing' on Cracoe Fell, witness for over an hour by up to three policemen who took photographs which appeared all over the world. Don't panic, research showed it to be a complicated effect caused by sunlight on angled, lichen-covered rock. Or Gaynor Sunderland's (and her brother's) sighting of a landed UFO and aliens in north Wales (the subject of Jenny Randles' book Alien Contact), which proved to be a hoax, sustained for over 30 years! There are many more. So, based on what we *know* about UFO cases, their causes, the witnesses and the explanations so far, it's reasonable to believe that even the closest sighting of a 'landing' is also likely to be a radical misperception or hoax. Were any close-up landing cases to be accompanied by clear and unequivocal photographs or examples of material scientists attest does not originate on Earth, then we might give many sightings more credence. But they don't, and indeed as camera technology gets better and more or less everyone has in their possession a camera capable of taking high quality photographs (your mobile phone) we should expect an increasing number of high-quality photos of 'landings'. Yet this does not happen and indeed quite the reverse is true. You might also say 'what about close up sightings of UFO landings by more than one person or by trained observers, surely they can't be wrong?'

Well yes they can, there are numerous UFO cases witnessed by two or more witnesses which have been subsequently 'solved' as being cases of radical misperception or hoaxes. And as for the myth of the 'trained observer', police officers, pilots and others who are supposedly trained in accurate observation are, when it comes to radical misperception, just as likely to misidentify phenomena as UFOs as anyone else. The above problems are multiplied when you take into account people often have a predisposition to a belief in the physical reality of UFOs, the influence of the media in suggestibility and the human psyche's desperation to experience 'the other', 'the supernatural' or whatever it is called, whether, as I note above, this is in the form of gods, elves, giants, UFOs, etc. So, whilst there *may* be instances of genuine landings of structured craft of unknown origin as yet there is no unassailable evidence other than the narrative of the human instrument/s who witnessed it and that instrument is, fundamentally, flawed and subject to many factors, both individual, historical and cultural which suggest the source of such experiences lies elsewhere.

Bob Tibbits:
Veteran UFO Researcher, who ran the Coventry UFO Research Group, edited several newsletters, including Syntonic, skilled compositor and typesetter by trade: currently assisting with the *Haunted Skies* project.
Assumptions are taken by researchers to help with coming to some understanding of what UFO landings represent.

These assumptions have to be applied as no researcher as far as I know, has the answer to the mystery of where these strange objects originate.

Current thinking about this phenomenon includes several possible origins. The Extraterrestrial explanation – curious creatures who, in order to scientifically explore our world, need to 'land' their vehicles and take samples; as witnessed by many people who watch these entities collect plants and soil, etc. If so, they have been doing this for a very, very long time indeed. Have they not learned enough yet? Or are there ever-increasing visitors from any number of origins who need to carry out the same experiments? Do they not talk to each other?

The Time Travelling crew who could be from our own future; from an extraterrestrial source but either travelling from some point in time, either before 'now' or beyond our 'now'; or perhaps a collaboration between our future selves and 'others', either conducting experiments in the past or trying to modify some form of future for both parties.

Inter-dimensional Beings. These are postulated to encompass an undetermined number that may include angels, imps, elves, fairies and the dreaded demons that appear to manifest currently as 'aliens' to unsuspecting humans who witness their antics in our 'plane' of existence. These beings have been seen to exert influence over us in many different ways. We may be tied to these elementals in ways that currently defy explanation but remember, organised religions base their views on interactions with these beings leading to many of the great religion books that millions adhere to! Take into account, also, the numerous cases of landings that involve the beings conveying apparent important information about mankind and our earth's future in the form of 'visions' while the encounter is in progress. Some witnesses have altered their lifestyle as a result but often the meeting with some of these individuals has been a negative event.

Earth Technology – both from current time but also from our own future. I have never fully understood why the phenomenon continues to 'show' itself by following cars and stopping cars by 'landing' or 'hovering' above the roads on which we travel. It almost appears that these 'people' wish to be observed carrying out these operations. If the earth technology is presumed to be top secret, why on earth display such craft to Joe-public? Is this just a blatant disregard for us or are the organisations that control these technologies placing new craft in front of us and in plain sight as mocking gesture?

In all of the above criteria one thing is apparent. Whoever is controlling these devices and landing them, there seems always to be an element of a 'change in reality' for the observer and sometimes even physical effects on the human body.

In the case of Cathie Connelly, who witnessed a landed 'craft' at Meriden, in 1940, the phenomenon exhibited effects on her that could suggest either the extraterrestrial; the time travelling/alien; or the inter-dimensional as the source of her encounters. There also appears to have been a 'religious' element to the case along with time travel where she witnessed several scenes from different epochs.

Warping the observer's sense of his/her place in our world and timeline seems to be a common side-effect of any encounter of a landed craft, to a greater or lesser degree. Often animals become overly subdued or sometimes extremely agitated while the episode is in full swing. The encounter with landed craft, whether remembered directly, or as a result of later revelation via normal recall or perhaps hypnotherapy, often results in a continued interaction and, sometimes, between the witness and seemingly different factions of the many groups of beings in control of the phenomenon. It can involve other members of the witness's family and sometimes clandestine 'military' involvement. That organisation deemed to be 'military' may well be controlled by a very advanced and aloof elite group who command massive amounts of funds and technology – a technology collaboration with certain groups from elsewhere – a technology well in advance of what we behold in our current times that has enabled exploration far beyond our horizons.

Given that the phenomenon itself has the ability to manipulate space and time and could go about its business unseen, it does make me wonder that perhaps in some instances 'they' wish to be observed and wish to invoke some sort of personal contact with the witness for reasons unknown at this time – almost as if in doing so may encourage us to ask questions about our life here on earth and question what we believe is real . . . tempting the imagination of mankind to progress.

This is a brief overview of what I consider relevant in trying to explain what I have learned over the years about the UFO and associated mysteries. The 'landing' of craft may be the result of all of the above possibilities but there could be other explanations that are far more bizarre than any of them.

Malcolm Robinson:
Founder Strange Phenomena Investigations (SPI), UFO/paranormal researcher/investigator, international author and lecturer.
Firstly, I would like to thank Philip Mantle for inviting me to lend my thoughts in regard to so called 'landed' UFOs. Of course, landed UFOs might be a bit of a misdemeanour as currently there is no acceptance coming from any government of this world that we should accept and admit to such things. But of course, let us not forget that we have countless thousands, if not millions of UFO sightings throughout man's history on this planet, to suggest that there are such things. To some they are 'flying saucers' to ancient man they were called 'Vimanas', or 'flying shields'. Many high standing academic people, from across the globe from pilots to navy and army personnel, to the man and women in the street, all at some point have had their own UFO experience.

Now that's as maybe, the vast majority of UFO sightings, as high as 95% can be explained away by a myriad of natural identifiable things, such as planets, satellites, weather balloons and a whole lot more. But this book is not talking about them; we are looking at so called UFO landing cases. Cases of high strangeness which of course, sets them apart from the normal 'lights in the sky.' I've been asked to give my own opinion as to what landed UFOs could be. Are they truly from outer or inner space? Are we dealing with a visiting alien race? Or are people seeing our own black budget technology being flown and then landing and being misconstrued as a fanciful flying saucer? I dare say there will be a number of my fellow commentators who will have their own ideas on this. As for me.

Well, I started off at a very young age to disprove UFO sightings, I honestly felt that there was no validity to any of them, how wrong was I! Yes, the vast majority could be explained, but there were a few puzzling cases that I just couldn't provide a satisfactory explanation for, and I refer to the Scottish A70 Case and the Dechmont Woods UFO Incident. In the A70 case, the UFO itself was not on the ground, but hovered about 20 feet off the ground and interacted with two shocked observers. The Dechmont Woods Encounter 'was' on the ground, a large 20-foot spherical object was seen by a startled observer which proceeded to emit two spherical balls, which rolled across the grass in front of the witness who subsequently fainted. (This case is featured in a chapter of this book). What are we to make of cases such as this? They are head and shoulders above any other case of their kind. But are they alien? Or are they our own technology? Or are we simply not looking in the right direction? Are we missing something? Are all these landed UFOs some kind of global psychosis? The UFO subject is covered in potholes which will bring the enquirer down, and at best confuse him, but within the quagmire of misinformation, there is an abundance of reliable information out there for digesting. But do 'landed UFOs' bring us any closer in accepting or reaching some kind of answer? I won't labour the point here other than to give you what I think is going on when we look to answer the landed UFO enigma.

I agree with the late British author Colin Wilson, who stated in the Daily Mail of December 9th 1997, that he believed that mankind was on the point of some great evolutionary change and that he was sure that the 'aliens' were very much interested in us simply because we were what 'they' once were, and that the 'aliens' were at this time, acting as some form of midwife overseeing our evolution. But apart from overseeing our evolution, they were adding to it. He felt that the 'aliens' are seeding the human race giving us different types of feelings, emotions, alterations in our consciousness, and manipulating us with genetic engineering. Sounds incredible, but who knows, he may not be that far off the mark! I firmly believe that we are being 'visited' by 'beings' from elsewhere.

Researching the subject of UFOs, you find that your opinions change throughout the years, you find that you bend with each new case, you think differently with each new photograph, and you take stock of all that is possible and some that is not. The sceptics will say that there is no real concrete proof that 'aliens' have visited us, that the photographs and movie film are all suspect and can be explained away. I would say different. I would say that the veracity of the evidence that has been accumulated throughout the years from countless thousands of individuals throughout the world, speaks volumes that 'something is going on'. There is no smoke without fire. The honest testimony that has been given, could, in other circumstances, send a man to jail. But the big question is, does this testimony prove to you the reader of this book, that UFOs are a reality? What do you, the reader, accept as proof? Is the collection of UFO landing incidents mentioned throughout this book sufficient to convince you that we are dealing with 'something from elsewhere'?

I have been researching UFOs for over 40 years now, which isn't really that long, and in that time my views have changed quite dramatically. I went from a believer to a sceptic, from a sceptic to a believer. There was a time when I felt that the earthlight hypothesis was the only answer to account for the UFO phenomenon, but now I realise that it is only a part of it.

And that's the thing with researching this subject, your views do change, you do see things in a different light. Meeting likeminded people and sharing information, all helps to establish a rapport of mind in which is an education within itself. Life is the proverbial school, and there is much to learn, but to turn our back on a subject like UFOs, would really not be in keeping with man's quest to learn more, or to try and find our place in the cosmos.

Colin Wilson could be right, that they, the 'aliens', are altering our genetic structure, that they are not taking things 'from' us but putting things 'into' us! And that is frightening. But my conviction, as to why I believe UFO landing reports to be true, is also due to the fact of the many countless thousands of good sound, and reliable testimony that we have coming from military and civilian radar operators. They have observed strange blips appearing on their screens to which their 'trained' eyes are not weather conditions or false returns. Let us not forget, these operators are in charge of equipment which is an extra eye for aircraft, and they wouldn't be in this job if they didn't know what they were doing, so I do accept the testimony that comes from trained radar operators. Let us not forget that we are dealing with a phenomenon that is mysterious as it is elusive, and of which is most certainly alien to our way of thinking. The dramatic turn of speed that these UFOs can achieve is breath-taking, and I fail to accept that any military power on earth at this time could match the agility and speed that these mysterious aerial machines can. We may laugh at poke fun at UFO witnesses. We laughed at John Logie Baird the Scottish inventor of television, we laughed at Marconi, the inventor of the wireless, we laughed at the Wright brothers as they took their first flight, and there were those that laughed at the possibility that we could ever set foot upon the Moon. Why does mankind laugh at things which might appear silly? Just because the tales coming from people who have witnessed a UFO landing may seem ridiculous, this does not mean to say that we should ignore them. I think that there are far too many people sitting in their comfortable armchairs and blowing hot air, if only they looked, if only they would get up, talk to the witnesses, if only they would look at this impressive data, then, they would clearly be in for a big surprise.

The evidence is there, it's only a case of looking. I hope that Philip Mantle's book, serves to whet your appetite in order for you to continue your own search into this fascinating subject that is ufology. Again, for me, some landed UFOs may be our own technology and we, (humans) misinterpret that as something else. But my research has shown to me, that we are dealing with some form of alien civilisation that are appearing in our skies and landing in our fields. I'm sure you will enjoy Philip's book. And as you traverse through Philip's book, your mind will wonder at the diversity of this incredible phenomenon. Philip and I go back many years and I have yet to meet a more grounded and important researcher working in this ufological minefield.

Chris Evers:
UFO researcher, editor & publisher of Outer Limits Magazine.
The Rendlesham Forest UFO incident, to the Dechmont Law (Robert Taylor) Incident, Margaret Fry's, Bexhill UFO encounter, and the Broad Haven UFO event, along with many other famous UFO landing cases, all share an account of at least one unknown 'alien craft' landing on the surface of our planet, specifically within the British isles.

Let it also be said that the British Isles are not uniquely alone in the history of such claims. Many reports share multiple witness accounts as a common theme. Some share reports of unusually reported radiation spikes on the ground and in the vicinity of the landing site. Some share multiple witness accounts with numbers of witnesses ranging from two or three to as many as thirty and more witnesses. Some share accounts of the crafts actual alien occupants, some being the classic Grey alien to reports of solid, moving machines emerging from their 'mother craft' that resemble world war two, naval mine like devices rolling across the ground and ripping trousers on the poor victim of a bizarre encounter in Dechmont woods. Witnesses have included police trained, as well as military personnel, businessmen, housewives, children, husbands, brothers and sisters and many more everyday folk. Since the modern global era of sightings began in 1947 these numbers must be considerable in scope by now, and more than likely in the hundreds if not thousands of credible witnesses, with credible reports. The question remains what exactly have the many different witnesses actually seen? The Rendlesham Forest incident of Christmas Nineteen Eighty alone contains reports of a solid craft, to a set of mysterious lights in the sky, to claims of alien like beings floating in a fog like mist. Are all these reports correct or is one particular witness report more coherent than any of the others? Is one witness more believable than another? The problem is of course that as UFO investigators, we DO NOT investigate reports of the actual UFO sighting or landing (although we do and should check out as many details as possible with local airports and other sources), we actually investigate reports of the reports of the landing or sighting and also as a natural part of the reports we also look to some extent at the witnesses own credibility. Clearly many of our witnesses are seeing something come into land, many witness, and experience a contact with the unknown's occupants of these vehicles. Many of these witnesses are down to earth, feet firmly planted on the ground individuals, with occupations that show them to be so. When we have investigated as much as we can and nothing else appears to provide a credible answer then we are left with perhaps no other option but to admit and say our witness did see something unusual, something not of this world, which visited our planet and landed and was witnessed by everyday folk. For as Sir Arthur Conan Doyle wrote in Sherlock Holmes "Once you eliminate the impossible, whatever remains, no matter how improbable, must be the truth."

The recent New York Times front page article on 17 December 2017, admitting that the Pentagon had investigated new UFO reports and that they had spent $12 million dollars investigating them, then finally admitting publicly for the first time in May 2020, that the credibility of UFO reports held some credence is a major step forward. Perhaps the next step is to admit we have and are being visited by intelligently controlled vehicles and their occupants from regions of deep space or perhaps some other dimension?

Dr. David Clarke:
UFO researcher, author, journalist and lecturer. Founder member of the Independent UFO Network (IUN) BUFORA council member. PhD in folklore and teacher of journalism at Sheffield Hallam University.
The idea of 'UFO landings' is entirely a social construct that occurred within the pop culture explosion of interest in flying saucers and ET contact that began in the West following the flap of 1947.

The initial sightings and experiences were mainly of distant lights and extraordinary objects in the sky - mainly from exotic locations in the Americas. The phenomenon did not really arrive in the British Isles until 1950 when national tabloids promoted the idea of ET visitations on the general public following the syndication of three influential books (Keyhoe, Scully and Heard) and celebrity backing (Mountbatten). But there is only so long that a new phenomenon can remain 'novel' and eventually people wanted more than just 'sightings', they wanted evidence that flying saucers had landed. Most importantly, a large proportion of the British public had been primed to accept the incredible. In 1953 this was provided by the Polish American contactee George Adamski and the Irish polymath Desmond Leslie, whose book title announced that 'Flying Saucers Have Landed'. This is the point that people began to report not just sightings of strange objects in the sky, but also close encounters with them and their occupants, some of which appeared to have landed. The French saucer flap of 1954 and others in South America included numerous accounts of 'landings' and occupant sightings that followed in the wake of the spread of Adamski's story. Yes there were plenty of pre-1953 accounts of 'landings' but a) many of these were not reported until years later within the UFO literature and b) a new breed of UFO enthusiasts like Desmond Leslie began scouring old manuscripts and newspaper cuttings to locate evidence that UFOs had landed in the past - e.g., the 1909 Caerphilly Mountain phantom airship landing and occupant story. There is evidence of this assertion in FSR's Special Issue No 1 The Humanoids, edited by Charles Bowen, which was first published in 1968. The first chapter 'Few and Far Between' bemoans the lack of close encounter/occupant reports from the UK before the mid-1960s and attributes this to the ET's reluctance to visit densely populated areas. So-called 'serious' ufologists like Bowen overlooked the many contactee stories that were common in the UK during the 50s and it was not until Betty and Barney Hill's story hit the tabloids in 1966 that the more familiar landing and contact narratives began to arrive here. The UFOIN files bear witness to the fact that the 1970s were the high-water mark for stories of classic UFO landings in the UK and elsewhere, with accounts of silver-suited humanoids emerging from craft and communications with witnesses by telepathy etc. These narratives took a more disturbing trajectory from the 1980s when they were replaced by abduction account - again influenced by pop culture and UFO books and TV programmes such as Fuller's Interrupted Journey and Budd Hopkins's Missing Time. UFO landing narratives have dwindled since the turn of the new millennium although not entirely disappeared.

But in my opinion this is not because aliens have stopped visiting Earth or have changed their modus operandi. A sociological phenomenon requires a sociological explanation and quite simply when our ideas of flying saucers are, what they and their occupants do and what their purpose is in engaging with us changes so do the narratives reported by those who claim to have witnessed or interacted with them.

Carl Nally:
UFO researcher, lecturer and internationally published author and member of UPRI.
The gods that created mankind are still amongst us. Note the plural gods and the small g. These gods, these beings, have access to life indefinite. The entities it seems could be immortal and though we were made in their image and likeness, we were not to benefit from extreme longevity or everlasting life. In Genesis 1:26 it states, 'Let us make man in our image according to our likeness.

The plurals 'us' and 'our' being used. Genesis 3:22-24 tells us that man was put out of the Garden of Eden to stop him from eating the fruit from the Tree of Life, so that he could live to time indefinite. Once man was prevented from doing this, a guard was posted at the east of the Garden of Eden, the cherub, and the flaming blade of a sword that was turning itself continually to protect the way to the Tree of Life.

Whoever these beings are, it seems that humans are so similar to them it may very well be difficult to tell us apart. It is almost certain that they are walking amongst us and that they could be involved in major projects that affect our progress or our very survival. For example, allowing us to develop technologically in some areas or, hindering us in other areas, such as discovering methods that would allow us to live for centuries, or to time indefinite. So, it would make perfect sense that they and their craft remain hidden from the public eye. They don't need anything from us, but we may be guided by them to discover what is necessary to help mankind to achieve a goal, and we remain totally unaware.

I would refer to them as the Gardeners of the Earth, and they are here forever, we are only passing through. The Old Testament tells us that even in those days these beings wanted to remain hidden from the people. In Exodus 40:38 it says that 'The cloud began to cover the tent of meeting and Jehovah's glory filled the tabernacle. Exodus says, 'that the pillar of cloud would come down' and it even 'stood at the entrance to the tent.' We are even told that Jehovah spoke to Moses saying, 'I am coming to you in a dark cloud.' Numbers 9:17 states, 'Whenever the cloud would go up from the tent, the sons of Israel would pull away right afterwards.'

Today these gods, these beings remain very much out of sight to us, most of the time. Except when they are observed by chance or they are seen and recorded on video, photographed or tracked on civilian or military radar systems.

American Ufologist Albert Bender was the founder of the International Flying Saucer Bureau (IFSB) in 1952. He also created 'World Contact Day' as the 15th of March in 1953. He wanted to contact the occupants of the Saucers by mental telepathy. He instructed each member of the organisation to memorise a message. On a designated time in a quiet secluded place, to lie down and repeat the message in their mind only. He suggested that if the occupants of the Saucers were able to pick up on mental telepathy, they would be able to pick up a telepathic message from hundreds of IFSB members. The experiment allegedly had immediate results

That night Bender woke up to find himself hovering above his own body. He was visited by three men in black, who communicated with him telepathically. 'We have been watching you and your activities. Please be advised to discontinue delving into the mysteries of the universe. We will make an appearance if you disobey.'

Ominously, they added: We are among you and know your every move, so please be advised we are here on your Earth.' Bender claimed that when he attempted to describe the experience, he would develop debilitating headaches. He did not manage to communicate the incident until 1962, when he published Flying Saucers and the Three Men. They want to remain elusive and out of sight as they go about tending to the planet.

When craft are observed landed, it could be that an abduction has taken place and medical procedures are in progress. It could be that the crafts power system needs to cool down. Or they are outside of their craft collecting samples of soil, vegetation or animal's etc. Whatever the reason, they want to remain out of sight and away from human interference to continue their undercover work here on Earth.

The author Jenny Randles refers to the high strangeness that people experience when in close proximity to a landed craft as the Oz Factor. There is a sudden strange quietness where the sound of birds singing, passing traffic, the wind rustling in the trees etc, cease to be audible. There is an eerie feeling experienced that cannot be rationally explained. The person may then make contact with entities while in this hypnotic state. It may be that the Oz Factor is induced by these beings on the unsuspecting human to maintain control as they go about their work plans undisturbed.

Steve Mera:
International UFO/paranormal, researcher, author, lecturer and publisher.
Statistically speaking there are over 300 well documented cases of UFO Landings world-wide. The locations where they come to rest vary dramatically, from forests, to farmland fields, from lonely rural roads to the flats of the desert plains. In almost each case there have been physical traces left behind that consist of hardened and dried out areas of earth demonstrating that a considerable amount of heat may have been applied. On a few occasions the sand covered earth had been turned to glass through the process of applied heat.

Unusual markings in the ground as if from the crafts legs or tripods have been discovered, burying themselves into the earth up to several inches in some cases. Radiation is seemingly a factor as well, with many reported claims from official investigators of radiation being detected in the vicinity. This assumably being associated with the crafts power or propulsion system. There is also the effects to trees, plants and grass in the vicinity. Apart from being burnt or showing signs of extreme heat, there have been unusual characteristics discovered in these plants.

Analysis carried out, which is referred to as 'Biological Traumatology', many of the plants were found to have been immersed in a thermo-electrical field resulting in a diathermic reaction in the plants. Such studies of magnetic and electric fields on plants have resulted in the stunting of growth and also the accelerated growth, depending on the type of plant, how strong the field was and the time it was immersed in the field.

As for the reasons why such craft land is speculative at best. Some would say that they do so in locations that are rural or void of onlookers so to collect samples from the environment. Others would suggest that its occupants are attempting contact for one reason or another. The most common theory is that the occupants need to carry out certain tasks on their craft and even possible repairs. There are stories that go back thousands of years, such as an incident that took place in the Death Valley, California. Modern days Native Americans talk of their ancestors witnessing a strange disc shaped craft in the sky that looked to be having difficulties. It descended quickly and landed. A number of figures were seen milling about outside the craft. A few minutes later a second craft appeared and landed beside the first.

After a short time, both craft took off together and flew away. It was assumed that the first craft had seemingly broken down and that a second craft appeared to offer assistance.

Strange crafts have also been seen to suddenly manifest close to or on the ground. Such incident have been reported several times and witnesses passing by in vehicles have experienced their car headlights bend towards the landed crafts. Others reported unusual faults with their vehicles. This could be evidence of a large magnetic/electric field, thus affecting the vehicles electrical system and the headlights bending towards the object as a result of a strong gravity well.

In modern day research, such gravity wells can be measured in locations where UFOs have been seen close to the ground, however such affects rarely last long.

Brian Allan:
UFO/paranormal researcher, lecturer, author and editor of Phenomena Magazine.
The problem with UFO landing cases is that it is difficult to classify them because they occur in many shapes and forms, and that is before we even consider the possibility of face-to-face contact with whatever is in them. Never mind where they actually come from, because there is absolutely no consensus as to whether they originate in other star systems or from other realities.

Here in the UK, there have been relatively few, irrespective of where they come from, that actually warrant the name of a fully fledged UFO landing. There have been many sightings of anomalous objects in the sky, some of them a close range and behaving a very odd fashion and seeming to interact with whoever saw them, but not all that many involving craft sitting on the ground. Of those encounters with either craft on the ground, or craft that did more than just vanish into thin air, there are maybe three that were not just fleeting encounters and deserve close inspection. These are what occurred at Rendlesham, The A70 Abduction and of course the Dechmont Forest encounter. Each of them, although well-documented and investigated, still have an indefinable aura of high strangeness about them.

One version of the Rendlesham case, and there can be no doubt the something unusual occurred there, seems to have involved some kind telepathic download of information, although that information did not emerge until sometime later and the other two, especially the Scottish A70 case, was an abduction that, fortunately, does not seem to have harmed either of the two men involved.

What they describe is almost dreamlike in nature, perhaps this was deliberately induced by what or whoever took them. I know and have interviewed one of the men at length and his story has never wavered or been enhanced in any way, he is sincere and believes what he is saying. As it happens so do I. The third case at Dechmont, well, the testimony of Robert Taylor, although entirely subjective, is unlikely to be a fabrication, because the man, now deceased, did see something but, despite the drawings he made, what it was can only be guessed at. There were some traces left at the site, but these quickly faded and are now long gone.

Were these encounters the work of some intelligence agency black-project, or were they actual encounters with extraterrestrial spacecraft and their occupants? If it was the second option then why, what did they want? In all cases the people involved experienced a sense of 'otherness' about them, that something was unreal, remote and not quite right, in some cases there also seemed to be instances of missing time. In other words, they all had an element of unreality and high strangeness about them.

Why this should be is currently unknown and we can only speculate, but, assuming that the abductors meant them no harm, perhaps it was to protect the experiencer from literally going insane, because the emotional shock would otherwise have been intense. Therefore, if the intention was to measure now they responded the feeling of remoteness and unreality may have deliberately induced to prevent any readings or measurements being affected, perhaps the missing time was due to the fact that the machines actually travelled in time or were inter-dimensional; but that is of course only speculation. In other words, as with so much that relates to the UFO phenomenon, we know little about this extremely important subject and the added dimension of unreality that surrounds the phenomenon only adds to this. It may be created by the phenomenon itself, either as an unintended side-effect of how it functions, or to protect anyone who encounters one. Perhaps we will learn in time, I hope so.

Sacha Christie:
UFO witness, researcher and blogger.
After we saw what we saw that night, I don't think we really talked about who the occupants were, I don't really recall. I am sure we didn't have any conversations about abductions. It was so shocking that the realisations took years to bubble to the forefront of my mind. It literally shattered me, so I have blank spots in events after that night. I tried to put it out of my mind so much I ended up not knowing when it happened. It wasn't until later when I found Steve again, he pieced those parts together for me. I had assumed it was October but now we are pretty sure it was early February. I suffered a descent into substance abuse and a bout of alcoholism, which doesn't do much to help remember, it helped me blank it out, but only for a while. PTSD can take years to fully blow up in our face, which was the case with me.

When I got a computer in 2005 and found others like myself and other well-meaning individuals who unfortunately filled my head with notions of abduction, experiments and implants. I assumed these people knew what they were talking about and took on board everything they said as if it were true. After a while I started to question these narratives and dropped all the assumptions because I realised they were just that, assumptions.

My son saw a hand that looked like it was made from sticks touch his foot, I heard something run behind me and actually bumped into me. I didn't see anything; in fact, as I ran I was utterly sightless. I have heard people say they took you up when they bumped into you and then you hit the ground running with the mental block still in effect, maybe they are right, I don't know. I cannot access that part of the event no matter how many times I mull it over, pick it apart and muse on it.

I will most likely never know, but because of that it is fair that I entertain the idea on occasion that it was aliens, and we were somehow marked.

I have had experiences all my life, but they were mostly ghostly paranormal with a UFO sighting and some strange "dreams", one of which turned out not to be a dream that happened in 1992 when I saw a short, wide, blue goblin with large black eyes in a brown hooded cape. So, I know I had experiences before this; it just took years for me to piece it together without adding to it with internet narratives.

Steve and I both recently went to see a hypnotherapist to see if we could be hypnotised and to see what recollections could be uncovered, alas, neither of us went under, I didn't feel safe and I didn't know the person I was talking to. I just ran through events as I recalled them and ended up bawling my eyes out. Steve was much the same without the tears.

I try to keep events as I remember them, but Philip has asked me what I personally think about what happened and this is not easy for me to say. Intellectually I argue with myself on this constantly. My whole-body screams that something else happened, I tremble like jelly on a vibro plate when I talk about it, my whole body is involved, not just my intellect. My intellect argues that I didn't see anything so I cannot say whether it was aliens or people. My body screams "something happened to us"!! Why were we all totally traumatised by it when I was the only person who ran for my life? In the end I have to concede that I don't know whether it was aliens or some black ops test with technology our powers that be hide from us, with people running around trying to freak us out, to what end? I can't even imagine. The noise of those running feet haunts me, shoeless and fast, very, very fast.

In the end the only safe place for me to be is hiding behind those three words "I don't know" because either side of the choice lays madness. People doing this to us is as unbearable as aliens doing it to us, although I can imagine why another race of beings would be so interested in us. That craft zeroed in on us, it was moving away to our right then stopped and came directly to us. Somehow whoever was in control saw us looking and came to our location, I have wondered if it was looking for us intentionally, I have wondered a lot of things but each road leads to panic and madness, so I hide behind I don't know. It is the only place I have to hide from what lies behind either option because the questions never end, and they potential answers are just musings.

I can never know my own life. I can never know these events, they are gone, and they are but memories. I am grateful to have found likeminded people; they have healed my heart and given me strength. Weirdly, even though it literally had me running in terror for my life and destroyed the person I was, I like who I ended up being and I like where I ended up, so for all of the nightmares and depression, I don't think I would change what happened. There is more to life than we are led to believe and I am glad that I am no longer oblivious to that. I would rather be aware and nervous than oblivious and locked in an illusion.

Philip Shepherdson:
UFO witness (encounter featured in this book) and author.
Thanks for your query email, regarding nature and origin; my viewpoint. It is difficult for me to add more than my detailed account that I had sent you and which featured in various magazines and articles you and others had undertaken.

Thanks again for that interesting artist impression of my close encounter which you had featured in one of them.

Nature of the Close Encounter.

My observation of the craft. First impressions was of how nuts and bolts it appeared. Although black, no markings, twin tail fins, transparent cockpit holding a headed shape within, it looked terrestrial. The overalls clad beings beside it were trying to drag and push it into the next field in an attempt to hide it from the nearby road where I was. It was then I realised that it had no undercarriage and hovered silent as a graveyard. I did not think we had that advanced form of technology. I think we still have not. My lasting impression was how silent the world had become. No bird song - nothing.

Time Dilation Effects.

Put simply, I cannot remember anything else after that - it was if the entire incident was wiped from my mind. Later as I carried on with my life, I was having frustrating incidents with my time keeping to a point where my friends poked fun at me about it. That came to a head when my current girlfriend was so angry that she dumped me on the spot because I had stood her up for an entire hour. My watch however displayed an absolute hour (I cannot be scientifically exact here for obvious reasons) had been wiped from it. She and her brother had gone looking for me, but I along with my car had mysteriously vanished from our rendezvous car park. Only years later when I was recovering from a bad motorcycle accident that my past Close Encounter experiences were jerked painfully back into focus.

Origin.

I cannot possibly comment here, but only can speculate. Were they ET, or from our future. Perhaps even a Roswell UFO being back engineered by our or USAAF military? That raises more questions than answers. The dinosaurs were on planet Earth for a lot longer than us. If they evolved like us to become super intelligent then they would have escaped the comet somehow.

Perhaps the Greys are this species? I wrote my EarthZoo book as a way of exorcising my troubled mind. It is fact and fiction, but I cannot tell what percentage that is: - only that it is a parable that I can live with within that comfort zone.

Ron Halliday:
UFO/paranormal UFO researcher, author and lecturer.
As investigators into UFO sightings are only too well aware the vast majority of reports relate to strange lights seen in the sky. There's general agreement that most of these can be explained by everyday objects misinterpreted including planes, stars, planets and so on. The insubstantial nature of these sightings is used to discredit the issue of UFOs. If you have had the experience - as I have had - of travelling miles to visit a witness claiming to have videoed a UFO only to watch an hour's coverage of the planet Venus, it's understandable how determined sceptics dismiss the subject as a mixture of fantasy and wishful thinking.

It's understandable that people can have doubts regarding the reality of UFOs if all there was to go on were reports of stationary or moving lights high in the sky. Distant objects in the heavens even in daylight can be difficult to identify. And even if there is no obvious explanation for a sighting it doesn't bring us any closer to solving or even confirming that a mystery exists.

However, there's one area where to my mind the subject of UFOs really does intrigue and cause serious questions to be raised. And that is in those situations involving a close encounter with an object, clearly not of earthly origin, and particularly where it is seen on the ground or hovering close to the ground. The number of these encounters form a small proportion of total UFO reports but taken worldwide they probably number in the thousands.

In these instances, you might believe that there could be no doubt about misidentifying an everyday object, but sceptics continue to search for 'rational' explanations no matter how unlikely and 'irrational' they seem. Responses to the Bob Taylor encounter in November 1979 on Dechmont Law near the town of Livingston demonstrate that those who don't want to believe in the reality of alien contact will come up with far-fetched explanations to disprove UFO encounters.

To recap briefly Bob Taylor came across a circular object in a forest clearing, grey coloured and partly translucent from which rolled two spiky balls which took hold of Bob's legs. He then passed out and when he came to the object had disappeared. In spite of the fact that Mr. Taylor was recognized as an honest person with no axe to grind on UFOs and had a close view of the object a variety of explanations have been trotted out over the past forty years to account for his experience. It was alleged to be the result of an epileptic fit or an undiagnosed medical condition, misidentification in the heat of the moment of some mundane object or even a remotely controlled device being tested by the military among others. The speculation which rages around this incident testifies to the awkward issues that a close encounter raises.

In 1976 a ten-year-old girl (I met her in the 1990s) to whom I gave the name Karen as she didn't want to be identified encountered several small blue beings in a wood close to her house.

She was then lifted by a beam of light into a hovering craft and found herself being scrutinised by an alien being, for want of another description. She was then returned on a beam of light to the ground and ran home where she discovered that she'd been missing for several hours, and her parents were on the point of calling the police. I met Karen when she was in her 30's and still troubled by this incident. I should add that following the event she felt unwell and spent some days in bed. I find this a particularly strange incident because it began with small blue beings more out of a fairy story than a standard UFO event but followed by a traditional close encounter with the witness being beamed aboard a UFO. Karen had by the 1990's a career as a social worker with a lot to lose by being linked to this strange event. She believed an implant of some kind might have been inserted in a tooth and was having it x-rayed by a dentist.

Admittedly, the Meigle wood event was experienced by a ten-year-old, but twenty years later the incident was still vivid in the witnesses' mind.

As UFO incidents go it was complex and involved several components including Karen being 'frozen to the spot' as she put it and unable to move. Dreams as we all know can be complicated involving all kinds of believable and fantastic aspects. But having an intense dream during the day and then finding yourself plagued by the experience for decades seems unlikely. In a way we find ourselves in a similar situation to the Bob Taylor encounter searching for an explanation to fit the event, but unable to solve the puzzle in a way acceptable to rational thinking.

Of course, with solo incidents, one solitary witness, it is always a cop-out to argue, 'it was an imagined event'. In the case of two or more witnesses, it becomes harder to account for it in that way though 'multiple hysteria' has been put forward as an explanation, as in the visions of the Virgin Mary at Medjugorje.

However, when the experience involves several components and may have lasted for an hour or more can imagination, hysteria and so on really be the answer. If we take the case of Gary Wood and Colin Wright - the A70 event for shorthand - putting it down to a kind of fantasy of the mind comes harder to sustain. To summarise: Gary and Colin were driving on the A70 out of Edinburgh to the village of Tarbrax when they encountered a shining object hovering over a bend in the road. The next thing they remember is emerging into darkness, but when they reached their destination at least an hour of time was unaccounted for. Controversially, both Gary and Colin underwent hypnotic regression and an account emerged of their being taken on board a spacecraft and undergoing some type of medical examination by alien entities.

Admittedly, hypnosis cannot be regarded as a scientifically reliable tool, although it is more favourably looked on in the USA, particularly as regards details, but if we accept that the broad outlines of what took place are accurate - that Gary and Colin underwent an encounter with a 'UFO' - then again we find ourselves in a position of dealing with an event which challenges our view of the nature of the universe. Quite clearly 'something strange' happened to Colin and Gary on the A70 as a significant amount of time was lost from their lives and there seems no reason why they would turn that into an imagined UFO encounter if there wasn't some basis for it - in other words the substance of it may well be accurate.

One aspect that is striking is that a close encounter doesn't guarantee that the issue of UFOs becomes any clearer. Frequently, it's the opposite and it raises more questions. The encounter with blue beings has been mentioned, but the sighting related by Tom Coventry (pseudonym) is equally puzzling. Tom was standing as a bus stop at 6am on Menock Road in Glasgow. This was a regular occurrence as Tom took an early bus to work. He caught sight of an object in the distance which he thought must be a helicopter as it was low down and moving comparatively slowly. As it approached Tom sensed an odd change to his surroundings particularly that everything had gone quiet. This sensation was for a time in ufology circles called the 'OZ' factor, promoted by author Jenny Randles, though this designation has largely fallen out of use. However, we want to label it there have been various witnesses over the years who have described the type of sensation experienced by Tom so perhaps an unexplained change in the environment or to the individual, mental or otherwise, does instigate a close encounter.

But what Tom saw definitely registers on the stranger end of the close encounter scale. He described the object which sailed over his head at a height of twenty feet as a flying' railway carriage'. Oblong in shape with porthole windows and flames spewing from the rear portion. He watched it move slowly across the city till it eventually disappeared from view. Tom's encounter raises several questions. One which stands out is why no one else reported seeing the object. Tom himself expected to see articles in newspapers, comments on radio, TV etc but not a peep. He confirmed that there were people about at the time and he was sure the object would become a talking point, but there was nothing. Tom was completely puzzled by this silence but insisted (I have him on tape) that he had seen the UFO as closely as he described.

But a UFO spewing flames? It seems unlikely that a craft from a distant planet or galaxy would be using a propulsion device of so crude a construction and in addition would be ignored or not seen by plenty of witnesses in a busy city. I have no intention of coming to a conclusion regarding Tom's sighting but recount it as an example of a close encounter which mystifies rather than explains UFOs.

Sometimes distant sightings of an object tie in with a close encounter. An instance is the case of Robert Lie (pronounced 'Lee') who lived in the village of Kinbuck a couple of miles outside the better-known town of Dunblane site of the infamous school massacre. Robert was a Norwegian who came to Scotland during World War Two and stayed. I first made contact with Robert when he rang me and claimed that he had witnessed several UFOs landing on hills a few miles from his house and disappearing inside them. He had watched these objects from a hill on the edge of Kinbuck many times, he told me. Not only that but one of these objects had flown over his house and he gave me a detailed description of what he had seen. There was a further twist to the account when Robert claimed an object of some kind had landed in his back garden and 'something' had actually entered his house.

From the hill using Robert's binoculars I could see the shiny objects sitting on the distant slopes. But what were we looking at? To get a better view we would have to get much closer, but there was no obvious route there so we would have to trek across miles of shrub and moorland to reach the site. With another UFO investigator a few days later, we set off.

I don't know whether I was unfit or another stranger explanation but after a few miles I suddenly felt sick and disorientated and had to come back. Robert carried on but eventually he too had to give up. So, the objects allegedly sitting on the hill had to be left to their own devices. But there was not necessarily any link between what Robert believed he saw twenty miles off and the object which flew over his head or the object he claimed actually landed beside his house. Robert believed the UFOs on the hill were monitoring him because they became aware he was watching them. But was he connecting up dots which shouldn't have been connected up? Or does Robert's experience indicate that the UFO phenomenon is more sinister than we think? Because according to Robert one of the UFOs lifted off and followed an RAF Hercules plane which crashed shortly after. The crash did take place, but no official admission of a UFO being in the vicinity.

However, Robert Lie's case emphasizes again that a landed UFO or a close encounter does not mean that we have been given a simple explanation to the phenomenon. In fact, as has been described getting up close can raise a host of questions which can twist the UFO puzzle in many directions. On 25th April 1984 Gwen Freeman was sitting in the back garden of her bungalow in Riverside Road in the Perthshire village of Blairgowrie when she suddenly became aware that her forsythia bush was shimmering with sparkling lights. She then watched a beam of light travel upwards till it hit a strange looking object; bulbous shaped about 150 feet long with five v-shaped projections below. Following this incident which they reported to the police at least two other odd incidents occurred.

The family witnessed twelve people all dressed in black, and distinctly odd looking, walk into the house next door, but when they inquired of their neighbours, as they were concerned about this strange group, they were met with a blank response as if it had never happened. Some weeks later a peculiarly dressed couple, a man and woman, came to the door, wearing clothes which looked like 1920's gear, and warned them not to talk about what they'd witnessed or 'a great evil would befall them'. I've summarized more extensive events, but even the basic facts are curious. Are they connected? Or was it a series of incidents which became linked in retrospect? This is what I mean by saying that a close encounter doesn't mean we get a straight answer. There's no doubt a strange object of some kind was witnessed albeit for a very short time span, but does the fact of seeing an unidentified object close up generate some kind of mental disorientation or excitement which links up incidents which might otherwise be discarded? Although not the first reported sighting in the Bonnybridge UFO 'wave' of the early to late 1990s the encounter by the Slogett family in March 1992 triggered a massive level of media interest. Their experience of an object which landed in a field then on the road behind them involving several witnesses lent the incident a level of credibility. However, the bulk of the sightings during the 'Bonnybridge phenomenon' appear to have been of objects in the sky with several good eyewitness accounts across the area including daylight video footage which I got closely involved in. I'd suggest that the fact that a _landed_ UFO was reported and publicised in the media and multiple witnesses were involved, albeit from the same family, gave the event a substantial basis it might have otherwise lacked, encouraging media involvement and witnesses to other sightings to come forward. The media certainly played it up for all it was worth, but the fact that the first event had 'close encounter' stamped on it gave the story legs and it really took off.

In UFO-land nothing is straightforward, and incidents seem plagued by the bizarre. As in the case of Arthur Moar from the Shetlands who witnessed a globe shaped object with flame all around it land in his back garden. He described the centre as a globe of the world with all the markings on it! Had I not spoken to Mr. Moar and received his written report I would have dismissed it as a prank, but he was serious about his encounter and convincing. But incidents of this nature - a close up sighting of a landed object - make little sense in terms of a 'rational' ufology. It's hard to say that we are looking for evidence that we're being visited by aliens from distant planets when you start to consider events which suggest that we are dealing with 'something' far more weird and strange than our day to day lives would prepare us for.

In 1973 Christine was a passenger in a car returning from a trip to Lochore in Fife. Out of the blue the car engine cut out and wouldn't move.

Neither could Christine, frozen in the back seat. However, she then witnessed two silver suited entities walk across the ground towards her and come right up to the car window. They then turned around and walked away. Shortly after she saw a beam of light shoot up into to the sky - the presumption being that this had been a spacecraft of some kind that had landed though she didn't see an actual object. The interaction between UFOs and car engines has been a reported feature.

In 1994 Andrew Swan observed a pyramid shaped object hovering over a field next to Armadale Academy, West Lothian. Driving along a back road to get a closer look. When he shone a halogen lamp at the object, the bulb exploded. Andrew, realising he was on his own with a strange object close by, decided to leave, but his car wouldn't start. Andrew rang the police, but in the meantime the UFO shot over his car and disappeared. The car, however, would still not start. The AA was summoned, but the mechanic couldn't get it going so it had to be towed away. However, in a strange twist the car started up again out of the blue some hours later. The AA man (who I spoke to) expressed his bafflement over the car's engine suddenly springing back to life after it had seemed down and out. Christine and Andrew's cases where other mechanical and electrical systems had been affected certainly convinced the witnesses that there had been interaction between the object seen and the car's engine cutting out. On the face of it, it does appear more than coincidence and suggests that a force of some kind may be generated by whatever it is that is encountered. Proof that maybe UFOs in these cases were 'real', solid functioning objects and not figments of the imagination.

Overall, there are a long list of close encounters of objects which can be described as 'spacecraft' of some kind, but as in the Tom Coventry case do raise issues hard to resolve in a rational way. In 1985 Angela Humphries was walking across a bridge over the River Tay in Perth when she suddenly observed hovering a few yards away from her what she described as a translucent circular object up to forty feet long with a large window which she likened to a viewing platform. Through the window she saw several small entities one of whom appeared to be using levers to manoeuvre the craft. There were people and traffic around, but it didn't look as if anyone else had seen it. However, according to Angela her life could never be the same after the encounter. It had a dramatic effect on her.

As it did on Allistair McNeill who in May 1976 with a group of friends observed from his Glasgow flat a large, silver, disc-shaped object hovering over a grassy space opposite.

He estimated it to be sixty feet across with porthole shaped windows. Suddenly the UFO hurtled in their direction and then soared over the building. Allistair described having a feeling of the 'divine' and that the incident 'blew his mind.' It's unlikely that a witness would feel so enraptured by seeing no more than an unexplained light in the sky. The impact of encountering an object difficult to fit neatly into a category certainly appears to change witnesses perception of what is 'out there'. It is more tangible evidence that we are experiencing a genuine functioning object which even if not perfect evidence that we are being visited by extraterrestrials at such events at the very least raise questions over supposed 'scientific' explanations, that UFOs simply don't, or can't, exist. Perhaps the truth is the opposite and a rational explanation is that we are, in fact, being visited by extraterrestrials!

Gloria Heather Dixon:

Long standing UFO researcher and Director of Investigations for the British UFO Research Association (BUFORA):

Philip's collation of narratives of UFO landing reports in the UK, beginning from 1767 to 2005 will be a fascinating addition to ufology, significantly for the new generation of researchers. I wish him well with the research and work that has gone into the writing of his book.

The UFO subject embraces a huge and diverse landscape, which encompasses some scientific disciplines, folklore and mythology, psychology, the paranormal, religion and, sometimes, neuroscience, to name but a few. As always though, within this subject of rumour and speculation, there are many more questions than answers in looking at reports from sightings of lights in the sky to the more complex landing and high strangeness cases. These questions centre around several key factors, memory, powerful beliefs and perception and how these will reflect how a person interprets a sighting. The 'human face' of ufology is a crucial component for an objective and robust approach by an investigator in assessing sighting reports, and those with up close and personal features as expressed by the witness.

Memory is far more inaccurate than we understand and unlike a video does not play out in the same way every time. Human memory is far more complicated and as it is laid down into our long-term memory banks, it can be edited and imperceptibly changed each time we access traumatic memories, so although the fundamental memory 'may' remain intact, there are minor, fragile changes taking place throughout our access into a specific memory, sometimes emotionally charged, even though we are unaware of this. In addition, UFO imagery recalled from the media, internet and many other agencies, may add to a memory that appears to confirm what we want to be true of our sighting or high strangeness experience.

In addition, and related to the problems with the accuracy of memory, are historical sightings from many years ago being reported to an investigator and memory can have a blurred lens in capturing an event from ten or more years ago, integrating many other memories that we have 'downloaded' to our long term memory banks over the years, which may echo our beliefs in the idea of an encounter with something of non-human origin. Powerful beliefs can lie at the core of how a sighting or high strangeness experience is reported, often unconsciously, and this may then change the accuracy of a report from being an objective understanding of our experience to one that is subtly changed to reflect what we believe to be true.

Beliefs in so many areas of our lives are a strong force and part of what it means to be human, but at times can, and do, have an effect on our understanding of the reality of our UFO sighting or experience.

Then we come to the controversial questions of the use of hypnosis to elicit the truth of a memory of a strange or unknown experience. There are serious problems in using hypnosis as a methodology to reveal an objective truth about a UFO experience. It does not do this. Someone who is under hypnosis is highly suggestible and imaginative and, significantly, highly telepathic. It should also be pointed out that hypnosis may also hugely reinforce any problems relating to the emotional and psychological well-being of the witness which have emerged from their experience.

BUFORA operate under a Code of Practice for all their investigators which identifies major problems with the use of hypnosis and therefore it is mandatory that hypnosis is never used during any investigation by a BUFORA investigator.

Finally, back to Philip's original question, '*The thrust of my argument is that in general terms that the closer a witness gets to a 'UFO' then the less likely it is to have a rational explanation, or in what Dr, Hynek called, has a degree of 'high strangeness'.* My response is that it is not necessarily less likely to have a rational explanation, as there are many limitations and possible problems in applying this statement to some cases and many other high strangeness cases from around the UK, as discussed above.

To conclude my thoughts on high strangeness events and experiences, it is my opinion and experience in my many years involved with the UFO subject, that it is critical we decipher, decode and become conversant with the multifarious parts of the UFO subject and how complex it has become. As technology has advanced, this has opened the gateway of 'UFO infrastructure' and what lies beneath all the hype and exposure that sometimes reveals such a superficial overview of the subject, including any kind of definitive insight to the reality of sightings and high strangeness events that remain unidentified at this time…or possibly any other time.

Philip Mantle (the author):
A long-standing UFO researcher and author from the UK. He was formerly the Director of Investigations for the British UFO Research Association and the MUFON Representative for England. He is the founder of FLYING DISK PRESS.
I dare say that when we look back at the case histories featured in this book that there are bound to be one or two that are hoaxes, others that will be a fantasy of some kind and several that will feature rare natural phenomenon. Having said all that I am convinced that the vast majority of these cases are the genuine article. So, what is the 'genuine article'? A good question. I have taken this opportunity to ask this very same question to a number of my colleagues here in the UK. Their comments precede mine. You will see that we have a variety of comments covering a wide range of possible explanations for these cases. I respect all of my colleague's comments irrespective of whether or not I agree with them. There are many things that puzzle me, and it is something that crops up time after time.

That is the lack of other witnesses in certain cases. Some of these case's took place where there was large population living around them, but no one else reported seeing anything. Why is that? The 'other worldly' aspect or 'OZ factor' also crops up on a regular basis. Again, what is this and why does it manifest in such a way? Another question that bothers me greatly is why are there no photographs of these UFOs on the ground, or should I say photographs that are deemed to be reliable and authentic? Do you notice another pattern emerging here? Yes, a pattern of questions. When trying to study these cases of high strangeness for me there is no one answer or theory that fits the bill. The more I try to study them the more questions I end up with and the more puzzled I become.

Another puzzling aspect is why did such cases peak in the 1970's? Why do we see so few cases reported now? It seems to me that there are more questions than answers. Even when you speak to some of the eyewitnesses they too have differing opinions and different points of view. What I can say is that the witnesses in question do undergo a genuine high strangeness close encounter which in my humble opinion does not have an obvious rational explanation. I envy those that are certain what lies behind these encounters and I am not sitting on the fence. I have personally interviewed some of these witnesses and have seen that look of bewilderment in their eyes. They have looked to me for an explanation but there is no way I can provide one. I know from experience that the vast majority of UFO reports do have a rational explanation but there is a tiny minority that does not. Within that minority are the types of cases featured in this book. I cannot tell you what the nature and origin of these cases is, but I can tell you what they are not. In general terms they are not misidentifications of astronomical objects, aircraft, drones, military experiments and so on. They are a mystery wrapped in a puzzle and encased in an enigma. They must therefore in my opinion simply still be labelled as **UNIDENTIFIED**.

*****

www.flyingdiskpress.com

FLYING DISK PRESS MERCHANDISE

Flying Disk Press and illustrator Ronald Kinsella have set up Flying Disk Press Merchandise and our online store is now open. We have produced a unique set of UFO/alien themed items for sale. This includes t-shirts, hoodies, mugs and a whole lot more. Our clothing is for all ages and comes in a wide range of sizes and colours. We will continue to add new items on a regular basis and even venture into other subject matter such as the 'paranormal'. Why not take a look and browse our shop at the web site below.

https://shop.spreadshirt.co.uk/flying-disk-press-merchandise/

Printed in Great Britain
by Amazon

87762809R00154